Alfred

Alfred

QUEEN VICTORIA'S SECOND SON

JOHN VAN DER KISTE

FONTHILL

Learn more about Fonthill Media. Join our mailing list to find out about our latest titles and special offers at: www.fonthill.media

Fonthill Media Limited
Fonthill Media LLC
www.fonthill.media
books@fonthill.media

First published in the United Kingdom 2013
Reprinted 2020

British Library Cataloguing in Publication Data:
A catalogue record for this book is available from the British Library

ISBN 978-1-78155-319-0

Typeset in 10.5pt on 13pt Sabon LT Std
Printed and bound in England
twitter.com/fonthillmedia facebook.com/fonthillmedia
#PrinceAlfredBook

Contents

Author's note

In 1981 I decided to begin research into the life of Alfred, Duke of Edinburgh and later Duke of Saxe-Coburg Gotha. I had long been fascinated by Queen Victoria's family and found it odd that there had not yet been a biography of her second son. He was after all by far the most widely-travelled prince of his time, having set foot in all five continents by the age of twenty-five, no mean feat for a man who died three years before the first successful flight; he was the victim of the first attempted assassination in Australian history; he married a Romanov Grand Duchess, daughter of the Tsar of Russia, in an age when Anglo-Russian relations were uncertain, not to say chilly; at the age of eighteen he was the overwhelming choice of Greek citizens for their temporarily vacant crown; and he was also responsible for starting the royal philatelic collection, long since acknowledged as the world's finest. In addition there was a local connection, as I lived near and worked at Devonport, where he had served as Commander-in-Chief.

As every biographer of the era will agree, he had his faults. Contemporaries found him a boring conversationalist, an amateur violinist whose talents were said to be overrated, and an ill-tempered prince whose heavy drinking shortened his life. His relations with Queen Victoria were often strained, and it comes as no comfort to any biographer of his to learn that his sister Princess Beatrice, as their mother's executor, destroyed thirty volumes of his letters to the Queen. However, it does him an injustice to focus on the more negative side aspects. He was an intelligent man, with an abiding interest in the arts, especially music and photography, as well as in mechanical devices, and a capable, conscientious naval officer who loved the service, and who had to leave it reluctantly to become a sovereign German duke, perhaps fortuitously at a time when Anglo-German relations were beginning to become strained.

A few months into my research, I contacted John A. S. Phillips of the Prince Consort Society, to ask whether he could assist with information on the Duke's years in Coburg. He put me in touch with Bee Jordaan, a retired librarian almost forty years my senior, living in Denmark, who had been working on a biography herself for some years. Although she had published one book some thirteen years earlier, she did not then have a publisher. I followed his advice, and several months of letters and swapping of ideas, long before e-mail, were the result, culminating in a meeting in April 1983 when she came to stay for two days while we hammered our collaboration into shape. We never met again, and Bee sadly took her own life after a severe illness in 1990. Many others who helped us in the course of our writing, as recorded in the acknowledgements, are likewise no longer with us.

The book, originally *Dearest Affie,* was first published in 1984 and reissued in 1995. Since then our knowledge of the Victorian royal family has expanded considerably; several relevant biographies and selections of royal correspondence have appeared; and the internet has made newspaper archives far simpler to research. It has long been my aim to expand and in effect rewrite the original work to a major extent. Almost thirty years after the original project was completed, I am delighted to be able to do so.

John Van der Kiste, 2013

CHAPTER 1

Nursery and Education 1844-55

Queen Victoria and Prince Albert were married on 10 February 1840, and during the next seventeen years she gave birth to nine children. The first were born within less than four years of each other, shared the nursery together, and would remain close to each other throughout their lives.

The eldest, Victoria, Princess Royal, was born on 21 November 1840. Twelve days before the princess's first birthday Albert Edward, Prince of Wales, was born, and seventeen months later, in April 1843, they had a baby sister, Alice.

In July 1844, when she was eight months pregnant, the Queen had to host a state visit to England from Tsar Nicholas I of Russia. Throughout her life she had an ambivalent relationship with her Eurasian ally, and her feelings were best summed up over a century later by her great-grandson, Earl Mountbatten of Burma. He considered that she feared Russia, with very good reason; as a very liberal-minded constitutional monarch, she believed 'that absolute autocracy was wrong and was bound to end in tears, which it did.'[1] However Prince Albert, who never shared her prejudices against foreign powers, welcomed such occasions as these when, he said, he not only saw 'these great people' at close range, but got to know them well. During the visit Sarah, Lady Lyttelton, or 'Laddle', as the infants called her, was concerned lest Her Majesty would over-exert herself in her condition. But she need not have been so anxious, for she had seen her 'tripping upstairs to chapel, and the vein of iron that runs thro' her extraordinary character enables her to bear up to the last minute, like nobody else.'[2] Throughout their lives, the children would feel this vein of iron in more ways than one.

One month later, on the morning of Tuesday, 6 August 1844, her second son was born at Windsor Castle. Ever the proud father, Albert wrote to his brother Ernest, Duke of Saxe-Coburg Gotha, that 'after much pain, she was confined this morning, ten minutes to eight o'clock. She let us wait a long time and consequently the child is unusually large and strong.'[3]

On 6 September the baby prince was christened Alfred Ernest Albert in the private chapel at Windsor. His sponsors at the ceremony were his aunt Alexandrine, Duchess of Saxe-Coburg (represented in her absence by the Queen's mother Victoria, Duchess of Kent), Prince George of Cambridge, and Prince William of Prussia. The latter, a tall, stern unbending soldier, accepted the invitation as he was hopeful of obtaining British support in the future. For his part, Albert hoped to establish friendship with a man whom he mistakenly believed to be a fellow-liberal in politics and therefore a useful ally in years to come.

Lady Lyttelton proved an ideal governess with her patience, a sense of humour and boundless love for children. Punishments she disapproved of, as 'they wear out so soon, and one is never really sure that they are fully understood.' Albert was a model father, and those who thought him unbending and aloof would have been astonished to see him playing hide-and-seek or turning somersaults with the youngsters. She frequently had to order him, only half in jest, out of the way when it was their bedtime or if she feared they were getting over-excited. The Queen was never such a frequent visitor to the nursery, and not solely for reasons of state and subsequent lack of time. She had been brought up exclusively in adult company, and because of this she tended to be ill at ease in her infants' company while they were small. Distinctly unenthusiastic about babies, she considered an ugly one a very nasty object, and even the prettiest 'frightful when undressed' until they were about four months old.[4]

The children were rarely intimidated by the more elderly or pompous officials that called regularly at Windsor Castle and Buckingham Palace, who were astonished by the gleeful impertinence that sometimes greeted them. It fell to the lot of Sir Hamilton Seymour, a former ambassador to Brussels and St Petersburg, to be 'entertained' by Affie. On a visit he walked up to the gentleman with his most innocent expression, asking if he would like to come and see a monkey. Sir Hamilton had been round many zoological gardens in his time, but Affie's persistent pleading was too much for him, so at length statesman and little prince walked hand in hand down a long corridor. At the end was a tall mirror, where the ambassador caught sight of his own reflection. 'There's a monkey,' piped up the gleeful youngster before scuttling away. Other gentlemen attending court experienced his lack of reverence in different ways. A favourite prank of his was to stick coloured flags on pins in their padded calves.

From babyhood Affie was much more even-tempered than the three eldest children. While they had their fair share of obstinacy and wilfulness, at eighteen months Laddle judged him to have 'a very good manly temper; and much more like that of most children than that of the Princess Royal or the Prince of Wales', and at four and a half he had 'very uncommon abilities; and a mind which will make the task of instructing him most smooth and delightful'.[5] Always quiet, he was 'not a great talker', and his customary expression for refusing to do something disagreeable was an emphatic 'Boys *never!*'[6] On his fourth birthday he was a 'great beauty, all blue and silver, bewildered with presents, and much preferring to all a penny trumpet' given him by Vicky, bought with her own money. He was also given two handmade silk balloons inflated with gas.[7]

Affie had inherited the Hanoverian high-spiritedness, and seemed oblivious of danger. As soon as he could walk on his own he climbed out of windows and balanced on ledges thirty feet or more above the ground unless restrained, or went jumping across fast-running streams before he could swim. Indoors he slid down banisters, falling off and concussing himself, once nearly fracturing his skull, and although given a severe scolding he would do just the same the next day. The customary punishments, such as being sent to his room, or 'a good whipping' (probably no more than a sharp smack) from his Mama, had no effect. Nearly every week he had a minor accident, but suffered little more than bruises or the odd black eye.

Nonetheless he was the delight of his parents and governess alike because of his cheerful disposition, willingness to share his toys with the others, and above all his aptitude for learning. Unlike the exceptionally clever Vicky he was no child prodigy, but he was intelligent and had powers of concentration so lacking in his elder brother Bertie.

From the beginning it was evident that Affie's future lay in the Royal Navy. He always had a passion for geography and anything to do with the sea, and learnt to read at any early age so that he could find out for himself all about ships and famous navigators. His knowledge of vessels in the navy extended beyond their names, right down to minute technical details. At drawing lessons he would sketch nothing but ships and naval battles. On his birthday one year Prince Albert gave him a ship's clock and barometer, and these became among the more highly-prized articles of furniture in his bedroom, which he decorated to look as much like a cabin as possible.

With this love of ships and nautical equipment went a fascination with anything practical. Affie always enjoyed taking mechanical objects to pieces and reassembling them with some minor improvement, or making toys for the younger children. He spent hours on end hammering, sawing and cutting pieces of wood, tin or leather to get exactly what he wanted, apparently unaware of the parents and tutors who were watching him at work. Once he made a musical box that played *Rule Britannia*, albeit after a fashion, but the fact that it only worked in fits and starts did not detract from his sense of achievement.

Affie had not remained the youngest for long. Before he was six, three more children had entered the nursery – Helena in May 1846, Louise in March 1848, and Arthur in May 1850. Shortly afterwards Lady Lyttelton resigned, to the regret of all. After more than a decade of what had been a very exacting job, she longed for the peace and quiet of her own home and her cross-stitch. She described the parting with 'her' children:

> The darlings all came up in succession, and a bad spot of road it was to get through....They all cried, and were most touching. The Prince of Wales, who has seen so little of me lately, cried and seemed to feel most. The Princess Royal said many striking and feeling and clever things.... Princess Alice's look of soft tenderness I shall never forget; nor Prince Alfred, with his manly face bathed in tears, looking so pretty.[8]

So ended the carefree nursery days and Affie's formal education began. It was important that he should be prepared for two eventual destinies, that of a Duke and a King. Assuming that he lived to a reasonable age, he would probably inherit the duchy of Saxe-Coburg and Gotha. Albert had agreed that if Ernest died childless his own second son should be his heir, Bertie naturally being his mother's successor to the British throne. After Alexandrine had suffered three miscarriages the possibility of her presenting Ernest with an heir seemed slender, and it was to their nephew that they looked for the future.

Wisely Albert laid down certain conditions that his untrustworthy brother had to observe. If the Prince of Wales died young, Affie might one day wear his mother's crown, so he had to be educated for both roles just in case, and the duchy was of considerably less importance than Britain. This gave Albert an excellent reason for keeping the boy at home in England, for Ernest's wish was to have him spending long periods with him in Germany. This was just what the fond father did not want, as he had no intention of letting Affie be initiated into his uncle's debauched ways. Like Ernest I, who had died in January 1844, Ernest II lived up to the customary title of German sovereigns, 'Father of his people'. His dutiful wife Alexandrine naively appeared to believe in his innocent explanations that the pretty young women he visited in a small house in the ducal park were only secretaries and translators.

Albert's own education had been supervised by a fellow Coburger, the dry and pedantic Baron Christian Friedrich von Stockmar. He had begun his career as physician to Albert's uncle Leopold, and was largely responsible for promoting the family's ascendancy to what would eventually be known scathingly by the German chancellor Otto von Bismarck as the 'stud farm of Europe', by persuading Leopold to accept the Belgian crown in 1831, and later arranging the marriage of Victoria and Albert. He remained attached to all three until Albert's death. It was he who had advocated the appointment of 'a Lady of Rank' – Lady Lyttelton – to the nursery, and after her resignation, putting both elder boys to the grind of the Coburg system. At the time Bertie was nearly eight and Affie was five.

The suggestions, arguments, debates and discussions which followed must have made the walls of Windsor rock. Papa insisted that their education must be as 'unlike as possible their maternal great-uncles' – the reprobate Kings George IV, William IV and their brothers. Mama had commanded that her heir must resemble 'his angelic father in every respect both in body and mind' – wishful thinking to say the least. With the preparation of Stockmar's two enormous memoranda on the education of princes, their fate was sealed.

A course of 'moulding' was initiated. In Bertie's case it was a tragic failure, turning him into a rude, frustrated and nervous adolescent, the despair of his parents. Even as a small boy Laddle had commented with concern on his 'passions and stamping'. As a second son Affie was fortunate. He could hide to some extent behind his elder brother as less exacting standards were required of him, and he had the advantage of knowing the profession he wanted to follow.

The first tutor or governor was Henry Birch, a young master of barely thirty years of age from Eton, engaged at a salary of £800 a year at Windsor. Seven days a week he taught calculating, geography and English in periods of thirty minutes each. Other visiting masters were responsible for religion, French, German, writing, drawing and music. Lessons were never discontinued for more than a few days at a time year in and year out, with holidays very few and far between.

Bertie was persistently inattentive and disobedient, and Birch hoped he might be stimulated to work harder by the efforts of his younger brother. Affie's attitude for serious study and concentration resulted in slight improvement, but Birch resigned in 1852 after being convinced he had failed in providing the heir to the throne with a satisfactory education. However he left behind him a volume of Affie's compulsory diary or Journal, which had been part of the curriculum. The original, now in the archives at Coburg, is inscribed: 'Dictated to Mr Birch by me. Alfred. Commencing October 1851.'

Even with so many ardent censors to hand all spontaneity is not quite lost, though Birch ensured that few personal comments were allowed. Preserved for posterity are impressions of the little boy who could not keep awake; who was glad there was a nice tea waiting at the end of a long journey; who thought his baby brother extremely fat; who was so pleased when he was allowed to have breakfast with his Mama, and when his Papa took him to watch shooting. There is a charm and naivety here that is altogether disarming, and over and over again one feels that Affie is on the verge of forgetting his mentors and will add something naughty and boyish. But the journal was written primarily for adult eyes, as was the one which had been kept by his mother as a young princess a few years previously, so almost at once the reader is back to essay-like descriptions and endless flat adjectives: pretty, fine, nice, glad, beautiful. Yet at least it gives a first-hand idea of how the royal children spent what leisure time they had – visits, important people met, presents received, and family life as a prince – as Prince Albert so rightfully regretted, 'not as other men'.

A few entries may be quoted to give some insight into Affie's formative days. For example, in November 1851:

> I was very much delighted when Mr Birch called me this afternoon to give me a most beautiful watch which Grandma had sent me. It came from the Exhibition [the Great Exhibition at Crystal Palace, which had closed on 15 October] and it was intended for a birthday present when we were at Osborne but then it was in the Crystal Palace. Mr Birch told me I make good use of my time, and that I had a watch which would show me how quickly minutes and hours fly away. I feel very grateful to Grandmama for being so kind as to send me a watch.[9]

Early in the new year he described the recent festivities at Windsor Castle:

> On the 20th of last December I returned from Osborne to Windsor Castle and passed a happy Christmas with Bertie and Mr Birch and I received many presents – a sword, a Tyrolese hat and belt, some very pretty soldiers which I shared with Bertie, an [*illegible*] case with paper and sealing wax and a place for stamps, a gutta-persha lion and some nice books. On Christmas Day I went to the kitchen with Bertie and Mr Birch and I saw the Baron of beef and boar's head, and I went down to the larder where I saw hares, pheasants, grouse and a great quantity of fat meat'; and we saw the pastry room and a model of Windsor Castle in sugar. In the evening Bertie and I supped with our sisters in the Oak Room and played with some of the presents. When I had finished playing I went to the great dinner and had a very happy evening.
>
> On the New Year's morning Bertie gave me a New Year's wish and Mr Birch as well. When I was dressing I heard some music on the terrace. I put on my Coburg costume and breakfasted with Mama and Papa, Grandmama and cousin George and my brothers and sister. I went to the Riding School to see people get their New Year's Gifts. The Gentlemen went into the riding school amongst the people. In the evening we heard

the Tyrolers sing and then dance. Then we had supper with our sisters. Afterwards I heard 'Aedipus' performed in the Waterloo Chamber and liked it very much. So ended that evening.[10]

Birch was replaced by Frederick Waymouth Gibbs, a barrister and Fellow of Trinity College, Cambridge. A stronger and more prim character than his predecessor, he began at the salary of £1,000 per annum. He immediately made the timetable more demanding, 'in exact obedience and subordination' to Prince Albert, with six or seven one-hour periods from 8 a.m. to 7 p.m., six days a week. The curriculum included Latin, French and German (short plays in the two latter languages were acted as well), and English classics; 'story books', including those of Sir Walter Scott, were prohibited as being thought too frivolous. Arithmetic, algebra and geometry, 'with direct reference to their applications to Gunnery, Fortifications and the Mechanical Arts', history and fine arts were also taught. Gibbs was ordered to ensure that his charges were exhausted at the end of each day mentally and physically; riding, gymnastics and drill saw to that.

Under Gibbs, Bertie was frequently ill-behaved, or 'excited' to use the tutor's own expression, and soon Affie began to imitate him. This was not so much following his example as self-defence, for when he became frustrated, Bertie took his feelings out on Affie, pulling his hair, kicking him, and on one occasion threatening him with a paper knife. Through sheer dogged persistence Gibbs eventually extracted some measure of obedience from them, though Affie began to show signs of slackness not in keeping with his earlier character.

The Journal was faithfully continued in Gibbs' handwriting. Among the next entries are descriptions of visits to the British Museum, Westminster Abbey, and an exhibition of lion hunter George Gordon-Cumming's

produce of his exploits in South Africa; all done by his hand and gun;....a boat which his brother gave him from the Carpathian mountains. He had skins and heads of deer, of lions, leopards, tigers and buffaloes. There were elephant's tusks – 2 very big ones. He put them up so as to represent an arch, and to decorate it at the top, three ostrich feathers so as to represent those of the Prince of Wales. There were missiles put up which the natives of South Africa used, in a kind of circle. There were 2 great elephant's feet.

He had a little Bushman; he was very funny; he played all sorts of tricks and imitated all the noises of the animals and birds. He lives in what used to be Mr Gordon-Cumming's travelling wagon in South Africa.[11]

The name Gordon-Cumming would return to haunt the family. In 1891 his nephew Sir William would be disgraced in the 'baccarat scandal' after a house party at Tranby Croft, Yorkshire, leading to an appearance in court in the witness box from the Prince of Wales, who had also been one of the guests and had carelessly allowed himself to become involved in the affair.

From this animated account of the exhibition, it can be seen that the boy of seven was fascinated by the display. Here the seed may have been sown of a determination to visit South Africa when he was older, and to build up his own very similar collection of trophies and souvenirs.

In July and August 1852 the family cruised on board the royal yacht *Victoria and Albert* along the south coast and across the North Sea to Belgium, where they were guests of the recently-widowed King Leopold and his family. Some of the expeditions were documented thus:

Yesterday morning [Saturday 13 August] we went to Uncle Leopold's palace at Brussels and spent the day there. We took a walk in the town with Cousin Leopold and Cousin Philippe [Leopold, later Duke of Brabant and King Leopold II, and Philippe, Count of Flanders]. In the afternoon we went to see the cathedral, the Hotel de Ville and then the Museum; some of the pictures I did not like because they were so horrible. I bought some pretty ornaments and some prints. After that we returned to Laeken.

This morning we started a little before nine for Antwerp. The cousins went with us in their uniforms. We saw the Exhibition of pictures. There was a great crowd of people there, who behaved very well. After that we went to the Cathedral; there we saw the finest picture in Antwerp. It was Christ being taken down from the cross. It was painted by Rubens. There were a great many people in the church who shouted 'Vive le Roi et sa couronne' and 'Vive la Reine'. After that we went to the Museum of pictures. There was a picture of a Dead Christ of which the eyes seemed to follow you. We had luncheon at the Palace and went on board the yacht. In the evening we anchored near the mouth of the river (Schelde).

Sunday morning we went a little way farther down the river intending to sail, but it was so rough that we returned and anchored opposite Terneusen a Dutch town. I landed there with Mama. We went to see a Dutch farm in a car without springs; after we had seen the farm we went back to the vessel and the river was very boisterous.

The next day we went to Dungeness, passing Calais. I made a net for the first time that day.

On Tuesday we returned and arrived at Osborne in the evening. The trip was very agreeable.[12]

That autumn, country and court mourned the death of the eighty-three-year-old Arthur Wellesley, Duke of Wellington, the greatest military hero of the age. Affie left an impressively simple account of the lying-in-state at Chelsea Hospital and the funeral procession:

> I could hardly believe it to be him who was so well merely a few weeks ago. It was very solemn and sad. It was so still that one could not hear any of the guards breathe who were leaning on their arms reversed. On the coffin were his coronet, cocked hat and sword. All his orders were fastened on a velvet pall hanging before the coffin. The windows were hung with black cloth and the only light in the room came from rows of tall candles.
>
> On Thursday the 18th November I saw the funeral procession of the Duke of Wellington from the front windows of Buckingham Palace. First came a battalion of Riflemen and the Royal Marines etc. etc., and then some cavalry and artillery, followed by Heralds and the carriages in which the officers were carrying the batons of the different countries in the armies of which the Duke was a Field Marshall; among which were three of Mama's and then came the band of the Grenadiers and again some Heralds, followed by the Household Trumpeters, and then, under the care of some grenadiers, came the bronze car on which was placed the coffin.[13]

The Journal is shorn of interesting events throughout 1853, and there is no trace of any entries for the following year, but in April 1855 (a month before it comes to an end) Emperor Napoleon and Empress Eugenie of the French paid a state visit to England. Affie describes fondly a military review given in their honour, and on 18 April the gifts each child received:

> ...to Vicky the Emperor gave a picture of a dog in tapestry – to Alice a peepshow which had some views of Paris in it, besides some very pretty landscapes. To Lenchen and Louise a large doll nearly as large as themselves, and a large box of games. To Arthur two tables full of soldiers – to Leopold two figures – a lady playing on a guitar – a doll which is wound up and moves its hands, and a Hussar and Vivandiere of his own regiments, which waltz and both run round the table and play; and to Bertie and me each a small cannon in imitation of the one which he invented himself. After this we were present at the Emperor's Investiture [when the Order of the Garter was conferred on him].[14]

In January 1856 Bertie and Affie attended lectures on metals given by the scientist Michael Faraday at the Royal Institution, as a change from book-learning. Three months later they were taken on a visit to the premises of De La Rue, the postage stamp printers in London. While they were there a special sheet of the 6*d* stamp due for issue later that year was presented to them, and this became the first item in the royal philatelic collection. In due course Affie became extremely interested in the new but already popular hobby, and as the first royal philatelist he began what would become the world's finest collection.

Gibbs was prepared to accept all aspects of the princes' education but one – he did not agree with their enforced isolation from other children. The Queen and Prince Albert always warned their family that they were no better than other boys and girls, but even so they still did not allow them companions from outside as they feared that any early friendships thus formed might have unforeseen consequences in future. Gibbs maintained that such contacts, in moderation, would be of some educational value, if not of psychological worth as well. It has since been suggested that many of the problems of Queen Victoria's children in dealing with other people in adult like sprang from the isolation during their formative years. The princesses always remained very shy, while in addition Vicky and Alice, who both married into families abroad, were inclined to be less than tactful with stupid in-laws, reluctant to suffer fools gladly. As for the princes, they were prone to rush headlong into their newfound freedom when they became adults and make unfortunate friends. Gibbs recognised the potential dangers in a way their parents apparently did not.

A few carefully chosen boys from Eton were invited to visit the royal children at Windsor Castle and Buckingham Palace. It had been decided that Charles Wynne-Carrington, later 3rd Baron Carrington and Marquess of Lincolnshire, would be a suitable friend for Affie, though instead he became Bertie's lifelong companion. His comments, though written several years afterwards, are interesting as the first observations of Affie from outside the domestic circle. 'Prince Alfred was the favourite but I always liked the Prince of Wales far the best. He was a very plucky boy and always ready for fun which often got him into scrapes.'[15] Even allowing for hindsight, this implies that Bertie's personality already had the winning attributes that were to make him friendly and popular, and the more reserved Affie was the opposite.

Prince Alfred was the favourite. It was a perceptive remark, for though he was only nine or ten years old at the time, his gifts had led the Queen and Prince Albert to expect great qualities in him that they could not see in Bertie. Yet for all his faults the Prince of Wales harboured no childish jealousy against his younger brother. Affie was devoted to him, and he was the only one of the children who could draw him into their games, thus keeping him occupied and holding at bay the boredom which was largely responsible for his fits of temper and bullying of the younger ones. This brotherly bond was to last throughout their lives.

Windsor Castle was forever to be associated with formality and even drudgery, but not so Osborne House on the Isle of Wight. Queen Victoria's official holiday residence had been the Royal Pavilion at Brighton, but the town expanded so quickly around the building that by 1840 it no longer afforded any privacy. A country dwelling where the family was within easy reach of London but could still relax was required, and Osborne proved ideal. On purchasing the estate in 1845 they replaced the only 18th-century house with a large mansion, the apartments of which were ready for occupation by September 1846 and the household accommodation a few years later. Apart from their Highland sojourns at Balmoral in Aberdeenshire, they spent as much time at Osborne as the Queen and Albert could spare from state duties.

All the children revelled in the comparative freedom of this island paradise, surrounded by luxurious gardens, open countryside and access to the sea. This last appealed especially to Affie, who loved swimming and going afloat in his father's yacht *Fairy*. When her engine gave trouble he gave a hand with helping to put it right, often with more success than his father. Had he been born about sixty years later, he would have doubtless been the kind of young man always fascinated by cars, ever ready to lift up the bonnet and examine the workings of the engine.

Another Osborne delight was the Swiss Cottage, brought in sections from Switzerland and erected in the grounds as a den, where the princes could learn carpentry and gardening, the princesses housekeeping and cooking. Affie was always useful to his sisters, who found him so good-tempered and helpful, unlike Bertie, when it was time for stoking the stove, carrying water, mending broken crockery, even preparing vegetables when they entertained Mama and Papa to their own meals. When the girls were not working they would watch him teaching the dogs tricks or busying himself at his carpentry bench, toying with an engine or making a model ship. Helena, his junior by twenty-one months, was his favourite sister, and they always remained particularly close. Next to each other in age, they had much in common; she was a tomboy, physically the toughest of the girls, ready to dismiss any brotherly teasing with a sharp punch on the nose. Though only moderate at art, sewing and music, she was good with machines and never minded getting her hands covered in grease or dirt. But all the younger children were devoted to Affie, and he in turn enjoyed keeping them amused. The two youngest children, both born after Lady Lyttelton's retirement, were Leopold, born in April 1853, and Beatrice, four years later.

Surprisingly for someone so mechanically-minded, Affie was also very artistic. All the royal children were encouraged to draw and paint, and his efforts were among the most successful. In May 1855 an exhibition of 'Royal Art' was held in aid of dependants of soldiers fighting at the Crimea. Drawings by him, Alice and Helena realised thirty guineas each, though this hardly compares with the 250 guineas paid for a battlefield scene by Vicky, easily the best painter of all. Three years later he painted a charming watercolour of Osborne from the sea, appropriately with boats in the foreground.

By now Affie was playing the violin, which he learnt secretly in his spare time as a surprise for his parents. In Prince Albert's opinion, nothing better exemplified his son's perseverance than this. When he was thirteen, the Queen's birthday festivities *en famille* included 'Alice and Affie on the violin a little composition of his own – very pretty and of which he is not a little proud'.[16] To the end of his days he treasured his instrument and would play in evenings to friends and relations. However, this was one area in which his talents were sometimes said to be limited, and few would dispute his claim that he was self-taught.

Throughout these early years, Albert sent regular reports on the progress of his second son to brother Ernest, who had to be reminded firmly that on no account could Affie be educated entirely abroad as he would know nothing of his subjects if anything happened to Bertie:

> If we have made a German out of him we shall have given him a great deal to live down, while on the other hand it could be a positive advantage to come from greater matters to the lesser affairs of Coburg.[17]

In spite of Affie's sheltered childhood, there were occasional excitements – and no less than two major events within the space of a month. He was eleven in September 1855 when the family received news at Balmoral that Sebastopol had fallen, one of the few British successes in the otherwise inglorious Crimean war. A bonfire had been prepared at Craig Gowan in anticipation of this event the previous year, and abandoned with regret. On 10 September it was lit in rejoicing, and Affie and also five-year-old Arthur were woken to watch this victory blaze on the mountain, where at midnight the elders 'performed a veritable witches' dance', inevitably 'supported by whisky'.[18]

Four days later they welcomed Prince Frederick William ('Fritz') of Prussia to the Highlands. The shy handsome young man had already been once to Britain, accompanying his parents as guests at the Great Exhibition in 1851. Now he wished to see Scotland, as Albert coyly informed the Duchess of Kent, but members of the 'older royal family' were not deceived. Nor was the satirical journal *Punch*, which noted that 'the bird of ill-omen has an eye towards Her Majesty's dove-cote'. By the end of the month Affie knew that Vicky, not yet fifteen, was betrothed.

Though she would soon be leaving the family circle, Affie would be the next to go. In the sweeping and rather cold-hearted style of the day, time was approaching when he would be 'set up in a separate establishment'.

CHAPTER 2

'A Passion for the Navy' 1856-60

In April 1856 Prince Albert informed Baron Stockmar that 'a great load' had been 'taken off his heart'. Lieutenant John Cowell of the Royal Engineers, aged twenty-three, had been chosen to superintend Affie's training for the Navy. He would join the royal household immediately 'to learn the workings of our system', and then take up his quarters with Affie at Royal Lodge, Windsor Park, during the summer. The purpose of this separation was twofold. Affie could study under a special tutor for his profession without interruption, and he would be kept away from Bertie, whose influence Albert felt was harmful.

Ernest viewed this development with suspicion, fearing his nephew's desire for the Royal Navy would make him disinclined to succeed to the duchy. The service would not be appropriate training for the 'limited quiet atmosphere of a small German court' or, he might have added, the soul-destroying boredom which Affie would find there one day to his cost. Albert had to pacify his brother in a long letter, undated but probably written early in 1857, recognising the problem but pointing out that the boy would not be swayed. The naval career was

a passion which we, as his parents, believe not to have the right to subdue. It is certainly not right to break the spontaneous wish of a young spirit.... He has a great inclination for natural history and mechanics and all that belongs to it. We gave him an Engineering officer as instructor, hoping to interest him in this branch, but his love for the Blue Jackets always turned up again, and always with greater force. With the remarkable perseverance this child possesses, it is not to be expected that he will give up the idea easily. An example of his perseverance is his violin, which he learnt to play secretly, in his free time, wishing to surprise us. He will not give it up any more. He gives every free moment to his mechanical constructions.[1]

In the Navy, he continued, Affie would see the world, and 'become more generally competent' than if he stayed at home or in Germany. If he was 'made a German', it would be extremely difficult for him should he succeed to the British throne, as Albert knew from bitter experience.

Affie and Cowell moved into Royal Lodge in June 1856. What had been a damp, dismal cottage in Hanoverian days had recently been renovated, because it reminded Albert of his beloved birthplace, Schloss Rosenau in Coburg. Before Osborne was 'discovered', it was considered as a country retreat for the Queen. Nevertheless its poky, stifling little rooms were too uncomfortable to be endured for long. Later they moved to a larger house, Alverbank, near Gosport, near the Isle of Wight and within reasonable distance of Portsmouth, heart of the navy. Here Affie studied under a retired naval chaplain, the Reverend William Rowe Jolley, who coached him in geometry and mathematics. At the same time he attended instruction in seamanship and navigation under Captain Robert Harris on board the two-deck training ship *Illustrious*, moored off Haslar Creek at Portsmouth.

Interruptions to this routine were rare. But in April 1857 he was sent to Geneva to improve his French, and in order to placate Ernest, Albert allowed him to spend a few days at the ancestral home. Affie returned to England full of enthusiasm for Coburg and the kindness of Uncle Ernest and Aunt Alexandrine, and his verbal accounts of what he had seen and done there made Albert feel more than usually homesick.

It was with his Coburg future in mind that Albert, who was created Prince Consort in June 1857, introduced Affie at Balmoral that autumn into the basic principles of methodical estate management. Together father and son looked at the problems of redesigning old farms, replacing bothies with stone cottages, making new tracks and keeping old ones in good repair, putting up fencing, and reclaiming marsh and waste land for agricultural use. For relaxation they went shooting and stalking together.

When they left Balmoral for Osborne and Windsor, Affie asked his father if he would teach him as he had taught Vicky. Albert had intended to introduce him to these lessons in due course, but he was delighted that his son should take the initiative in asking. Though Affie was no bookworm, and his quick thinking and concentration did not match those of his remarkable sister, he still proved himself an excellent pupil, always keen to learn. It would be unfair to charge Albert with favouritism, for Arthur and Leopold were much too young to share the activities of their father and second brother, but if he had a 'favourite son', Affie was obviously the one. At least the duchy would eventually be in good hands, he believed, even if the British Empire was to be the inheritance of 'poor Bertie'.

Affie had begun writing regularly to Aunt Alexandrine since shortly after taking his leave of her and Ernest that spring, and in December he wrote from Alverbank:

I wish you many happy returns of your birthday, & may you live to see many, many more. I hope that you and dear Uncle are quite well and have enjoyed yourselves at the 'Rifs'; did Uncle Ernest have good sport? When I was in Scotland I shot my first stag and my first roe dear. I am hard at work preparing for my examination & I have very little time for writing letters; I will give you some ice dried flowers when you come for Vicky's marriage; you do come do you not?[2]

Over Christmas and the new year, the nine children and their parents were together for what would be the last time. On 25 January 1858 Vicky and Fritz were married at St James's Chapel, and they left for Prussia a week later. Bertie and Affie accompanied the Prince Consort and the young couple on that heartrending journey from Windsor, braving the bitter February snow in an open carriage so that well-wishers might wave them goodbye, to embark upon the royal yacht at Gravesend. All the family were deeply affected, the boys weeping bitterly on their ride back while Albert was too overcome with emotion to say a word, until Affie unintentionally brought a sad smile to their faces as he exclaimed through his tears that Vicky was so fond of the Navy.

After the wedding festivities Affie returned to his studies at Alverbank. The Queen was pleased that her 'dear, good, clever promising child' was not too far away for her to see regularly. Only occasionally did he let her down, as on the occasion when he forgot to congratulate his parents on their eighteenth wedding anniversary. 'Naughty Affie took no notice whatever of the day till I telegraphed to him to ask if he remembered what day it was!'[4] she wrote to Vicky. But it was still quite an occasion when he was allowed to come and spend the afternoon with his parents and siblings at Osborne. In May she wrote to Vicky of a grand tea they had enjoyed at the Swiss Cottage – 'and imagine good Affie by way of amusement exhibiting his air pump and steam engine (puffing and blowing all the time – in the tool house) to Grandmama, the others and the little Greys [the children of the Prince Consort's private secretary, Lieutenant General Charles Grey] – and pumping over himself and Arthur!'[5] The Prince Consort was in Coburg at the time, and discovered that the boy was 'much talked about here, and that the people have taken a great fancy to him.'

During the summer Affie had a first brief taste of his chosen life on a cruise to Ireland, on which he was very sick and 'much teased about it'. By August he was considered sufficiently advanced to take his naval entrance examination. His parents were visiting Germany at the time and arrived home at Dover on 31 August. At Portsmouth they were told that he had passed with very high marks; he had gone to report to his first ship HMS *Euryalus*, and would meet them at Osborne. He came to see them as they disembarked at the private pier, dressed 'in his middie's jacket, cap and dirk, half-blushing, and looking very happy', reported the proud father. 'He is a little pulled from these three days' hard examination.'[6]

A few days later the Prince Consort sent his son's written papers to the Prime Minister, Lord Derby, commenting that he solved the mathematical problems almost all without fault, and managed the translations without a dictionary. On returning them, Derby remarked how grateful he was 'that no such examination was necessary to qualify Her Majesty's Ministers for their offices, as it would very seriously increase the difficulty of forming an administration.'[7]

From Osborne, Affie wrote proudly to Aunt Alexandrine that his exam pass was 'a great load off my heart, and (I) have now got the two letters R.N. fixed to the end of my name as the old maids say that it is all right now because I have come back to the Royal Nursery.'[8]

Following his initial appointment to *Euryalus* he was granted six weeks' special leave. Part was spent shooting at Balmoral and the rest in Germany with Vicky who was pregnant for the first time, very homesick and far from comfortable at the stiff Prussian court. She was thrilled to have her brother with her again, and although she was expecting her first child at the time, they were almost like small children again, playing merrily around the gloomy corridors of Babelsberg Palace. They also went riding and taking picnics, boating on the Havel, exploring historic Berlin together, and playing croquet. Queen Victoria chided her gently for indulging the lad in his 'aquatic propensities'. What did she mean by letting him on the water so much, 'making a fool of himself as I fear he has done, by playing the sailor on the Havel' at Babelsberg?[9] Why was she not making sure that he was sampling Teutonic culture to the full, which he would need to counterbalance the philistine life which he would undoubtedly be leading very soon when he went away to sea?

Within a fortnight scolding had given way to irritation, mingled with sadness, at Affie's imminent departure. The Queen had been 'shamefully deceived' about the plans made for him. Her second son, she said, was

> to go away for many months and I shall not see him God knows! When, and Papa is most cruel upon the subject. I assure you, it is much better to have no children than to have them only to give them up! It is too wretched.[10]

Papa may have been 'most cruel', but it was with a heavy heart that he and Bertie accompanied Affie to Spithead on 27 October. Sobbing bitterly, the fourteen-year-old cadet was escorted to *Euryalus* by pinnace, while his father and brother watched from ashore until they could no longer see her tall masts against the darkening summer skies. To Albert the departure of 'the second child lost to our family circle in one year' was 'another great trial'.[11]

HMS *Euryalus* was a screw steam frigate of 400 horsepower, armed with 50 guns, commanded by Captain John Tarleton who had previously served in the East Indies and North America. As she sailed down channel for the Mediterranean, calling in at Gibraltar *en route* to land mail from home, Affie had a first prolonged taste of life on the ocean wave. Cowell reported back to the Queen and the Prince Consort that he was a bright, amiable, capable junior officer; the cheerfulness and inability to be bored as a youngster had prepared him well for the service. Doubtless he was contented, even a little bewitched by this, his very own achievement, but not yet counting his blessings in escaping from the drudgery that was to be his elder brother's lot.

From his parents' point of view, if not his own, Affie was fortunate never to see active service in wartime. Britain was enjoying a long age of peace, lasting from the post-Napoleonic era to the Boer campaigns, interrupted only by the brief Crimean war. This last conflict had proved the ineffectiveness of the Royal Navy's wooden warships, which could not stand up to prolonged shellfire. The service therefore launched the world's first ironclad warship, *Warrior*, in 1860.

But Affie soon learnt that being a 'snotty' was no bed of roses. Royal orders had decreed that Prince Alfred had to be treated exactly as the rest of the crew, and he was given no respite from the primitive conditions endured by the other midshipmen, and there was no question of showing any privileges to him while they were afloat. Space was cramped, with a tiny hammock for bed in quarters that must have seemed more like a dog kennel after the comforts he had left behind him. Privacy there was none, and the often coarse, brutal treatment of his mess mates and senior officers had to be borne in silence. The navy was not distinguished for making gentlemen out of royalty, and in an earlier generation Affie's great-uncle Prince William Henry, later Duke of Clarence and King William IV, had been described by his fastidious elder brother Frederick, Duke of York, as 'unpolished, excessively rough and rude' after a long spell at sea. The food at sea was appalling and Affie often went hungry. As there was no refrigeration on board, any fresh rations were soon eaten. There was cocoa and biscuit for breakfast; salt-beef and duff, or salt-pork, and pea-soup for dinner; and tea and biscuits for supper. The biscuits were neatly always full of maggots which had to be knocked out before each meal, hence a weekly 'Maggot Derby' in which the snotties raced their pets, kept in pill-boxes and trained to compete against each other on the mess table. Small scuttles were let into the side of the ship for air and daylight, but they were so grimy that lamps or 'pursers dips' in the tops of old gin bottles had to be kept lit all day. The Queen was surely unaware of such conditions when she complained to Vicky that his letters were 'too shockingly and disgracefully written'.

One wonders if Affie, like his companions, ever affixed pictures of his relations inside the top of his sea-chest. Was ever a likeness of Her Majesty in such an insignificant position? One snotty of the time had a pin-up of Psyche in her bath, and stood proudly beside his open chest on rounds one morning. 'What's that?' rapped his commander. 'My sister, sir,' came the innocent reply. Rather startled, the commander continued his rounds in silence.

Affie too had to learn to be quick on the uptake. Once when coming alongside, Number One on the fo'c'sle was having some difficulty mooring up. The captain sent a snotty down to ask how much longer it would take. The snotty returned to say, 'About five minutes, sir.' Twenty minutes later the boy was sent down again. Number One's bull-like roar was blown back to the bridge: 'Tell that bloody captain if I get any more tomfool messages from him I'll come and boot him off the bridge.' The snotty came back to report: 'First Lieutenant nearly finished, sir.' 'Come here, boy,' said the captain. 'Was that what the First Lieutenant really said?' 'Words to that effect, sir.' 'You'll go a long way, my boy,' the captain replied.

By the end of December 1858 *Euryalus* had reached Malta. At Windsor the newspaper reports of Affie's reception were studied with interest, though the Queen thought *The Times* rather impudent at thinking 'fit to disapprove him being properly loyally received'. It wished that he might

> learn his profession – not in a vapid, half-and-half, Royal Highness kind of way. He was sent out to be trained to salt water, and it is upon rose water that his first lesson in navigation is taking place. What has a Middy to do with royal receptions, and royal salutes and royal fiddle-faddles of every description?....He was greeted by the slogan 'Viva Alfredo'. But why not 'Viva Midshipman Easy'?[12]

The other midshipmen were equally indignant at the Malta harbour authorities greeting Affie with a royal salute, and expressed their feelings by picking him up and bumping him as each cannon was fired. Whether he complained home, or whether the leader-writer's remarks had already bitten deep enough, is uncertain, but the end result was the same. The Queen issued an order forbidding any further salutes in her son's honour for the time being.

Yet if there were disadvantages in being a prince of the blood, there were benefits too. The Coburgs were never slow to exploit ways of making or saving money, and in selling Mama's letters Affie was to prove himself no exception. Apparently he placed a higher value on some than on others, and the story goes that he waved a particular one (the contents of which it would be interesting to know) in front of his mates, declaring that they should give him £5 for it, as there was 'such a *lot* of good advice in it'.[13]

As a unit of the Mediterranean Fleet, *Euryalus* spent much of the following year carrying out normal exercises with the other ships. This enabled Affie to train as a naval officer when not visiting foreign ports, a programme arranged partly for his education (as a future sovereign duke, if not a future king) and partly to show the Queen's son off around the world. On 26 April he wrote to Aunt Alexandrine from Rhodes, an island off the coast of Turkey:

> Since I write to you last which I think was from Gibraltar [a letter which has not survived] I have been in Morocco, Malta, Tunis, Egypt, Palestine and Syria. The most interesting of all the expedition was that to Jerusalem and all through Palestine which Journey was entirely performed on horseback and sleeping in tents being sometimes 16 hours in the saddle. I send you some dried flowers from some of the places which I visited to your collection...[14]

At this time the shadow of war hung over him, as France and Austria were about to cross swords over Italian territory. 'Poor dear boy he may see fire before long!'[15] lamented the Queen. But the French army defeated the Austrians in a lightning campaign and declared peace, and Britain was spared the prospect of involvement in a more widespread conflict.

In February 1860 *Euryalus* sailed home into Portsmouth. Despite the arguments over Affie's reception at Malta, the Queen was determined that he should be greeted by a royal salute. The port authorities baulked at paying him such an honour, fearing the right royal wrath, but they could hardly disobey their sovereign's orders. It was therefore suggested to the Prince Consort, blissfully unaware of such plans, that he should join the ship and accompany his son onto land. A salute could thus be fired without any awkward questions being asked.

After passing his midshipman's examination, again with such high marks that his father could barely find fault with the written papers, Affie was to be prepared for confirmation. The Queen was overjoyed to have him home again. Letter after letter to Vicky dwelt on his capacity for hard work, her delight in having him back, and the 'sad contrast' between him and his elder brother.

Affie was confirmed at Windsor on Maundy Thursday (as were all his brothers and sisters – in this case, 5 April). His examination by a naval chaplain, the Reverend William Onslow, later rector of Sandringham, passed off very satisfactorily. True to form, he was 'much impressed' and shed many an emotional tear. He kept to his room all day and only came to wish his parents good morning before breakfast. The Queen was profoundly moved as she wrote to Vicky of 'the young sailor, inured to life; its trials and hardships – its dangers and temptations who has been in foreign lands and to the Holy Sepulchre itself – standing there before the altar.'[16]

On 2 May he sailed again, this time as a genuine royal ambassador. Throughout her life Queen Victoria never set foot outside Europe, but she was adept at sending members of the family to various corners of the globe in order that the monarchy should be seen – and her second son was destined to travel furthest of all. In a few months' time he was to lay the foundation stone of the breakwater for a new harbour at Cape Town, while the Prince of Wales was to open the St Lawrence Bridge in Canada.

'What a cheering picture is here of the progress and expansion of the British race, and of the useful co-operation of the Royal Family in the civilisation which England has developed and advanced!'wrote the Prince Consort to Stockmar on 27 April. 'In both these young colonies, our children are looked for with great affection, and conscious national pride.'[17]

After his short peaceful interlude at Windsor, Affie's return to HMS *Euryalus* and the lengthy voyage was indeed, as one admiral likened it, tantamount to being 'pitchforked into a den of ravening thieves'. On board it made little difference for prince or commoner alike. Between them Cowell and Tarleton had to ensure that he was worked hard, with little respite from keeping watch, scrubbing decks, painting, coaling and going aloft, in addition to learning seamanship and marine engineering.

It was at this time that Affie really came into his own. Now almost sixteen, he felt more at home than before in the navy, and he thoroughly enjoyed being feted in port – as would any boy of his tender years – even if sometimes he was not there 'officially'. These visits to places that had once been mere names on the large globes and maps of is schoolroom made life afloat much more tolerable.

HMS *Euryalus* had tossed her way across the southern seas for over two months when the look-out sighted land ahead. There, rearing its singularly awe-inspiring bulk, was the flat massive of Table Mountain, a backcloth to the beautiful curve of Table Bay and the city at its feet. The name Cape of Good Hope was a familiar one to Affie from geography lessons, but to those on board and anyone who had sailed in those waters, the old name Cape of Storms was more appropriate. On 24 July the ship dropped anchor at the naval base of Simonstown, in False Bay – despite its name, a much more sheltered place with proper facilities. As they boarded the frigate, the harbourmaster was surprised to discover that the duty midshipman waiting at the gangway to receive him was the prince himself. There followed several consultations with Cowell. What should his young charge say, and when? Should he keep his cap on when three cheers were called for the Queen? Should he wear his gloves the whole time?

This was the first British royal visit to South Africa, and it would be the precursor to several more in years to come. Cape Town went wild in its welcome. The mixed population – families of colonists from nearly every European country, especially Britain and the Netherlands, Hottentots, Malays and Chinese – all vied with each other to make it a visit to be remembered for many a year. July was midwinter in that part of the world, and Affie's arrival coincided with a sparkling, champagne-like day when everything glinted and shone, from the bridles and horses of his official carriage to the choppy waves in the bay. The drive onto Cape Town was over too soon. Bowing and smiling, cap in hand, he alighted in one of the still gracious suburbs of Claremont – a name from home. From there he rode into the city on horseback, through streets seething with people and decorations.

Having no precedent, the city fathers had gone to considerable trouble during the preceding months to ensure that everything was *en fête* for their illustrious visitor. Never was there such a show of precariously-tottering triumphal arches, forests of flags (any that were available, regardless of national design, appear to have sufficed), tattered bunting swathed around anything vertical or horizontal, masses of flowers, deafening eternal salutes, clanging of church bells, speeches and dreadful verses, eternal presentations, bands, parties, balls, luncheons and dinners. A splendid wardrobe of costly stinkwood had been made for use in Affie's bedroom at Government House.

Two pieces of music had been composed specially: *The Prince Alfred Polka*, and the *Euryalus Schottische*, dedicated to the officers and members of the Cape Town Rifles. By the time he left Cape Town, Affie must have known these tunes by heart after having heard them performed so many times. There was also a *Prince Alfred Grand March*, dedicated to him 'By Permission' which must have made him very proud. This last was in honour of his visit to the Paarl, then a Boer stronghold. Though Cowell might have entertained reservations as to the reception such a potentially hostile area would give him, the people were determined not to be outdone by the rest and opened their hospitable doors wide to this chubby, blue-eyed youngster and his entourage – and its bottles. Paarl was, and is still, noted for its excellent wine, and it was probably here that Affie began to sample the delights of the grape.

Before his official task at the breakwater, he was taken up country to see the neighbouring republics, the Orange Free State and the Transvaal, as well as the eastern borders of Basutoland and Natal. Like Bertie in Canada, Affie was being used politically, but on each trip he won the hearts of all. He was even pronounced the Child of Heaven by a group of 'barbarians waving assegais in the usual tribal rush', doubtless an unnerving experience to any European seated yards away. One dreads to think of the ragging he must have had on board ship afterwards.

In the Free State Affie rode around on horseback and by wagon. Sensibly he changed his short jacket and naval attire for a proper hunting coat, breeches and top boots. A photograph of him in this outfit might equally have been taken at Balmoral, if it was not for the cart and his rough indigenous 'staff'. Here he took part in what was known at the time as a magnificent hunt – and would be recognised today as nothing short of downright slaughter – of wild game. His party shot over six hundred head, 'all larger than horses'. In all, a bag of over 1,000 head of game was proudly reported by one of the huntsmen. Like most of the family, Affie was even at that age a very accomplished shot. In Africa he had to be, for hitting one's target in the endless veldt was far harder than at home.

Travelling south again, Affie visited Durban, and then East London and Port Elizabeth, where he celebrated his sixteenth birthday, with the usual repetition of all the festivities which had greeted him in Cape Town. At Port Elizabeth one of his hosts was a Mrs Kettle. He politely asked her whether she had boys or girls in her family. 'Oh, boys,' she replied eagerly, adding that all her little kettles 'had spouts'.

For a fuller account of his sojourn in the town, posterity is indebted to an unknown housewife, whose letter – for all its style of writing, pronunciation and spelling – is practically hysterical with excitement and wants her recipient to share in their fun to the full. A trifle incoherently she wrote that 'the little middie was a thorough triumph', but thought that he was being worked too hard on his birthday. After the usual addresses when he came ashore, 'at one o'clock he held a levee at three he went to the museum at four he laid the foundation stone of the church that was a very imposing sight and it was a very long time I never saw such a crowd in my life. It was such wether – but to our joy it gently cleared away and after we had very fine wether.' There were six or seven arches and 'the multitude went out to meet him and we all got places very near.... Thousands appeared to rush forwards at his approach....There were 3,000 school children....with Banners of silk....all white gold letters the sight was imposing and told well of the Prince. In the square the daies was very Handsome....ten steps carpeted out on the ground below couches chairs of rosewood velvet. The Prince I should say went down amongst the people ten times. He planted an oak in front of the daies.' Tickets for the grand ball that night cost £3, a formidable sum in those days. 'Each gentleman could take two ladies....three hundred sat down to Supper at one time.' Apologetically she referred to the city's 'illuminations which were all that could be done with our gass.' The prince had a 'cavalry guard-of-honour who look well. He received the address made his reply and passed on Bouncing (?) as only a Child like himself could do all the way through the throng high.'[18]

On 17 September Affie was back in Cape Town for the main purpose of his African travels. A large crowd of spectators watched on shore as he titled over a truckload of rocks with a specially-inscribed silver trowel, to form the foundations of the Table Bay Breakwater. Though in time he would perform dozens of similar duties laying foundation stones and the like, he took this first example very seriously. To see tons of rock careering over the side at a single touch of his gloved hand was a strange experience, reflected in the preoccupied look on his face captured by a photographer. To this day, the occasion is remembered by the naming of the Alfred Basin and Alfred Docks in Cape Town.

Next day he opened the Cape Town Public Library, now simply the South African Library. A stately, classical building in the gardens at the foot of Table Mountain, it was to become one of the most famous libraries in the world. Shortly afterwards, the people of Cape Town raised a public subscription which enabled the artist F. R. Say to paint Affie's portrait, which still looks down on 'his' room. Many a young researcher has gazed up into his blue eyes, while branches of oaks outside, mere saplings when he was there, brush gently against the windows.

A day later *Euryalus* set sail once more for England. His hosts were sorry to see the Prince depart. 'In their eyes,' wrote Sir George Grey, Governor of Cape Town, 'the most admirable of all the many things they saw was the sight of a number of hardy barefooted lads assisting at daybreak in washing the decks, foremost among them in activity was the son of the Queen of England.'[19]

On 9 November Affie arrived at Portsmouth, and later that week Bertie returned from Canada. After a joyful family reunion at Windsor, the Queen wrote glowingly to Uncle Leopold about the fascinating accounts of his expeditions, to say nothing of animal trophies and photographs. Cowell had given an excellent report of him; 'He is really such a dear, gifted, handsome child, that it makes one doubly anxious that he should have as few failings as mortal men can have.'[19]

To his already considerable skills Affie had just added another, that of the then infant science of photography. The Prince Consort had engaged a professional photographer, Frederick York, to show him the rudiments before his journey to South Africa so that he could have something to occupy his mind apart from navigation and seamanship during his leisure hours, and enrich royal photograph albums at the same time. Perhaps he felt that his young companions would take more kindly to the sight of Affie with camera in hand than the sounds of a violin at his elbow. At any rate he became an enthusiastic amateur, and before long he could undertake the processing himself.

December 1860 was the coldest of the century so far. With twenty-eight degrees of frost, there was skating and ice-hockey for all at Windsor. Festivities were kept in the German fashion as usual, with presents laid out on tables and distributed on Christmas Eve to family and servants alike.

But one shadow had already fallen to mar the gaiety. In September the Prince Consort's stepmother had died. Though it was with a characteristic sense of world-weariness that he sent his customary new year greetings to Baron Stockmar – 'may you have every reason to be satisfied with 1861' – nobody could have foreseen quite how ironic those words would appear within twelve months.

After Christmas Affie visited Ernest and Alexandrine at Coburg, and then spent a short time with Vicky and Fritz at Berlin. They saw him onto the train on new year's eve before hurrying to the deathbed of their pitifully insane invalid uncle, the childless King Frederick William IV of Prussia. Though his demise was a merciful release from his twilight existence, it was but a prelude to two deaths which were shortly to strike at the very heart of the family, and directly at the security and happiness in which Affie had been born and raised.

CHAPTER 3

'Day turned into night' 1861–66

For Affie, the year 1861 opened promisingly enough. On 8 January he was appointed to HMS *George*, a 90-gun screw steamship commanded by Captain Francis Egerton. She left Devonport a week later on 'particular service', a term applied to certain seagoing ships not attached to any specific naval station. For a while she cruised in the English Channel, then went to join the North American and West Indies station, commanded by Rear-Admiral Sir Alexander Milne. Though this was less important than that of the Mediterranean, Affie was thrilled to be cruising in the same historic waters that Drake, Nelson and other British naval heroes had themselves sailed.

The news of Affie's safe arrival at Barbados in March after heavy winter gales coincided with the last hours of his grandmother the Duchess of Kent. Her death overwhelmed the Queen, whose severe nervous prostration added to the burdens of her already desperately overworked and prematurely ageing husband. Not the least of his problems was trying to counter rumours spreading throughout Europe that she had taken after her grandfather King George III and become mentally unhinged.

Writing to Ernest on 6 August, Albert commented how his second son, whose seventeenth birthday it was, had become 'a dear fellow and very agreeable in society and always ready to learn and get on. He may become a very excellent man, but he will have to go through a hard school if he is not to perish in spite of all his good qualities,'[1] There is a disturbing air of finality in these words, as if the Prince Consort had a premonition that he was about to see him for the last time and was subconsciously wishing him well for a future in which he would be deprived of paternal guidance.

Twelve days later Affie arrived at Osborne, and they all went north to Balmoral for one last glorious holiday. The Queen had been utterly miserable since her mother's death, and the Prince Consort was under increasing strain, but in Scotland their spirits lifted temporarily as they and their children savoured the joys of the Scottish Highlands.

For Affie, these four weeks of leave sped swiftly by, and on 20 September he sailed from Liverpool for the American station once more. He never saw his father again. For the weary Prince Albert, the deaths from typhoid of two Coburg cousins in Portugal during November and an affair of Bertie's at the Curragh military camp in Ireland, which he only learnt of from Stockmar in Germany after it had become common knowledge throughout the courts of Europe, were the final blows.

Affie was several thousand miles away on 14 December, the night that his father succumbed to typhoid, or possibly stomach cancer, at Windsor Castle. Apart from Vicky, who was convalescing at Berlin from pneumonia, Affie was the only one of the children absent from home. Although he did not arrive back until February 1862, nearly two months after the funeral, he was granted an extended period of compassionate leave.

Affie had been stunned by his father's death. Both had shared a common bond in their love for Coburg, for the boy had discovered on his visits to the duchy that he found the same feelings of contentment and tranquility at Rosenau that Albert had experienced at a similar age. It distressed him even more that his father had died while they were so far apart, and that he did not know exactly what had happened except from second-hand accounts of the last few hours. Moreover there was nowhere on the ship where he could give full rein to his grief and healing tears, no brothers or sisters with whom to share the burden of misery. Even Cowell, devoted and sympathetic as he was, could be no more than a substitute for the family.

The widowed Queen Victoria was likewise shattered, having earnestly hoped and prayed in happier days never to survive her husband. Now she was certain that she would soon follow him. For several days after his death she had refused to see anybody by her lady-in-waiting and her daughters Alice and 'baby' Beatrice. Bertie, she was convinced, had broken his father's heart, and at first she could hardly bear the sight of him. He was sent packing on a tour of the Holy Land after the funeral with almost indecent haste.

By the time Affie was home she had got over the worst paroxysms of grief, but the change which had come over the once happy home astonished him. Life there was now 'day turned into night', as she wrote under one of the several family groups photographed in mourning beside a bust of the Late Lamented at this time. Affie was too young to understand and appreciate full what she was going through, even though his own sense of loss was hardly less than hers, and his reluctance to observe every little detail of mourning sadly began to drive mother and son apart. At the age of seventeen he was almost an adult, and with the resilience of the young and hardy he understood that life had to go on for those left behind. He felt that she was taking matters a shade too far every time she reproached him for whistling, laughing or playing his violin, as if he was a disobedient little child. It was useless to argue that he too missed Papa desperately and was not trying to be heartless, but all the longing in the world could not bring him back. In view of the way in which the Queen had sung his praises only months earlier, and considering the deep affinity which had existed between father and son, it was ironic that Affie's brave attempts to be cheerful should have irked her so much.

Nevertheless he gratified her by sobbing bitterly throughout the wedding of Alice to Prince Louis of Hesse on 1 July. The melancholy little ceremony took place privately in the dining room at Osborne House, beneath Winterhalter's portrait of the Queen, and the Prince Consort with the five elder children, painted in 1846. Though the prince was gone, his spirit – represented in the painting, and by the general feeling of gloom and desolation – somehow dominated the occasion. The Queen looked upon all weddings after his death as 'terrible moments', and she was determined that this would be no exception. 'After a great struggle,' she recorded in her journal with a hint of self-congratulation, she was calm throughout.

No sooner was one wedding accomplished than another loomed on the horizon. In September 1861 Bertie and 'Alix', Princess Alexandra of Denmark, had met in Germany at a rendezvous carefully arranged by Vicky who thought she might make a suitable Princess of Wales. Alix had been considered by the family as long ago as December 1860, when even the Prince Consort had declared that, after seeing her picture, he would 'marry her at once'. Since Bertie's 'fall', the Queen was adamant that his only moral salvation lay in marriage as soon as possible. On the strength of Alix's photographs alone, Affie made no secret of his wish to marry her himself if his strangely hesitant elder brother declined her. Should this be the case, the Queen was prepared to recommend Affie becoming engaged to her within the next three years. In the event such speculation was futile, for in September 1862 Bertie and Alix were officially betrothed.

During the spring of 1862, even before Bertie had made his mind up about Alix, Queen Victoria was beginning to look at the possible brides for Affie. Vicky was keen that he should be given a chance to consider Alix's sister Dagmar, but the Queen would not hear of it. She did not wish her to be kept for Affie, as she disliked the idea of two brothers marrying two sisters. There had already been such an outcry in Germany against Bertie's 'anti-German' marriage that it would never do for the future Duke of Saxe-Coburg to take the second sister, as it 'would be really courting abuse and enmity'.[2] In any case, she knew Tsar Alexander II was considering his eldest son, Tsarevich Nicholas, as a bridegroom for her; 'let the Emperor have her.'

Just as Bertie had thus begun to redeem himself in the eyes of his Mama, Affie cast another shadow over her dark existence. Soon after rejoining HMS *George* in July and reaching Malta, he followed in the family tradition of his ducal uncle, elder brother and Hanoverian great-uncles, and succumbed to the temptation of the opposite sex. In view of the other midshipmen's behaviour, and lack of other leisure facilities on the island, it would probably have been a greater cause for concern had he not had an affair – if indeed matters went this far. If ever girl loves a sailor, as it is said, what girl could resist a handsome eighteen-year-old royal tar? For his part, Affie was doubtless swept off his feet by many a young beauty. Compared with Bertie who paid many a private visit in a closed cab at dead of night in London, Affie was reasonably safe abroad. But he was certainly not immune from the gossipmongers whose chatter got back to the Queen and spread around Europe like wildfire. She was shocked by his 'heartless and dishonourable behaviour', and it was left to the ever-understanding Vicky, so often the peacemaker when family differences arose, to smooth matters over. 'How could Affie be such a goose, to play such a silly trick and stand in his own light?' she wrote to the Queen 'I feel so pained to think that he should have been so thoughtless as to add to your grief by misbehavior. It is so disheartening as he had been going on so well in every respect, and is such a darling.'[3]

When he returned to Osborne on leave, the long-suffering Cowell was immediately sent for. After consulting him the Queen was much impressed with his 'noble conduct in remaining with Affie and touching grief about Affie only bring back too vividly all the agonies and miseries of last November.' Her son had no excuse, and could not even 'give utterance ever to anything'. It was hardly surprising for a young man of his age practically insensible with nerves, facing the right royal wrath and aura of an angry Mama, who had the gift of freezing at ten yards. Fortunately she could forgive, to the extent that he was 'quieter and subdued – and such an amiable companion' only three days later. However it was with tremendous relief, for mother and son in equal measure, that he left that same week for Lisbon and the Mediterranean Fleet once more.

Affie's indiscretion had come at a most inopportune moment, for the Queen was then embroiled in discussions with her ministers about an extraordinary affair of very different complexion. She had been utterly dependent on her husband, even to the extent of letting him draft her official letters and choose her bonnets. Within less than a year of losing such guidance forever, she was confronted with a situation that would have taxed even his powers of thought to a considerable degree.

In 1830 the crown of newly-independent Greece was offered to the then Prince Leopold of Saxe-Coburg, who rejected it although he accepted the Belgian crown in hardly dissimilar circumstances a year later. The Greeks accordingly chose Prince Otto of Bavaria instead. Too pro-German in outlook, surrounding himself exclusively with Bavarian troops and advisers, he had made no genuine effort to endear himself to his subjects. In October 1862 they rebelled against his rule and he fled, abdicating in favour of his brother Leopold. The revolutionary leaders and provisional government rejected the latter, at the same time making clear their intentions of 'adhering to the monarchical form of rule'. The protecting powers of Britain, France and Russia, who had established and undertaken to respect the sovereignty and independence of Greece, were asked to nominate another King. Under the terms of the 1830 London protocol, members of these ruling powers' families were ineligible, although they were slow to acknowledge the fact.

As early as 29 October, it was rumoured in Greece that 'a son of Queen Victoria' was to be chosen, and on 18 November *The Times*' Trieste correspondent noted that 'the choice of Prince Alfred for the Greek throne is regarded as certain'. Even before the revolution, he had been mentioned as a possible successor to the childless Otto, and the consul of Greece in Corfu had proposed his nomination. Though Affie himself was little known, the advantages of choosing a British prince were inestimable. Much capital and prestige, it was assumed, would follow him into his new kingdom. Moreover the Greeks, according to Lord Palmerston, were 'panting for increase of territory'. They apparently believed that Britain would make King Alfred a coronation gift of the Ionian Islands, a British protectorate since 1815, and persuade the Turks to add Epirus and Thessaly to their territories. Britain's friendship with and support of Turkey as a bulwark against Russian expansion was legendary.

On 24 November *The Times* published a letter signed 'Digamma':

> The choice of (Prince Alfred) annihilates the bugbear of Russian preponderance, and offers the surest guarantee against aggression on Turkey. It can scarce be doubted that the latter feels the inefficiency of her sway over Epirus and Thessaly, nor that she would be glad to see those districts in hands which would not make them the fulcrum of further invasion. The ambitious designs of Russia on Turkey would render a Greek kingdom under a Russian Prince as insecure a tenure as Turkey itself, and indicate projects of territorial aggrandizement which could not be charged against an English dynasty.[4]

Though it was unlikely that his views would have varied much weight with the politicians, it can be assumed that Affie was extremely worried at the prospect. Flattering as it was to be offered the crown, he was as personally committed to the Navy and eventually to Coburg. Moreover, what the volatile Greeks had done to Otto, they could just as easily do to King Alfred. More than ever he missed the father whom he would have so readily consulted. Despite her grief the Queen was of similar mind; 'she could not understand why people seemed to think there was the *possibility* of Prince Alfred to accept the Crown, and she wished it to be contradicted.'[5] The Prince Consort would have agreed. In 1849 he had dismissed a proposal that the Saxon and Thuringian states of Germany should form a federation and ask for his second son, then not quite five years old, to be their king. Though circumstances were now different, he would never have welcomed such an interruption to the young man's career.

Thankfully for all concerned, the British government made it plain that Prince Alfred had to decline the vacant throne. After the candidature of Russia's nominee Nicolas, Duke of Leuchtenberg (a nephew of Tsar Alexander II, who had received over 2,000 votes in the plebiscite), had likewise been declared invalid, Lord Palmerston and King Leopold proposed submitting Duke Ernest as a candidate. The prospect of a crown, albeit such a potentially unstable one, appealed greatly to his vanity. He declared himself willing to go to Athens, while at the same time retaining his title Duke of Coburg, along with its accompanying privileges. His nephew, he proclaimed loftily, could live there and act as his regent.

Though he could hardly have expected the family to agree to such selfish provisions, Ernest had his champions among those who considered him the best possible choice after his young nephew. In January *The Times* published a letter from one M. E. Mavrogordato, who obviously knew little about him as a person, writing on behalf of the Greek mercantile community in England. He hoped Ernest would accept the crown as it would bring the advantages of British friendship to Greece, as well as a close alliance with the royal family. Moreover the Duke, he continued, was cherished by England as the champion of constitutional liberty in Europe, and chief of that powerful dynastic connection which stood at the head of continental free governments – 'in fine, we discern in Duke Ernest the same noble character for which England honours the memory of his lamented brother, the Prince Consort, and we discover in him the personal qualities...which, in our opinion, the King of Greece ought to possess.'[6] The ghost of Prince Albert would probably have been less than flattered by such a testimonial.

Some weeks later the Greeks settled the issue by choosing another, hardly less well-connected, royal sailor to reign over them, namely seventeen-year-old Prince William of Denmark, the younger brother of the Princess of Wales. He took the title of King George I and arrived in Greece in October 1863.

Having outlived Affie by twelve years, in 1913 he was assassinated by a madman who turned the gun on himself before he could be brought to trial.

Affie's relief at the conclusion of the Greek throne affair was unbounded. After nearly a year of the unwanted crown hanging over his head, he could concentrate once more on his naval career. Under normal circumstances he would have been allowed to take his lieutenant's examination on completion of his qualifying period at the age of eighteen, but because of his royal duties and responsibilities he was often absent from training, and it was felt necessary to make an Order-in-Council permitting him to take the examination as soon as possible, notwithstanding his age and the regulations. In January 1863 the Admiralty informed the Commander-in-Chief of the Mediterranean Fleet, Vice-Admiral Sir William Martin, that on passing the examination the prince should be appointed acting Lieutenant in HMS *Marlborough*, Martin's flagship, and then sent home on leave overland via Marseilles. Affie's commission was to be prepared but left undated, and delivered to him the day after he passed. HMS *Magicienne*, a corvette commanded by Prince Ernest of Leiningen, son of Charles, Prince of Leiningen, Queen Victoria's half-brother, was to take him to London so they could attend the wedding of the Prince of Wales on 10 March 1863.

However Affie was suddenly taken ill. A week before the examination he went down with a feverish cold at Naples, and plans were made to send him straight home by sea. But then ominous symptoms appeared; he had contracted the dreaded typhoid which had robbed him of his father. The Queen was horrified lest her eldest son's wedding might possibly be overshadowed by the death of her second son – and her third major bereavement within two years. How could Affie be so ill so soon after the death of his Papa? She besought the Almighty to 'spare our darling boy; so like his beloved Father, so clever and talented and so excessively amiable.'

Under the fatherly care of Cowell, Affie's tenacity pulled him through, but he had to enter hospital at Malta as he was too ill to travel home, and consequently missed the wedding. While Bertie and Alix stood at the altar in St George's Chapel, Windsor, Affie was only just starting to take meals and outdoor exercise again several thousand miles away. He had insisted on taking the examination on board ship first, the day he was taken seriously ill, in the presence of three senior captains. True to form, he passed through without any trouble. When the Admiralty was notified, he was promoted to acting Lieutenant and appointed to HMS *Racoon* with orders that he should join the ship at home when fit. *Racoon* was a twenty-two-gun steam corvette of 1,476 tons and 400 horsepower, then refitting at Chatham, commanded by Captain Count Gleichen, younger brother of Prince Ernest of Leiningen.

On 16 March Affie wrote from the Royal Naval Hospital at Malta to Aunt Alexandrine:

> I hope to be able to start for England some time this week as I am already strong. I have been out walking already the day before yesterday but unfortunately the weather is so bad that it keeps me in doors & makes it rather longer than otherwise should be.[7]

Two weeks later he sailed for Dover, calling at Marseilles, and was eagerly welcomed at Windsor, still thin but in high spirits. In May he passed his examinations in gunnery and navigation, for confirmation in the rank of Lieutenant. The tests were confined to inspection of work he had already done and a *viva voce*, in view of the interruption to his studies caused by illness. Yet still he managed to displease the Queen once again.

London society, which had been without a leader since the heyday of the Price regent some sixty years previously, was about to acquire another figurehead in his great-nephew, the newly married Prince of Wales accompanied by his lovely Danish wife. The 'smart set' had had no time for the Prince Consort, and vice versa. They looked to his son, obviously a prince of very different character, for an example in the art of enjoying life to the full. His London home Marlborough House immediately became the centre of society, and it was hardly surprising that Affie should head there when his naval duties permitted. Like Bertie he was old enough to choose his own lifestyle and cut free from the eternal mourning of his mother's palaces in which the younger children were still cocooned. Moreover he was devoted to his sister-in-law. Queen Victoria wrote acidly to Vicky that she did what she could to keep him away from Marlborough House, as he was 'far too *epris* of (infatuated with) Alix to be allowed to be much there without possibly ruining the happiness of all three, and Affie had not the strength of mind or rather of principle and character to resist the temptation and it is like playing with fire'.[8] Her remarks were all too clearly coloured by disapproval of the 'Marlborough style' – so very different from her quiet *Gemutlich* life with Albert.

Affie may have been a little jealous of his brother who had married the princess he once secretly thought might be his; perhaps this helps to explain his questionable behaviour in giving the Queen mischievously-exaggerated accounts of Bertie's expensive alterations at Sandringham, the Norfolk country estate recently purchased for him. On the other hand Bertie must have unconsciously envied Affie his freedom at sea, far away from the disapproving maternal eye. But it would have taken more than such trifling jealousy to disturb the bonds of brotherhood. Alix in turn adored her brother-in-law, who was only four months her senior, and shared his love of music.

The brothers were similar in many ways. Both were well-built, though Bertie became increasingly corpulent with age, and was a few inches the shorter, and both sported neatly-trimmed beards from their mid-twenties onwards. They enjoyed the good things in life – wine, women, cigars, amusing company, parties well into the small hours, and keeping a safe distance from the gloom of their Mama's court. Inwardly, however, they were quite different. Affie took after their Papa in being shy and ill at ease, especially with strangers. At a dinner party given by Bertie and Alix in April 1863, the future Prime Minister Benjamin Disraeli was seated next to Affie, and perceptively described his 'bronzed and manly countenance, with a thoughtful brow; altogether like his father.'[9] He had been much closer to the Prince Consort in his zeal for learning, aptitude for mechanical objects, science and art – even in their common love for Coburg. Father and second son had loved to share each other's company in the activities they enjoyed together, and the father was sorely missed. On the other hand Bertie had always been a little afraid of the father whom he realised he disappointed so much, and the loss had probably hit Affie much harder. Almost overnight the cheerful youngster had become a somewhat withdrawn, even touchy adult, possibly with a chip on his shoulder.

According to Roger Fulford, Affie 'developed into one of the most unpopular and disagreeable of all English princes'.[10] That he lacked the gift of making himself popular is evident, but contemporary opinions of him varied sharply. As a young man the future Prime Minister Lord Rosebery apparently 'detested' him. Even the Prince of Wales, who was always devoted to him, was once moved to describe him as 'a crashing bore'. Lord Clarendon, formerly Secretary of State for Foreign Affairs and one of the most lively of Victorian correspondents, noted in March 1863 that he had heard Prince Alfred was to leave the navy on health grounds, 'a pity as he is a baddish fellow and will give trouble at home.'[11] Whether he meant the Prince was mischievous (a term which might have equally been applied to Clarendon himself) or actually unpleasant is not clear, though he may have been referring to Affie's imperious treatment of his mother's servants. On the other hand Prince Alexander of Hesse, brother of the Grand Duke and father of the Battenberg princes, called him 'frank and jovial'. From these comments one must conclude that he was better company at Marlborough House and high society elsewhere, where he enjoyed himself, than at Osborne or Windsor where he did not attempt to conceal his boredom.

Among Affie's closest friends from the Marlborough House set were the Duke and Duchess of Sutherland. Although the Duke was son of Queen Victoria's much-loved Mistress of the Robes Harriet, 2nd Duchess of Sutherland, the Queen often deplored the Duke's behaviour. 'He does not live as a Duke ought,' she wrote disapprovingly, referring to his passion for driving fire and railway engines and, later, to his open partisanship of the Italian revolutionary patriot General Garibaldi. Both Bertie and Affie were regular guests at the ducal estates of Trentham in Staffordshire, Dunrobin Castle in Sutherland, and their London home, Stafford House. But Affie was closer to the ill-used Duchess, whose poor health and unhappy married life led her to return increasingly to their Devonshire home, Sutherland Towers in Torquay. Both kept up a regular correspondence until shortly before her death in November 1888.

In June 1863 Affie was pronounced fully recovered and fit enough to join *Racoon*. At this time he was in Scotland, visiting Edinburgh to choose apartments at Holyrood Palace where he would stay during his session at the university, beginning in November. After returning briefly to Windsor, he joined the ship at Portsmouth on 20 June for a three-month cruise around the Scottish coast. At Dundee he had the novel if not altogether welcome experience of being greeted by such eager crowds that he had to take temporary refuge in a bookshop. On the Shetland Isles he played at quoits and went trout fishing, a new hobby he had recently taken up with great enjoyment. Already he was as familiar with the pools around Balmoral as any of the local keepers, and had a reputation as one of the most skillful and tenacious anglers on Deeside.

The highlight of his cruise was a visit to Lews Castle, the seat of Sir James and Lady Matheson, in the Outer Hebrides, where they entertained him, Count Gleichen, and guests from Stornoway with a dinner and dance. Within the fortnight he was back at Osborne celebrating his nineteenth birthday with the family, and accompanied the Queen on a visit to Germany before going to study in Edinburgh.

Affie must have missed the sea, but his days as a scholar were made more bearable by the company of another student one year older and related by marriage, Prince William of Hesse, son of Prince Charles of Hesse, Alice's brother-in-law. Together they attended classes in chemistry, natural history, philosophy and history. At the end of their session the people of the city presented the university with a bust of Prince Alfred 'in commemoration of the high esteem and golden opinions which he had won among them'.

A letter of 27 November 1863 from Affie to 'Dear Lord Alfred' – Lord Paget, then chiefly equerry in the Queen's Household – reveals what else occupied the royal students' minds. After assuring him that they were both 'grinding away here pretty stiff at our studies' and mentioning that he was about to go out of town for some shooting, he issued an urgent appeal:

Would you kindly tell Benson to send me 600 more of those cigars you ordered for me in June; I found the last box excellent and I am sorry to

say that my friend did also, so that I am completely run out and shall
have to stick to a pipe until I get some more.[12]

This supply of cigars worked out at about four a day between them. *En
passant* one wonders how many crates Affie would take with him on long
voyages.

Early in 1864 Affie went on to attend the University of Bonn, an old ton of
great charm, which in itself would have bored him stiff had it not been for
students' clubs and beer halls where they all drank, duelled, and enjoyed
endless 'high jinks'. There were also various excursions in the picturesque
countryside, particularly boating and canoeing on the Rhine, local theatre
performances, and seasonal carnivals. It was a carefree life while it lasted,
and Affie was doubtless glad to be far away from the stern eye of his
mother for a while.

In the light of this, it was surprising that he should have told her at the
beginning of the year that he no longer wanted to be heir to the duchy of
Saxe-Coburg, even though he had been brought up to expect it since his
childhood. Shocked as she was, Queen Victoria and her advisers decided
not to put any pressure on him one way or the other, in the hope that he
would change his mind. They knew that there was no really satisfactory
alternative. Bertie suggested that perhaps Leopold should be made heir
instead, leaving Arthur free to take up the career in the army for which
he was showing great enthusiasm. The Queen dismissed this idea, on the
grounds that Leopold was not nearly strong enough for such a destiny,
and he would be far more use to her in England as a patron of the sciences
than the military-minded, more Germanic Arthur, who would become
frustrated if his idea of an army career was thwarted. Affie was adamant
that he wanted to stay in England to follow in his father's footsteps and
help his mother with her work. He was warned by Sir Charles Phipps,
Keeper of the Privy Purse, that this would need 'immense dedication',
and that attendance on Her Majesty would become his first duty,
overshadowing his profession and his pleasures.[13] Queen Victoria feared
that her second son was too fond of England and would be ill-fitted to
rule a German duchy. Howard Elphinstone, Arthur's tutor, blamed it on
what he called the Prince's 'peculiar education on board a man of war'.
She was also alarmed at apparent differences between Affie and Cowell,
whose religious devotion was starting to irritate his young charge, and
found it necessary to try and urge the tutor 'to be as cordial with Prince
Alfred as he can'.[14]

After a while, no more was heard of Affie's resistance to his eventual
destiny. At weekends he sometimes paid visits to his sister Alice and Louis

at the unpretentious palace in Darmstadt, and in June 1865 he performed an investiture on behalf of the Queen. She had conferred the order of the Garter on the Grand Duke, but he begged that the function should take place at his own court. The ceremony was conducted by Affie and his brother-in-law Louis in grand style, though both of them and Alice were much amused that the Grand Duke had received them dressed in his *Lederhosen*. After the large dinner which followed, however, he told them that he felt the honour 'utmostly'.

There was another reason why Affie had cause to remember his days at Darmstadt, for among other regular guests were the Battenberg family. Prince Alexander of Hesse had married morganatically and his children were looked down on as *parvenus* by most European heads, with the significant exception of Queen Victoria, whose championship of the talented and good-looking princes would eventually prove of inestimable benefit not only to the royal family but also to Britain as a nation in peace and war.

Unconsciously Affie took the first step in furthering their cause. The eldest boy, Louis, was spellbound by the sight of Lieutenant Prince Alfred in his glittering naval uniform, and the stories he told of life in the Royal Navy, unquestionably the world's finest. Affie was equally impressed by the lad's keen interest and encouraged him in his ambition to join the service. In spite of his parents' dismay that he should opt for a remote and probably very rough alien force instead of a German military career, Louis was not to be dissuaded. A couple of years later, at the age of fourteen, he went to England, became a British subject and joined the Navy. Not the least of Affie's services to his profession, therefore, was his responsibility for recruiting a future First Sea Lord and his son, the latter born within six weeks of Affie's death, likewise destined to become First Sea Lord, and later Chief of the Defence Staff – Louis, Earl Mountbatten of Burma.

In May 1864 King William of Prussia conferred the Order of the Black Eagle on Affie – 'a very questionable honour' commented *The Times*, much to the fury of Queen Victoria, who wrote to Vicky that she was 'quite bursting with indignation' at this 'shameful and utterly disgraceful observation'.[15] Prussia was very unpopular at the time in Britain on account of her successes in the Prusso-Danish war; the Princess of Wales was much loved by her adopted country which shared her anger that 'perfidious Albion' should remain neutral and not lift a finger to aid the hapless Danish armies. For the family it was the beginning of sharply-divided political loyalties which were to plague nearly all of Affie's brothers and sisters in turn, not least Affie himself.

Already the question of his marriage had concerned the Queen for some time, and she was at pains to ensure that Vicky should introduce him to the princesses from whom her second daughter-in-law might be chosen. She must be German – 'I think a Princess of a Saxon House particularly desirable – so thoroughly and truly German, which is a necessity!'[16] The Queen was already convinced that having a Danish princess among them had been a grave political error, and the sooner Affie married the better; it would prevent him from 'getting into mischief' with Alix. At first she thought Marie of Saxe-Altenburg, daughter of Grand Duke Charles of Saxe-Weimar might make him a good wife. Affie was introduced to her and afterwards he remarked unenthusiastically that her hands and feet were not too large and she only had one bad tooth. Two years hence, the Queen discovered that dental shortcomings were not the half of it. Marie was 'everything most undesirable' – though whether on moral or health grounds was not clear. By now Affie was thought to be more than a little in love with Lady Constance Grosvenor, youngest daughter of the 2nd Duke of Sutherland, and the Queen feared this was making him reluctant to marry.

An earlier infatuation with Princess Frederica of Hanover had passed. Queen Victoria had looked aghast at the prospects of such a match. It was out of the question for health reasons – 'three generations of blindness and double relationships'[17] and the state of enmity between the King of Hanover and Duke Ernest, which would provoke further family disharmony, was another reason why this could not come to pass.

Princess Elizabeth of Wied was also under consideration for a time. She had a reputation for being clever and intelligent, and the Queen sometimes regretted that she had not had an opportunity to become Princess of Wales. Affie was sent to make her acquaintance, and he would be eternally grateful for being warned in time of the family's eccentricities. Her mother set great store by faith healing and spiritualism. Elizabeth, however, seemed comparatively normal until she discovered that her suitor played the violin. Mother and daughter accordingly arranged an expedition into their favourite beech woods, so he could serenade them under the trees. Gallantly he complied with this extraordinary command, silently vowing the whole time between clenched teeth that he would definitely search elsewhere for a wife. Queen Victoria's unsympathetic verdict – with which he would surely have taken great issue – was that 'he did not behave well there'.

The difficult relationship between mother and son made it important for both that Affie's matrimonial future should be settled sooner rather than later. She encouraged his visits to Vicky at Berlin, but looked coldly on weekends spent with Alice. If he was merely helping her with charity work in Darmstadt, and selling goods at stalls in her fund-raising bazaars, all very well – but it did not end there. What irritated her was the belief that Alice was trying to bring a little gaiety into Mama's family life, corrupting Affie and Louise to this end, and by implication conspiring behind her back to make her appear more in public. It was unjust of the Queen, as she did not appreciate that Affie felt it was time that she should gently put mourning aside and allow him to enjoy himself more. He and Louise confided freely in Alice, and confirmed her suspicions (gleaned from other European courts) that Her Majesty's seclusion was harmful to the English monarchy.

Affie did not dare to do anything that might have been construed as trying to coax his mother out into public life, unlike Alice who could write tactfully from a distance of 'the brave example to others not to shirk from their duty' when congratulating her on having opened Parliament in February 1866 for the first time in her widowhood. Unfortunately he lacked the tact to allay her suspicions; unlike Bertie, who was 'really very amiable' to her despite his faults, Affie made her 'very unhappy; he hardly ever comes near me, is reserved, touchy, vague and wilful and I distrust him completely....he is quite a stranger to me.'[18] She was convinced that Alice had 'ruined' him with her love of 'amusing herself and of fine society'. Equally trying was a slack habit which the Prince Consort had hated in young men; 'really to see Prince Alfred never with his hands out of (trouser pockets) would be enough to cure anyone. He walks into dinner and sits at dinner with his hands in his pockets.'[19] Watching him eat like this must have provided a remarkable display of supernatural powers if both hands were placed thus all the time.

In August 1865, what could have proved an insurmountable problem was solved when Affie reached the age of twenty-one. Cowell resigned his position as governor, doubtless with some relief. He was knighted by the Queen for his services, and appointed governor to the frail twelve-year-old Leopold.

Although Cowell and others had their reservations about Affie, for all his faults and lack of consideration, he was deeply devoted to the family, and just as anxious as anyone to smooth over disagreements between his brothers and sisters. In August 1865 all nine, and Queen Victoria, were together for the first time since Vicky's wedding seven and a half years earlier, a the unveiling of a statue to the Prince Consort at Coburg. Vicky had carefully arranged for Helena, now aged nineteen, to meet Prince Christian of Schleswig-Holstein. Marriage prospects for them both were far from encouraging. He was prematurely bald, penniless, and with his ponderous manner seemed much older than his thirty-five years, while she was plain and generally considered 'wanting in charm'. Aware of their shortcomings, they knew that if they turned each other down they might well regret it, though Christian had been so ill informed about the rendezvous beforehand that he had apparently believed himself destined to become the second husband of Her Majesty. By Christmas he and Helena were betrothed.

The match initially caused much ill feeling in the family. The Queen and Vicky were pleased, while Alice and Affie objected, as they thought their sister's happiness was being sacrificed to their mother's convenience. It was quite obvious, they felt, that Mama wanted to keep Helena at home – or at least within very close distance – and this was the only reason she was marrying her off to an otherwise totally ineligible prince almost twice her age, who would become a foreigner dependent on the English exchequer and therefore unlikely to improve the monarchy's already tarnished image. The Prince and Princess of Wales were so affronted that they threatened to absent themselves from the wedding ceremony altogether, for Christian's brother Frederick had been the self-proclaimed Duke of Schleswig-Holstein, territory regarded by King Christian of Denmark as his own – at least until Bismarck had neatly settled the issue in 1864 by defeating the Danes in war and was and claiming them on behalf of the German Confederation – and they saw it as an open rebuff for the Danish cause.

When Alice learnt of this she immediately wrote Bertie an affectionate letter trying to reconcile him to the marriage, gently reminding him that Mama had risked antagonising the Germans by sanctioning his betrothal to Alix. Vicky weighed in as well, and Affie wrote in more down-to-earth terms that, as the engagement had taken place, 'we must put a good face on it. Of course, the relationship is painful to you, but you must try to accept him for what he is worth personally, and don't look at him with a prejudiced eye for he is really a very good fellow, though not handsome.'[20]

Such diplomatic skills on his part helped to ensure that the wedding took place without rancour on 5 July 1866. Despite the age differences between bride and groom, their marriage was unique among those of Queen Victoria's children in that they were the only couple who lived long enough to celebrate their golden wedding together. By the time Prince Alfred was there watching them standing at the altar, he had become a Duke and a Captain.

CHAPTER 4

The First Cruise of HMS *Galatea* 1866-68

In February 1866 Queen Victoria signed an Order-in-Council authorising the Admiralty to promote her second son to the rank of Captain, and subsequently to flag rank, thus bypassing that of Commander. Although this made Prince Alfred at twenty-one a very youthful Captain, a precedent already existed in the case of his great-uncle Prince William, who had been similarly advanced in rank at a like age in 1788. Parliament granted him an income of £15,000 a year, unbounded wealth in comparison with his pay as a Lieutenant of £1 a day. On the Queen's birthday, 24 May, he was created Duke of Edinburgh, and Earl of Ulster and Kent. At the same time he was made a Knight of the Garter and Thistle, awarded the Grand Crosses of the Orders of St Michael and St George, and the Star of India and the Indian Empire. The Lord Mayor of London presented him with the Freedom of the City, and he was appointed Master of Trinity House.

All these honours formed a prelude to considerable responsibility, for shortly afterwards he was appointed to the command of HMS *Galatea* with orders to take her on a world cruise such as no British prince had yet undertaken. A wooden screw frigate, *Galatea* was reckoned to be one of the fastest and best-equipped vessels of her time. Launched at Woolwich in 1859, she had already served in the West Indies, Baltic and Mediterranean Seas. With a tonnage of 3,227, she had a steam engine of 800 horsepower, a top speed of thirteen knots, twenty-six guns, and provisions including 700 tons of coal and seventy-two tons of water. Fully rigged with sails, her engines were only used in emergencies.

In September 1866 Affie wrote to Sir John Pakington, First Lord of the Admiralty, that he was glad to hear *Galatea* was ready, and he hoped that when he returned from the obligatory autumn visit to Balmoral they would be able to 'settle the definite time at which I am to commission her.'[1]

On 16 November, he sent Sir John a summary of 'The proposed arrangements for *Galatea* cruise 1867'. The itinerary, which concerned for the most part only the brief preliminary journeys in Mediterranean waters, proposed that the ship was

to be commissioned the 3rd or 4th January. Leave England about 22nd.
Calling at Lisbon to Gibraltar staying there about three weeks.
Then to join the Admiral at Malta & to arrive on coast of Italy calling
at Naples, Civitavechia & Leghorn? Genoa arriving at Marseilles about
28th March leaving 2nd or 3rd April.
Cruize homewards calling at Gibraltar & Cadiz arriving at Spithead
about 1st week in May.
It will then be necessary for me to go to Germany for a few weeks and
to be in London for a time during the session of Parliament. It would be
agreable to the Queen and myself if the ship could be stationed at Cowes
at (as) Guard ship to Her Majesty during her stay at Osborne in the
summer.

The further proposals for the *Galatea* cruises would depend upon the
state of relationship between the different countries and Her Majesty's
feeling at the time, but the Queen had thought that a visit to North
America would be advisable.[2]

When a ship is commissioned, she has to get used to an entirely new crew
– from the proverbial ABs, up through the lowest of the low in the form of
junior officers, the midshipmen; the sub-lieutenants; the acting commander
and commander; and lastly, the man responsible for everything and
everyone, the captain. He sets the tone of his ship, beginning on the first
day of commission with an address. In Affie's case, on speaking to the men
in the first week of January 1867, he doubtless dwelt on virtues such as
duty, discipline, Queen and country.

After the brief Mediterranean cruise, plans were made in earnest for the
tour that would take in ports of call such as Rio, Cape Town, Adelaide
and Melbourne. In view of the work involved, it seemed a little churlish of
Queen Victoria to have remarked on Affie's undertaking the responsibility
'with such reluctance and suspicion'. One can understand his being
nervous about the mission, and despite his love of naval life not altogether
happy at being separated from family and friends for so long. The latter
was just what his mother wanted – 'I hope the responsibility and the
separation from his London flatterers will do him good'.[3] He wished 'to
come home for the Season, which did him so much harm last year. But
I and the Admiralty will be firm and do only what is for his good and
the good of the Service.'[4] Already she and Alexander of Hesse had had to
turn down firmly his request for the twelve-year-old Louis of Battenberg
to accompany him.

Apparently the last few months had gone to Affie's head, for he had
begun to take advantage of his rank by flying the royal standard in port.
This, the Queen complained, was contrary to the regulations. He must

understand that he 'went in command of *Galatea* as a Captain in her Navy and not as a Prince. He must not hoist the Royal Standard in general and never in the presence of his Admiral…but merely when he landed as a Prince…the Admiralty must make no difference in their treatment of her Son if he does not conform'. Fortunately he did conform in time to avoid any official reprimand.

After attending the international exhibition at Paris in the spring, Affie went to Marseilles where *Galatea* had lain in dock. It was a very unhealthy area, where sewerage from the dockside slums ran into the sea and caused an intolerable stench in hot dry midsummer, several of the crew were ill, some with typhoid, by the time their captain joined them. In addition a sudden gale blew up, and as a French passenger steamer was entering harbour her engines broke down. She was swept against a jetty by the waves, and Affie sent some boats and working parties of sailors to her aid. The provincial governor came on board *Galatea* to thank him in person, to offer him the Freedom of the City of Marseilles, and to bring several cases of champagne for distribution among the crew.

Leaving the infested port behind them as soon as possible, the ship set sail in the first week of June, skirted the Balearic Islands and Spanish coast, and landed at Gibraltar a few days later. Here she took charge of fresh food and coal supplies, and Affie was given confirmation of Admiralty orders to travel to the lands of South America, the Cape Colony, China, India, Australia and New Zealand.

From Gibraltar *Galatea* proceeded to the island of Madeira, then almost unrivalled as a producer of sweet dessert wine, and collected presentation samples of various wines. In August she reached Rio de Janeiro, where Affie became the first member of a British royal house to visit Brazil. Pedro II, a representative of the Portuguese dynasty of Braganza, was the only reigning monarch on the American continent, and he laid on several parties and receptions for his guest.

Next they called at Tristan da Cunha, then the most remote of all British colonies, an island consisting of the cone of a submerged marine volcano, with a population of fifty. The ship's chaplain, the Reverend John Milner, felt that the settlement with its little stone cottages had the appearance of a group of Highland crofts. Affie was taken on a walk to see the large colonies of seals and albatross, and the party was entertained to lunch by William Glass, chief of the community. Before leaving he arranged or a distribution of gifts – including freshly baked bread, rum, tobacco, vinegar, sugar, treacle, tea, coffee, sailcloth and serge – to the islanders, and Glass thanked him on their behalf. He declared that henceforth the settlement would be named Edinburgh in commemoration of the visit. Appropriately, and especially in view of his philatelic interests, in July 1967 the postal authorities of Tristan da Cunha issued a set of four pictorial commemorative stamps to celebrate the centenary of the Duke's visit.

En route for the Cape, the men spliced the mainbrace in celebration of Affie's twenty-third birthday and he gave a dinner attended by twenty-two of the officers. Nine days later they sighted land again.

This second journey to the Cape was not nearly so demanding as when Affie had been a high-spirited midshipman. No longer the wide-eyed teenager and pampered darling of all the hostesses, or child of heaven to the natives in the north, he was now a slim young man with a pronounced Hanoverian pout, and the ghost of moustaches and the customary naval beard just beginning to grow. He wore the captain's heavy gold epaulettes and exuded an air of dignity as befitted the most senior officer aboard. In other words, this visit was not officially a royal one, and perhaps not so much fun.

After dutifully paying his respects to the city fathers and their families and listening ad infinitum to two more 'musical offerings' specially composed, namely *Afric's Welcome* and *The Duke of Edinburgh's Waltz*, Affie embarked once more. *Galatea* docked at Simonstown, and he took his old ship *Racoon* on a cruise to the deep harbour of Plettenburg Bay, embarking on the smaller *Petrel* from Knysna, reminiscent of Devon with its high cliffs and delightful wooded areas right down to the sea.

In these dense hardwood forests he followed with glee the sport of wealthy South African gentlemen, elephant hunting – or what would be dismissed in a later, more wildlife conservation-conscious age as sheer slaughter. It was midwinter again, and he wore his velvet Balmoral/Sandringham 'Norfolks', flat bowler with cocked feather, and soft buckskin high boots. The party camped out with great enthusiasm in the rough, and Affie narrowly avoided being trampled on – but he shot his elephant. After the excitement was over, he dispensed gifts in true royal fashion. Each member of the expedition received hunting knives with hilts made of ivory from his 'kill'. To his host George Rex he gave a gold watch and silver tankard, and to one of his sons a blue-grey onyx ring inscribed with his name and the date, 13 September 1867.

George Rex was the main reason for Affie's coming to this part of the Cape. He was said to be the son of a morganatic marriage between Prince George, later King George III, and the East London Quakeress Hannah Lightfoot. Little is known of her, but the boy's presence was an embarrassment to crown and government alike. In 1797, an East Bahamas Indiaman left England under sealed Admiralty orders, 'bearing into life-long exile…a King's son.' The founder of the Rex family still extant in Knysna, he died in 1839 and was buried in a little Victorian churchyard full of family graves, quiet and isolated among the lush fields of the then Rex estates.

His son, who was also Affie's host, was the head of this now wealthy family of shipbuilders, timber merchants and agriculturists, owning four thousand acres of crown land. Affie's reception was certainly in lavish style as befitted the son of the Queen of England. Knowing all about this extraordinary story, he was full of questions and eager to see everything Mr Rex could show him. In his host's mansion he seemed to be surrounded with 'likenesses' of his own ancestors just as he had been at Windsor. The resemblances were remarkable; there was one portrait that looked exactly like his great-uncle King William IV. There was also one of George Rex's daughters, Caroline, who looked as if she could have been Mama herself...

While on board *Racoon*, Affie found a few moments to write to the Duchess of Sutherland:

> You will by this time I suppose be at dear old Dunrobin where we spent such a happy month last autumn & this letter will probably find you on your return. We had a prosperous though rather slow passage out as far as here & ever since our arrival have been very gay, plenty of balls, dinners etc. all very fatiguing things. Yesterday I started in this ship (strangely enough the last one I served in) on a trip up the coast where I am going on an Elephant hunt which will be both new and exciting to me. In about a fortnight I leave for Australia. The 'Malabar' one of the large Indian troopships which arrived a week ago brought me a most unwelcome letter from the Admiralty telling me to remain away six months longer than was originally intended; but I am writing to My Lords [of the Admiralty] proposing another plan which splits the difference with them, my plans being the fearful weather I shld. encounter rounding the Horn at the season they wish, which will I hope bring me home by the beginning of August next year & if you have a spare bedroom at Dunrobin that autumn I hope Stafford & yourself will invite me...[5]

From the Cape, it had been planned to sail for Mauritius, until the party received reports of a typhoid epidemic on the island. Two of the crew had died of the disease since leaving Marseilles, and in order not to tempt Providence, it was thought advisable for *Galatea* to head immediately for Australia.

An unusually pathetic yet charming story was told of an event occurring on this leg of the cruise, as the entourage worked their way under the Westerlies in October. It shows the Royal Navy with tongue in august cheek, but fiercely adhering to Queen's Regulations, in respect of a unique member of the Captain's crew – a monkey named Jacko:

We were running before the wind that morning, when suddenly the officer of the watch was heard to call out "Hard a starboard!" and everybody rushed on deck, knowing that something unusual must have occurred. The ship was rounded to, in order to lower a boat and try to save poor Jack, who had just fallen overboard. The men jumped into the port cutter, and were all ready for lowering away. On the bridge everybody was looking out to see if he could catch a glimpse of poor "cookems" struggling in the water; but the "wake" of the ship was right under the sun, and in the glare of the broken water it was impossible to detect where he was. Nobody had thought of letting go a life-buoy to mark the spot where he had fallen. After a short pause of suspense the boat was kept fast, the ship once more brought before the wind, and Jacko was left to his untimely fate, sincerely lamented by everyone on board. 'Poor little fellow!' said the Duke; 'if I had been on deck, I think I should have gone overboard after him; we shall never get another like him.'

He lost his life from a habit, which he had recently contracted, of biting a hind-leg when in a passion, holding it in his hands, and hopping on the other leg to keep his balance. He happened at the time to be skylarking on the hammock-netting, and when interfered with flew into a rage, bit his leg, hopped the wrong way, and disappeared over the side. Jacko was brought from Gibraltar in December, 1865, and was taken to England in H.M.S. *Racoon* with another monkey called Jinny. He was dismissed from that ship 'with disgrace,' for throwing overboard some valuable papers belonging to the Captain. He then joined the Queen's yacht, whence he was sent to the *Galatea* with a regular blue-jacket's transfer sheet.[6]

Strong winds in the Roaring Forties blew *Galatea* towards South Australia, and on the morning of 30 October she entered the port of Glenelg near Adelaide. Affie's equerries visited Government House shortly before midday while he remained on board, and were presented with an extensive list of official engagements which had been optimistically drawn up by the royal reception committee. They insisted that he had no intention of coming ashore that day, let alone visiting the city. Nonetheless the South Australian authorities promptly proclaimed that the next day would be a public holiday.

The temperature was in the nineties early on 31 October as Affie landed. At first the massive crowds which had gathered since first light did not recognise him in his morning coat and top hat, instead of the glittering naval uniform they had expected. After a brief address from the civic dignitaries and an even shorter one from their guest himself, the royal coach drove into Adelaide to the sound of exuberant cheering and a regular pelting of flowers.

That evening the main buildings were illuminated by gaslight. The streets were decorated with hastily-constructed wooden triumphal arches and gas-lit transparencies bearing what was supposed to be the ducal likeness, but an absence of authentic portraits meant that most of them did not resemble him (or even each other) in the least. Affie commented wryly to his chaplain that he doubted if his own mother would recognise him from them. The Adelaide Gas Company, which had only recently installed its lighting system in the city, was convinced that its lights and transparencies would provide a memorable public spectacle. Insurance firms were not alone in thinking gloomily that they might be horribly right. It was fortunate that in the end there was insufficient gas to provide all the planned illuminations.

For the next three weeks the pattern of Affie's Australian tour was established with a round of state banquets, military reviews, and other civic functions. At one dinner the Mayor declared in his speech that he wished to open his heart to the Prince, and a journalist subsequently reported that he was planning to indulge in a rather curious piece of surgery. The local German community organised a *Liedertafel*, a male voice choir in which torchbearers dressed in German national costumes paraded before him as they sang. He laid the foundation stone of Prince Alfred College, the first of many, and went to an operatic performance at the Adelaide Theatre where only half the seats were occupied, as a local stockbroker had bought several dozen tickets in the vain hope of selling them again at inflated prices to the more ardent royalty-worshippers. At the botanic gardens he impressed his guides with his scientific knowledge of the names of most Australian plants, familiar to him since childhood. Between the rounds of these official functions he was escorted by the governor and his party into the rural areas of South Australia and took part in a possum shoot.

Apart from an incident when Affie's temporary valet absconded with some jewellery and silverware stolen from on board ship, this stage of the tour passed off without trouble. The euphoric editor of the *Adelaide Advertiser* proposed in his columns that a federal union of the Australian colonies should try and obtain British approval for proclaiming Prince Alfred as their sovereign, an idea that was not taken up elsewhere but indicated nonetheless how widespread was enthusiasm for their guest. Though nobody else entertained the idea seriously, it was of some interest as being the third time in twenty years that Affie was considered as a possible sovereign (and the second time for a non-existent throne), so great was the prestige of being reigned over by the second son of the Queen of England.

As yet the spectre of Irish republican agitation was not close enough to cast its shadow over the royal tour. Yet it was an unhappy coincidence that on 23 November, just as *Galatea* was entering Port Phillip Bay and bound for Melbourne, three members of the Fenian Brotherhood were paying with their lives in Manchester prison for the fatal shooting of a policeman. The Brotherhood had been formed in 1858 in the United States of America by Irish immigrants to promote armed struggle for Irish independence. In Britain there were rumours of plots to kidnap or even kill Queen Victoria and members of the royal family, and to blow up the Houses of Parliament. Fears that she sovereign was going to be captured while staying at Balmoral in October 1867 resulted in a squad of armed undercover police officers being sent to Deeside and posted in a cordon around the castle. The Queen was dismissive about such threats to her personal safety, but her private secretary Charles Grey warned her respectfully to return to the castle after visiting the estate at a reasonable time each evening, as well as issuing security passes to all family, guests and servants present. Fenian activity was not merely confined to both sides of the Atlantic and Irish seas, but was also evident in Australia where almost a quarter of the population was of Irish birth. Though news of the Manchester executions could not have reached the community until the new year, to one man in particular the appearance of Queen Victoria's second son was a providential target for revenge.

None of this can have concerned Affie, or even crossed his mind, as *Galatea* headed south-east along the coast, appropriately, for the state of Victoria. Port of call was Melbourne, then the largest city in Australia, with a population of over 200,000. They intended to land at Queenscliff, but a group of borough councillors waiting at the harbour was so anxious to present the first loyal address of welcome to him in Victoria that some of them boarded a pilot boat and arrived on deck just at the moment that he assumed command. Angry at being taken by surprise in this way, he told the pilot bluntly that he wanted no addresses just yet, and promptly decided the next morning, but on his coach procession into the city he passed each vellum-bound declaration of loyalty to his equerry without bothering to open it first.

That night, Melbourne came to life with a variety of illuminations – gas brackets, transparencies, and flame pots on the roofs and exteriors of shops and business premises. Two contained portents of what was to come; St Patrick's Hall was decorated with a large glowing green harp and the Gaelic greeting *Caed Mile Failtichs* (A hundred thousand welcomes). In nearby Stephens Street was the protestant Hall, headquarters for the city's Ulstermen, provocatively displaying a transparency of King William III putting to flight the Catholic troops of James II at the battle of the Boyne.

Two days later, Affie attended a governor's ball, which was tragically marred by what was to be known as the Stephens Street outrage. The 'King Billy' decorations had been fiercely denounced by the Irish-Catholic community, and during the ball demonstrators gathered outside the Protestant Hall shouting abuse, singing Irish songs, and throwing stones at the shattered windows. Eventually an upper window was thrown open and shots were fired at the crowd. Most fled to safety but some were injured, and one youth was taken to hospital with fatal head wounds after what was to be the first serious outbreak of violence in Australia triggered off by Fenianism. It was not to be the last.

Even if he had not felt the stirring tensions of political agitation, Affie would hardly have been human if he had not grown a little weary of the endless pomp and ceremony everywhere he went. It was hardly surprising that his patience snapped at a dinner he attended after laying the foundation stone for the new Melbourne town hall. The mayor was following his colleagues in delivering an unbearably long speech of thanks, when Affie was handed a written note to the effect that a *Liedertafel* was waiting outside ready to burst into song. Leaning across the table, he barked out in his sharpest quarterdeck manner: 'Cut it short, Mr Mayor – the Germans are burning their fingers,'[7] and left the table to join them outside.

If Affie did not shrink from issuing the occasional embarrassing rebuke, he was not always free from censure himself. A few days later he presented £500 in sovereigns as prize money in the 'Duke of Edinburgh stakes' at a Melbourne race meeting. The presence of the clergy at such a function was strongly deprecated, and Affie was likewise criticised in the press for encouraging the vice of gambling.

It was a relief for the royal entourage to leave Melbourne behind and visit some of the smaller towns and villages in Victoria, where there was little formality. Nonetheless lack of organisation brought problems in its wake. At Colac their coach was met by a rabble of mounted horsemen, local councillors and citizens, but in the noise and confusion Affie and his retinue did not stop. The assembled multitudes were angry at being ignored, but apprehension of poor security was probably responsible. Ever since the Stephens Street episode and subsequent distribution of leaflets at official Melbourne functions calling on Britain to 'Give Ireland back her Parliament and set her churches free', Affie had been concerned about the possibility of being a terrorist target. It was noticed that he became uneasy when villagers at the other towns threw bouquets into the coach. They could so easily be bombs in disguise.

For relaxation between long hot dusty journeys he was taken on rabbit and kangaroo shoots by local landowners who entertained him. At a lakeside shooting expedition the only game available was a solitary black swan, which he promptly shot, to the anger of the local press. One writer claimed that the bird had been conveniently doped and was as drunk as most of the onlookers, while another called for the Duke's prosecution on a charge of shooting swans out of season.

On 9 December they reached Ballarat, the largest inland Australian city. Here they were received at the specially-erected Prince Albert Hall, the building of which had caused some problems. The committee had insisted on a 'Greek basilica made from local timber', but to its surprise found that Australian builders and craftsmen were not generally conversant with the finer points of classical Greek architecture. In the end an artifice of vague Greek influences was ready, though the Melbourne press pooh-poohed it as 'a rather hideous joss-house'.

On the train journey to Bendigo, the next major town visited, Affie gave further evidence that he was tiring of the endless formalities. As they stopped on the way he refused to leave his seat but left one of his staff to receive the declaration of loyalty, informing the angry councilors that he would reply in writing.

At Bendigo the tour was dogged by two accidents, one tragic. On his arrival at the station Affie inspected a large, skillfully-constructed model of *Galatea*, made of wood, tar-paper and canvas, with miniature sails and a crew of small boys on deck dressed as sailors. They saluted him and he returned the compliment, to the crowd's delight. After a councillors' dinner he went to the town centre to watch the torchlight procession. Among the floats none was watched more eagerly than the model, mounted on a steam-traction engine. A member of the local volunteer fire brigade stood on deck, ready to supervise the firework display planned for later that evening. The spectators were indiscriminately throwing fireworks around, and the inevitable happened. A dozen boxes of Roman candles and sky rockets had been opened on deck, and one firework thrown by the crows landed in the idle of them. Within seconds the sails of the model were alight, and rockets piled around the deck were igniting. The screaming children jumped into the crowd, their clothes ablaze, but three were trapped by the fallen charred sails. The procession broke up in confusion and the injured were taken to hospital, where the three most severely burned died that night.

Affie and the royal party returned immediately to the hotel and stayed there for two days as a mark of respect. He did not attend the funeral of the victims, but sent wreaths and a donation towards the headstone. Festivities were suspended, and in mourning the town hoisted all the bunting at half-mast.

After what was considered a decent interval of nearly a week, the council entertained Affie to a ball at another specially built Alfred Hall. The authorities had obviously not learnt their lesson, and once again there was an extraordinary lack of fire precautions. Shortly before the guests arrived, calico sheets decorating the hall were caught by a gas racket, and in less than an hour the entire building was gutted. An improvised bucket-brigade saved the neighbouring town hall and with it the supper, set out on trestle tables in the banquet room – the only part of the evening's preparations to survive. As soon as Affie heard about the fire he drove to the smoking remains, where the unhappy mayor was telling guests that the proceedings were cancelled. Affie suggested that instead they should have a makeshift ball in the supper room. After eating, the tables were removed and he brought his piper, who provided them with Scottish reels to which they danced until the small hours.

Affie returned to Melbourne for Christmas and the new year, carefully refusing all invitations from ambitious politicians and social leaders who competed for the hour of having him to stay for the festive season. Inevitably there were complaints that he and his suite were too fond of their own company. On Christmas Eve they went shopping in the main city stores, and – perhaps by design – missed a council deputation led by the mayor on board *Galatea*. Nobody appreciated this embarrassment more than a satirical journalist who wrote that 'in place of the Babylonian repast, they were given an accidental biscuit'.

Nonetheless he attended the council's Christmas fancy dress ball that evening, although his royal naval uniform was hardly fancy dress. He stayed until the small hours, and his piper piped him from the hall at the end. Such enthusiasm did not mark his unpunctual behaviour at a Boxing Night concert. The city's musical and choral societies had rehearsed a programme including a Mendelssohn oratorio (which alone involved four hundred singers), an overture by Meyerbeer, and a *Prince Alfred March* composed for the occasion by a Mr Schoot, whose music was generally considered as being more remarkable for its volume than for any pure melodic qualities. Affie missed the national anthem and arrived during the overture, whereupon the singers promptly stopped and sang the anthem again. He stayed for the first half of the show, but glanced at his watch several times with an expression of acute boredom and left at the interval.

After a final rush of Melbourne functions, *Galatea* sailed for Tasmania. Though Affie's lack of punctuality was bitterly criticised after his departure – which, it was noted, was on time for once – his tour of Victoria had been remarkably busy, and his excuses of tiredness after late nights in the hot dusty climate were convincing enough. The fortnight in Tasmania provided welcome relief, with a minimum of official receptions and several drives through rural areas in the north of the island. With green, largely unspoilt terrain and torrential rain (a pleasant change from the previous weeks), he could almost imagine himself nearer home at Balmoral or Coburg.

By the end of January 1868 they were back on mainland at Sydney, New South Wales. Seemingly endless functions crowded in on Affie, sometimes up to four a day. Most were nearly identical to those laid on for him at Adelaide and Melbourne, and it was hardly surprising that he should have betrayed occasional boredom and impatience – curt words to pompous councillors, or a glazed look during lengthy speeches. The invitation he accepted most eagerly was to the towns of Hunter Valley, an area renowned for its magnificent vineyards.

The itinerary had been planned for a month at Sydney followed by a visit to New Zealand, but after an outcry by press and governors in Queensland it was changed to allow Affie a few days there. A last-minute decision was taken to dry-dock *Galatea* for overhaul and put the royal party on a British warship, HMS *Challenger*. Affie's sojourn in the state was marked by petty arguments between rival politicians, and more ominously by a tussle between Protestant students carrying an Orange banner and a procession of Catholic teachers, which had to be broken up by police.

It was with some relief that Affie sailed back into Sydney harbour on 29 February, hoping for only a few days before engagements before leaving for New Zealand, and then home. But news of the Manchester executions in November had inflamed the Irish Catholic communities, and the Catholic press was openly sympathetic to the cause of Fenianism. In addition Sir Henry Parkes, Prime Minister of New South Wales, was involved in arguments with the Catholic hierarchy over state aid for local education and other regional issues; politics, religion and the question of Irish independence became hopelessly intertwined. Affie's titles coincidentally included that of Earl of Ulster, but he was careful not to be drawn into any controversial discussions. The detachments of armed police chosen by Parkes to guard him on his next public appearances were ample proof that the danger he faced was real enough.

The one important function to which he committed himself was a grand picnic to raise funds for a sailors' rest home. It was held at the ironically-named Clontarf, an attractive grassy area overlooking Port Jackson, on 12 March, a baking hot day. After taking luncheon in the marquee, Affie and Sir William Manning, one of the appeal organisers, walked across the plain to admire the view. He was holding a cheque comprising his personal donation to the fund, a cause dear to his heart. A small crowd followed part of the way, and just as Affie and Sir William paused, an Irishman, James O'Farrell, detached himself from the group. Increasing his pace, he reached arm's length, drew a pistol from his coat, aimed sharply and shot Affie in the back.

The excited buzz of conversation and music of the bands ceased sharply at the sound of the shot. Dignitaries rushed to the aid of Affie, writhing on the ground in agony as he cried out that his back was broken, while others threw themselves on O'Farrell. He fired a second time and shot one, a Mr Thorne, in the foot. The wounds of both men were fortunately classed as no more than 'trifling'. Affie enjoyed a healthy constitution, and three nurses had providentially arrived in New South Wales from London that day, trained by Florence Nightingale. Suffering from severe shock and loss of blood, he was placed on an improvised stretcher and taken by sea to Government House, where he arrived safely in spite of coming close to being thrown in the water when his boat was violently knocked by a passing steamer.

An inspection revealed that the bullet had been deflected from his spine by his heavy leather braces. It had entered his back and was lodged in the front of the abdomen. During an operation two days later it was removed and he was pronounced out of danger.

Like most sailors, Affie was good at telling a story. When he had got over the unpleasant experience, he would spin a yarn about his faithful old servant Smith, who had incidentally taken to his heels at Knysna when his master's elephant charged the party. Smith looked after Affie's guns, and was very fond of digging out bullets from dead game in order to see 'the form of the projectile'. He was one of the first people to see the Duke after the shot had been extracted, but his ruling passion seemed to be almost greater than anxiety for the invalid. He immediately demanded to see what the bullet looked like after it had been embedded in the princely flesh.

Public reaction veered between fury, hysteria and gratitude for the salvation of Australia's royal guest. Once again there was ample proof that nothing boosted loyalty to the crown so much as an attempt on a royal life, and Sunday 22 March was proclaimed a day of thanksgiving throughout New South Wales and Victoria, with churches offering prayers for the Duke's full recovery. Funds were opened as a gesture of thanksgiving for the sparing of his life, and as a result several hospitals bearing his name were built in Sydney and Melbourne. Parkes, who was intent on refuting rumours that he himself had been shot as well, spoke emotionally of a deep-rooted Fenian (if not Catholic) conspiracy to kill the Duke.

On 3 April Affie was well enough to appear in public again. He left Government House in a heavily-guarded carriage and rode through packed streets of wildly cheering crowds. For his part he and the suite were no less affected by these demonstrations, and were close to tears. Mr Thorne was presented with a gold watch personally inscribed with a message of thanks from the Duke.

It was then announced that he would be sailing for Britain the next day, without stopping to visit New Zealand first. Everyone agreed that it would be tempting providence to continue the itinerary, which had been published in advance, as planned. There had already been pro-Fenian demonstrations in Hokitika, South Island, and the authorities could not guarantee his safety. Yet an assurance was given that the tour would be resumed at a later date.

As *Galatea* sailed out of Sydney Harbour with its rich farewell display of fireworks and bonfires, across the South Pacific, around the Horn and across the Atlantic, echoes of the first attempted assassination in Australian history slowly died away. O'Farrell, the son of an immigrant Irish butcher, had a record of mental instability. After his arrest he successively claimed and denied membership of a Fenian group in the sub-continent. At first he claimed that he had acted on instructions from a band of Fenians in Melbourne, but later he retracted this and said that, from continually thinking and talking of the wrongs committed against Ireland, 'I became excited and filled with enthusiasm for the subject, and it was then under the influence of those feelings that I attempted to perpetrate the deed for which I am now justly called upon to suffer'.[8]

While being held in custody, he told the police that he did not care for death, and that he was sorry he had missed his aim. When Parkes asked him why he had done such a thing, he replied, 'Come, come, it is not fair to ask me such a question as that; the Prince is all right; the Prince will live; you need not fear about that, it's only a side wound. I shall be hanged; but the Prince will live.'[9] No evidence was produced at his trial before the Supreme Court on 18 March to substantiate claims of a widespread conspiracy against the Duke or any other public figure, but it was clear that he had been inspired by a spirit of revenge against the crown because of the Manchester executions. Though he was working alone, had he not succeeded in his attempt, there were other Irishmen in Australia who might have done the same if given the opportunity. The Duke of Buckingham, Secretary of State for the Colonies, had been warned that O'Farrell had been 'sent with others from England and they drew lots, but this must be *kept secret*'.[10]

The would-be assassin was found guilty of assault with intent to murder, and sentenced to death. Affie personally interceded with the governor, the Earl of Belmore, for the man's life to be spared. However, it was thought by the authorities 'that clemency, in a case so atrocious, would have a bad effect.'[11] He was hanged at Darlinghurst Gaol on 21 April 1868 and his body was buried in the Catholic section of Rookwood cemetery.

By coincidence his brother Peter O'Farrell, a solicitor by profession, was also convicted of an attempted assassination attempt in Australia some fifteen years later. On 21 August 1882 he shot at and wounded Archbishop James Goold, after a dispute over legal matters. This O'Farrell had originally decided to go into the church and had received deacon's orders as a young man, but had a dispute with one of the bishops and was never ordained.

On 25 April, while at Osborne, Queen Victoria received a telegram with news of the shooting. At first she was anxious lest Affie's health might have been permanently impaired, but after her initial shock she was more concerned that he should 'come back an altered being!' His presence and high-handed behaviour at home the year before, she told Vicky, had been 'a source of no satisfaction or comfort.' He had 'displeased high and low, and made mischief. In short he was quite a stranger to me.'[12]

HMS *Galatea* arrived at Spithead shortly after midday on 26 June. On dropping her anchor, she exchanged salutes with HMS *Victory* in Portsmouth harbour. The aldermen and councillors presented him with a brief address of congratulation on recovering from his wounds. As he looked along the faces of the crowds who had come to greet him, he recognised Mr Anderson, the conductor of Queen Victoria's private band, and shook him heartily by the hand. It was observed by the press that he looked in suitably robust health, and that he appeared somewhat stouter than before, increasingly resembling the Prince of Wales.

CHAPTER 5

The Second Cruise of HMS *Galatea* 1868–71

Affie was delighted to be home again, tired and still a little sore, but contented and proud of his experiences. Queen Victoria was relieved to see him safe and sound with only a slight bullet wound and scar, and though him 'decidedly improved'. However, once he had rejoined friends and relations at Marlborough House – especially Bertie and a now rather careworn Alix, exhausted by four pregnancies in quick succession and a severe attack of rheumatic fever which had left her permanently lame and exacerbated a hereditary tendency to deafness – he became once again the old Affie the Queen knew but did not love. During the summer, her letters to Vicky were full of complaints that he had become so conceited, and receiving ovations 'as if he had done something – instead of God's mercy having spared his life.'[1] Two days later, he had 'become so noisy and excitable that it is all I can do to bear it.'[2] It was not only a tendency to be pleased with himself that irritated her, but also the fact that he wasted little time after his return to England before he resumed his womanising. In August she was bitterly lamenting that he was 'a great, great grief – and I may say source of bitter anger for he is not led astray!' His conduct was 'gratuitous', and he was so different to his elder brother, who was 'so loving and affectionate, and so anxious to do well'.[3] It took a severe letter from her to make him 'quite himself again, affectionate, kind and amiable to higher and lower'.[4]

Galatea was still in commission, and in November 1868 Affie, his staff, officers and men set sail once more. Before he left, Vicky paid him a visit at his London home, Clarence House, and sensed that he was not altogether looking forward to it. She found him in very low spirits; 'he was busy packing up all his things, paying his bills – the place was in great confusion.'[5]

However, there would be compensations. To his delight, one member of the Marlborough House set, Lord Charles Beresford, who was to brighten (or damn, according to his mother) his life for many a year to come, would be joining him. Charlie B, as he was generally known, had recently been promoted to the rank of Lieutenant, and as such was to become an officer on board his ship.

Thanks to him, this second part of the voyage of *Galatea* would be full of colourful hair-raising incidents. Whichever side he was on, he was both an asset and a disaster, but as the unpredictable, wild and fun-loving Irishman that he was, Affie heartily welcomed him aboard. He was the second of five sons of the 4th Marquis of Waterford. All were hard riders, daredevils and courageous charmers, always ready for adventure. Life would never be dull afloat with Charlie B on board. Perhaps it is significant that the reports of this second stage of the cruise that appeared in *The Times*, which are not only very sedate but rather uneven in their coverage, do not mention him once. For his part, he thought his Captain 'an admirable seaman, with a great natural ability for handling a fleet', who would have made a first-class fighting Admiral – a chance he never had. He always remembered Affie's 'many acts of kindness', and after his youthful experiences in other ships, was delighted to be 'afloat in a crack sailing ship, smart and well found in every detail'.

With sails set and bunkers full, *Galatea* touched at Madeira where there was an episode with a goat during a wild night ashore, the animal being captured by some of the junior officers. No details are to hand, but one can imagine who was responsible. Next stop was the Cape, where Affie sailed into Simonstown for the third time on Christmas Day 1868, one of the hottest times of the year down there. Though he missed the festive tables and presents of his family, the tree and all the heavy Mrs Beeton seasonal fare, he made sure that all on board stuffed themselves with turkey, Christmas plum pudding and extra rum rations.

Early in the new year *Galatea* sailed again to Australia. According to Charlie B, the fact that an attempt had been made on his life there was one of the reasons why Affie chose to pay the colony another visit. At first glance this appears rather a paradoxical remark, but his return could be put down both to good manners and a desire to show off his wound with pride – or at least prove how fully he had recovered. It could also have been a gesture of courage, in that royalty would not allow fear of the assassin to prevent them from carrying out their duties and obligations.

The party arrived at Melbourne on 22 February 1869. It had been announced in advance that Her Majesty the Queen had wished for His Royal Highness's visit not to be 'attended by the sort of demonstrations with which he was welcomed last year'. There was therefore no officially-organised public welcome on his landing, but it was far too much to expect that he would be given a quiet reception, for crowds gathered to cheer loudly as he stepped from barge to jetty. Though he had to attend the inevitable dinners and theatre performances with the governor and other local dignitaries, he was left more to his own devices. The Melbourne correspondent of *The Times* commented that 'his present freedom from restraint evidently affords him a very enjoyable contrast to his Victorian experiences of last year', when the authorities 'ruthlessly devoted him under that tremendous programme I feel very sure he can never forget'.[6] The lesson had perhaps been learnt that he had been subjected to some pressure, and those officials who had experienced his outbursts of bad temper may have advised that a less demanding schedule would be in order this time.

Nevertheless Affie still kept his promise to visit New Zealand. To the joy of the officers – and doubtless the lower deck too – this stage of the tour was marked by plenty of hunting, especially wild cattle and boar. The irrepressible Irish lieutenant joined in, not with a rifle, but using his dirk instead. For once his expertise did not help him; he admitted making 'an awful mess of it' and if it had not been for the heavy mastiffs he would have been badly cut. As it was, the boar merely bowled him over into the mud. They also had a delightful time bathing in hot springs, with the Maoris, where 'you stand in the water, warm as milk, close beside the springs of boiling water, and occasionally a jet of steam makes you jump'.

In June 1869 they reached the Fiji Islands and Tahiti, to be greeted again by a formidable array of native beauty. The islands enjoyed perfect climate, hot without the stiflingly dusty atmosphere of Australian midsummer. Nobody seemed to work, but just sat in the sun all day, occasionally carried bananas, and swam in the clear blue sea. For once the officers and crew of *Galatea* were in no hurry to move on, and enjoyed every minute of the time. Here Charlie B's perpetual daring was almost his undoing, in another attempt to do everything better than anyone else. He shot down a fifty-foot waterfall head first, not knowing what was at the bottom. Luckily he ended up none the worse, and proud thus to initiate a new 'game'.

There was another reason why everyone remembered Tahiti for a long time afterwards. At Sunday service in the local church, tobacco was distributed around the congregation in the middle of the service. The Queen of Tahiti was an inveterate smoker and this was her idea. After an allotted time for enjoyment of the weed, she clapped her hands and the service continued.

The next idyllic port of call in the Pacific was Hawaii, where Charlie B met another friend. This was Queen Emma, whom he had escorted to England four years earlier for an audience with Queen Victoria. The latter thought her royal sister a 'savage' to look at, but 'peculiarly civilised' – as usual coming to the root of the matter in only a few words. This time Beresford was to make the return call. Driving his tandem, a light carriage with two horses, without which he never went on land or sea, and turning into the gate of the royal residence, he took the corner too sharply, the wheels locked, and down came driver, tandem and all. Queen Emma rushed out at the alarm and jingling of Canadian sleigh bells attached to the harness, to find her visitor sprawling on the ground in very lowly undignified obeisance.

In July 1869 *Galatea* left the enchantment of the South Seas for Japan, a visit which was both official and royal – and therefore more formal. Affie's apartments were in the Mikado's summer palace at Yedo. They were completely furnished in European style, while the walls were covered with curiously painted Japanese paper. In his sitting room stood a magnificent bronze vase covered with beautifully-executed birds and dragons, a gift from the Mikado. He met his host in person, the first European royal to be thus honoured, on what was possibly the last time the Japanese court was presented in full costume – their sweeping, lavishly-embroidered silk robes and jewels with foreign delegations in European uniform, sitting back in a barouche, 'a modern of the moderns'. Even then the Japanese were fast learning and adapting to western ways.

Here the hospitality of the far east embraced a very full programme which Affie must have found a little irksome after the free-and-easy Pacific Islands. He spent hours watching performances of the Nō theatre; sweaty wrestling and sword-play; extraordinary dancing and howling music; and wherever he went, he saw the populace either falling to their faces in homage (as nobody was permitted to 'look down' on him) or banging their windows shut as he passed.

It was not surprising that as a result of his travels Affie became a great collector of curios. He and his senior officers would visit the bazaar in search of souvenirs, where all would spend generously; he knew what he liked, and made no pretence as to whether it might be considered a connoisseur's piece or not. But as a prince of the blood royal, he was in the enviable position of not having to purchase everything he wanted. Among the gifts with which he was presented were ten sumptuous volumes of a history of Japan, each fourteen inches square by four inches deep; large porcelain bowls of exquisite workmanship and painting; a priceless set of Nō masks, made from painstakingly carved and painted wood; and various bronzes, silks and satins. When they eventually set sail, after about five months in the east, the holds of the ship were filled almost to capacity.

For once Charlie B appears to have been kept in the background, as there are no tales of his hair-raising escapades at this stage of their travels. But both he and his captain went through the agonies of tattooing, presumably just (in his own words) 'for the hell of it'. In those days the Japanese and oriental method was white upon dark, working on the skin round the chief design. The occidental way was the complete opposite;

dark design upon white, using the natural skin as background. Posterity does not record where either man was 'illustrated'.

More oriental entertainments awaited them as *Galatea* steamed northwest across the Yellow Sea to dock at Tientsin, the port of Peking. A photograph of Affie at this time shows him in his Norfolks, sporting the beginning of the full beard he would have in later life. By the time the ship reached England some eighteen months later, officers and men were by no means 'clean', luxuriating instead in the new Admiralty permission for cessation from the daily chore of shaving. After the formality of the Japanese court, Affie was glad to be entirely incognito in China. He and the party stayed in the British Embassy in Peking, and spent their days either riding and hunting, or shopping in the city for more curios.

Another form of relaxation which all – especially Affie – enjoyed until the small hours was the game of bowls. When they were back in port he staged a grand tournament – navy versus shore, eight-a-side. The challenge began at 9 p.m., but the captain was not on board again till 4 a.m. One senior officer reported that the match was 'a Spirited and hardly-contested game, the Shore, however, beating the Navy five successive games, HRH backing his side until he had lost nearly 400 dollars. Then he pluckily challenged them double or quits, which he won.'

Such activities obviously gave Affie a healthy appetite, and on board ship at this time it was recorded that he made an omelette with 200 eggs. It was served in the wardroom for breakfast, and worked out at about ten eggs per officer. One Sunday in China, after attending church, 'HRH, to whom it was a novelty, partook of a regular Chinese feast – bird's nest soup, eggs that had been kept 100 years or longer, shark's fins etc.' To western ways of thinking at least, the omelette must have been rather more inviting than the venerable eastern fare.

At Manila and the Philippines, such was the custom of a less squeamish age, the main entertainment was cock-fighting. Affie and Charlie B were hardened to such barbaric displays, and the latter wrote quite calmly afterwards of watching birds armed with steel spurs shaped like scythes and sharpened to a razor edge. Heads were sliced off, and chests slashed open – 'the use of the artificial spurs affected the betting, making the fight very much more uncertain and therefore more exciting.'

Christmas 1869 found Affie beginning a three months' 'progress through India' as a guest of the viceroy Lord Mayo. The Prince of Wales had insisted that his brother must go there not as a naval commander, but as a prince and son of the sovereign. As no son of any British sovereign had been there before, Affie would have to travel in great pomp, so it would have 'a beneficial effect on India'. Australia, Bertie tactfully pointed out, was an English colony, whereas India was 'a great Eastern country conquered by the English',[7] and for the tour to have any political status would be ill-advised.

On 22 December *Galatea* docked in the Hooghly near Calcutta, where Affie mounted an Arab charger and took part in a long procession of horsemen and carriages through a multitude of people, European infantry and native regiments. When they reached the lawns of Government House, seventy elephants were drawn up as a guard of honour. Mayo reported in Major Cowell-style to Queen Victoria that HRH had already won golden opinions from everybody, and although they had found him courteous, considerate and 'sincerely desirous to please', he had no doubt that the Duke would 'comport himself in a way worthy of his position, and in a manner which will be satisfactory to Your Majesty'.[8]

What, one wonders, made him write thus? Affie was twenty-five and a man of the world, having travelled a good deal further than his mother ever would. Perhaps that was the trouble, and the Queen had warned her Viceroy in advance, knowing her son and his weaknesses too well.

So began Affie's earthbound progress over thousands of miles. In trains and carriages, on horseback and elephant; cursing the heat on the plains and joyfully relaxing in the hills. Duty bound, he visited Bombay, Madras and countless smaller cities. In Nepal and the upper provinces of the Punjab, Rajputana and beautiful Kashmir, the native princes took him big game hunting which put his little Cape elephant to shame. He shot tigers with hundreds of mounted elephants as beaters, played polo, went pig-sticking and watched wild beast fights. In these activities he was joined from time to time by two Beresfords, not only Charlie but also his younger brother Bill, who was aide-de-camp to several viceroys in India.

In Affie's honour many grand levees were staged, watched by thousands of natives 'in all their finery and variety of colour', and the oriental splendor of maharajahs and worthies from all walks of Indian life. There were the customary displays of fireworks and accompanying illuminations. By the time he had done his duty for almost thirteen years viewing such spectacles, and still had to look as if they were his first. Nonetheless he behaved himself in an exemplary manner which gave the sharp-eyed Viceroy no cause for reproach, and was duly invested with the insignia of the Knight Grand Cross of the Star of India. As was noted in London at the time, although these royal visits were meant to 'stimulate personal loyalty to the Queen, the pleasurable features…were not to be ignored.' It was a kind thought, but easier when travelling incognito than cognito as was the case with Affie just then.

At Ceylon he was presented with a young elephant called Tom, although the possibility remains that the ship's crew acquired him by less certain means. Charlie B immediately took charge of him, and taught him to pipe for meals. Over and above his legitimate rations, he appreciated the most curious food – pea-soup, paper, wood shavings, tea leaves, champagne, beer, whisky, a daily ration of rum (as he was considered a member of the crew), brandy, gin, wine, soda water, and of course tobacco. Although he had been quite small when he joined ship, he grew enormously with this varied, not to say princely, diet. Anticipating the age of automated labour by a hundred years or so, he could do the work of twenty men. One of his duties was to help to clew up the mainsail with a rope in a bowline around his neck, walking on until he was told to stop. Everybody adored him, and a house was built aft in which he slept. He would hoist Charlie B up on his shoulders circus-style with a fore foot, or upon his back with a hind foot.

Unlike many seamen, Tom was never sick. One night when the officers were having supper on deck and had to leave the meal to trim sails, he obligingly finished it for them. He ate everything on the table, put his foot on the plates and smashed them, and squashed a large coffee-can quite flat. Then, according to the officers, he looked at them just like a naughty child. On their return to England he was sent to London zoo in a truck, but sadly the marine artilleryman who was appointed to take charge as his escort was pinned against the side of the vehicle and killed.

Affie's Indian sojourn was marred by an unsavoury episode over which he had no control. An exchange of correspondence purporting to be between him and the Prince of Wales was made public. Bertie's letters were full of comments on his hopes to visit India one day 'if *la mère* approves', the distress caused him by the Mordaunt divorce case in which he was implicated at the time, and various items of small-talk – quite harmless apart from allusions to the beauty of Alix's conveniently still-unmarried sister Thyra. Worst of all, though, were remarks on how the Prince Consort's name was 'constantly held up….I must not do this or do that, I must always be goody because he was so good….Here nine years after poor father's death I am expected to sit in sackcloth and ashes to his memory'.[9] All this and more was published initially in an Irish newspaper and then in the *Madras Mail*, and extracts were published in translation in *L'Independence Belge*. They were so convincing that even Bertie's other siblings wondered if they were genuine after all.

On 6 June 1870 *The Times* confirmed that these letters were indeed forgeries, but not before many European readers had been astounded by the apparent indiscretions of the heir to the British throne. The hoax had no severe results as far as Affie was concerned, beyond inspiring in him contempt for the press in general, but it was one of several incidents which did Bertie no little harm in Germany.

By this time, on 24 May 1870, *Galatea* had docked at Mauritius, where Charlie B attempted to climb Sugar Loaf mountain. They all went shooting with the natives, which turned out to be a nerve-racking experience, 'one of the most dangerous amusements' in that part of the world, with bullets whistling in the air around them.

From that 'pearl of the Indian Ocean', Affie sailed on 3 June for the Cape of Good Hope to fulfil yet another obligation which he had begun as a white-gloved midshipman. This was the official inauguration on 12 July of the new harbour, breakwater and docks at Table Bay, where everything was conducted with the usual blaring accompaniment. With this, Cape Town was on the road to becoming one of the most important ports in the world.

Despite his programme of functions and devotion to hunting activities, Affie found some time to help at least one man less fortunate than himself. This was clear from a letter to Gladstone, written on behalf of a senior army officer in South Africa who was now seriously ill, written from on board *Galatea* on 13 July:

> Allow me to interest you in favor of a great friend of mine Sir Walter Currie, who has long served in this Colony & has recently owing to exposure & hard work lost his health & his mind partially. I am in hopes you may be able to give him some pension or allowance on the part of Her Majesty's Government which would greatly assist him in his present state...[10]

Later that summer the ship proceeded in leisurely fashion across the south Atlantic. At the Falkland Islands Charlie B found another friend – 'a good fellow' on a ranch who bred bulldogs and bulls for bull-baiting, which had by then been forbidden in England.

On 11 March 1871 they landed at Montevideo in Uruguay. Here Affie formally paid his respects to the President, Don Lorenzo Battle, and visited the city museum and cathedral. The British consul, Major St John Munro, entertained him with a banquet at his house, and he was invited to play billiards at the English club. While he was there he impressed the local community, who were skilled horsemen, 'by the cool daring and finished dexterity with which he managed a team of four thoroughbred South American horses in an English mail break'.[11]

Before sailing out from the Rio de Plata on 17 March the last homeward stretch, Affie found to his consternation that the ship's deck seams had been badly strained by rough seas, and water was streaming into their cabins. The following conversation would be heard: 'How did you sleep last night? It was pretty rough.' Answer: 'I woke up at one o'clock and saw them reefing tops'ls' (lying in their hammocks the men could see 'clear through the seams'). Charlie B had learned sailmaking as a boy, and solved the problem by making an awning – not only for himself and Affie, one trusts, but also for their mates.

On 19 May 1871 the extremely weather worn *Galatea*, her captain and crew – not forgetting Tom the elephant – docked at Plymouth. Affie was now a full-grown man of nearly twenty-seven, by all accounts an excellent if strict captain, and certainly experienced in the ways of the world, the Royal Navy, and the hazards of both. Three days later *The Times* announced that he was leaving Plymouth by train for London, and would proceed north to Balmoral next day. As ever, the presence of Queen Victoria loomed in the background.

CHAPTER 6

'The Murder is Out!' 1871–3

Affie's homecoming coincided with a critical time for the British monarchy in more ways than one. Queen Victoria's prolonged seclusion and the Prince of Wales's indiscreet social behaviour had an adverse effect on the standing of the crown at large. With the overthrow of Napoleon III, Emperor of the French, after his defeat in the Franco-Prussian war, radical opinion was sufficiently encouraged to contemplate the possibility of a British republic. Internal divisions between the Queen and her children only served to complicate the family relationship.

The elder children were increasingly alarmed by their mother's indifference to the public mood. For nearly a year Alice had been discussing it with them, and though it had come to the Queen's notice and a sharp exchange of letters between the two had followed, Alice refused to be cowed. When Affie came back to England he was quickly acquainted with the situation, and agreed with Bertie that a tactful note ought to be written warning the Queen of the danger posed to the monarchy by her absence from the public eye. Vicky, who was on holiday with Fritz in London after the war with France, was alone in thinking that such a move could be counter-productive and only make her more obstinate still, but as the eldest and most literate of all and the inveterate family peacemaker, she reluctantly accepted their decision that she should draft the letter for all of them to sign. By the time it was written and ready for their approval the Queen was seriously ill with a combination of gout, neuralgia and an abscess on the arm. Never had she felt so ill since an attack of typhoid at the age of sixteen; her servants had to do everything for her, feed her like a baby and even help her to blow her nose. Sir Thomas Biddulph, Master of the Royal Household, dismissed a suggestion that her children should be sent for, as their presence 'would have killed her at once!'[1] In the end it went no further, and what might have been an irretrievably damaging rupture to family harmony passed into oblivion.

As if Her Majesty's illness was not trouble enough, the domestic situation was soured further by a succession of 'Brown rows' in which nobody incurred her displeasure more than Affie.

John Brown had started his unique career as the Prince Consort's Highland ghillie, and was now the Queen's personal servant. His honesty and blunt outspoken manner amused her, surrounded as she was by relations, members of her household and obsequious ministers who were generally a little afraid of her. He helped her onto her ponies, lifted her into the carriage when she was too stiff to walk, saw that she was properly wrapped up in bad weather, and ensured there was 'a wee drappie' in her picnic hampers instead of 'old woman's tea'. The elder children had no time at all for Brown. Bertie had always detested him, but in happier days Affie had used him on deerstalking expeditions around Balmoral and happily shared his pipe tobacco. But as Brown's power and confidence increased, and whispers throughout the country of 'Mrs Brown' grew louder, Affie came to share his brother's opinion. Much as the Queen might blame everything on her second son, thinking he had become too overbearing since he was appointed to the command of *Galatea*, there is no doubt that Brown's willful arrogance and drunkenness were equally responsible for the feud.

The two men had been enemies since a ghillies' ball in the summer of 1871 when the revelry threatened to get out of hand and Affie ordered the musicians to stop playing. Brown, it is said, told him angrily, 'I'll not take this from you or from any other man,' but on being questioned another day when he was sober, claimed that he had misunderstood at first, and then told the fiddlers that they were quite right to stop on the Duke's instructions. The quarrels were made no easier by jealousy between Brown and John Grant, who had entered royal service at the same time. Grant, the Queen suspected, had been poisoning Affie's mind against Brown.

When Affie arrived at Balmoral in September, he ostentatiously made a point of shaking hands with everyone except Brown. After complaints from the latter, the convalescent Queen told her private secretary, Colonel Ponsonby, to try and arrange a reconciliation. Affie agreed to see him as long as Ponsonby was present as a witness. 'If I see a man on board my ship it is always in the presence of an officer,' he explained. 'You have, I believe, the same rule in the Army.' The Queen was furious, insisting that Balmoral was not a ship 'and I won't have naval discipline introduced here.' Nonetheless Ponsonby brought both men together. Asked why he had been so angry, Affie told Brown that he was 'surprised at the extraordinary language' used at the ghillies' ball. Brown apologised for losing his temper and begged forgiveness. At length Affie expressed himself satisfied with the meeting, whereupon the servant mischievously said he was too. Ponsonby hastily ushered them out of the room before they could start arguing again, and wrote to his wife that he thought they were both lying – 'neither is satisfied.'[2]

He knew too well the faults of both. Though loyal to the family, in his view Affie lacked his brothers' charm, and had a look in his eyes which somehow did not inspire trust. Moreover he was almost as partial to the bottle as Brown, and his musical skills could be overrated. One evening at about this time Ponsonby dined at the Prince of Wales's Highland home Abergeldie in the company of both princes and Gladstone. Afterwards three of them and another guest played whist, while Affie and a friend serenaded them on violin and piano respectively. Though both out of tune, they kept up 'an appalling din' for an hour, until even the long-suffering Prince of Wales was driven to suggest tactfully that 'I don't think you're quite right.'[3]

Others would also express their reservations as to Affie's musical prowess. Some years later the Liberal minister Viscount Goschen asked Joseph Joachim, head of the Berlin Academy of Music, if the Duke of Edinburgh could have earned his living as a professional violinist. Joachim said that perhaps he could – on the sands. On the other hand the pianist and conductor Sir Charles Hallé, founder of the orchestra which would bear his name, had given him lessons in composition as a young man, and declared that he was a much better musician than he was frequently given full credit for. In the absence of any recorded evidence, nobody is in a position to pronounce with authority on how proficient or otherwise the Duke of Edinburgh was on his chosen instrument. It has to be accepted that where the second son of the Queen was involved, there was bound to be a degree of sycophancy from those who wanted to invite him to play at public concerts and were aware that the presence of a senior member of royalty in the orchestra was a great honour. Nevertheless, it is perhaps only fair to give him the benefit of the doubt and accept that the standard of his playing was variable, but as a musician and also the composer of occasional pieces, such as the *Galatea Waltz*, that he did not altogether lack skill.

The Queen's interest in the 'Brown row' did her health a power of good, and it was considered more than mere coincidence that from that time onwards she began to recover from her indisposition.

For Affie and Bertie, there was another problem to be handled with discretion. When they visited the international exhibition in Paris four years earlier, they were introduced by the duc de Gramont to Giulia Beneni, 'La Barucci', who proclaimed herself 'the greatest whore in the world'. In September 1871 Bertie received a letter from her brother in Italy, Pirro Beneni, saying she had died of tuberculosis, that all her intimate and highly compromising correspondence with *'votre Altesse'*, was in his hands, and that such documents could be reclaimed for a sum approaching £1,200. Affie had apparently been just as indiscreet as his brother, and was approached in similar fashion. Bertie's private secretary Francis Knollys was asked to deal with the matter, and he took it upon himself to negotiate through Monsieur Kanne, a royal courier in Florence who had previous experience of such delicate transactions. It was suggested to Kanne that the letters might be forgeries, but he was allowed to examine them and had to conclude that the writing and 'intimate gossip' furnished sufficient proof of identity. Nevertheless, in the second week of November he was able to conclude a satisfactory purchase for a little less than a quarter of the original asking price. The royal brothers' minds could rest easy once again – though not without a tactful warning from Kanne, through Knollys, that they should be more careful in future.[4]

Affie and Bertie had had one narrow escape, and for the latter there was about to be another. In the first week of November 1871 Sir Charles Dilke, Liberal Member of Parliament for Chelsea, delivered a speech at Newcastle fiercely attacking the monarchy and advocating a republic. Queen Victoria's seclusion and the dissolute behaviour of her two elder sons were doing the crown no favours. On 9 November, the day that Kanne completed the purchase of the notorious letters, the Prince of Wales celebrated his thirtieth birthday at Sandringham with a ball and then retired to bed with what was thought at first to be no more than a severe chill. As Dilke stumped the land with his speeches, invariably disrupted by hecklers so persistently that at Bolton a man was killed when a volley of nuts and bolts was hurled through the assembly hall windows, the heir's condition deteriorated. Queen and family hurriedly descended on the Norfolk house where he lay delirious with what had been diagnosed as typhoid fever.

Most of them sat hushed around the invalid anxiously awaiting some improvement in his almost hopeless condition, but Affie and Arthur went skating on the Sandringham pond. If their behaviour might have seemed heartless, it was nonetheless practical. In his down-to-earth manner, Affie knew there was nothing to be gained by sitting around a cramped bedroom, merely getting in the way of the nurses. To the Princess of Wales's lady-in-waiting Lady Macclesfield, it was 'quite impossible to keep a house quiet as long as it is swarming with people and really the way in which they all squabble and wrangle and abuse each other destroys one's peace.'[5] If he chose to avoid these tensions from time to time and go outside, Affie could hardly be blamed. Yet at the same time Bertie and Alix were among his closest friends, and the prospect of losing his favourite brother so young was one which he dared not contemplate. He was moved particularly by the patient's 'wonderful kindness and courtesy and consideration for everyone, even in his wanderings.'

To Gladstone, he wrote on 27 November that his brother

continues to go on favourably in his illness which being a very severe one makes us very anxious. We are now in the very worst moment of the illness, but his strength and pulse keeping up & having taken a great deal of wine and nourishment today, the Doctors pronounce time to have been gained which is every thing in this disease.[6]

Two weeks later, everyone despaired for the heir's life. Dean and Lady Stanley met Affie while waiting for a train at Windsor, and reported him 'terribly overcome' when they asked him about the nature of the attack. He could only point to his chest and burst into tears.[7] On 14 December, the ominous tenth anniversary of the Prince Consort's death, grim expectations of another royal passing from typhoid were in the air. Nevertheless it was on the same morning that doctors reported encouraging signs of recovery. The son had a will to live that his father had conspicuously lacked. Affie recommended the addition of pale ale to Bertie's diet, though his claims that he thus saved his brother's life were surely somewhat exaggerated. From his bed Bertie asked who had thought of such a novel medicine, which had apparently revived him. On being told, he commented, 'That was a good idea of his but won't it make me too fat?'[8]

The Queen had no time for Affie's boasts of miraculous powers of healing or his unseemly devotion to outdoor pursuits, and he was one of the first to be sent packing once Bertie's life was out of danger. If typhoid did not claim the life of a prince, it helped to dampen the fires of the British republican movement. While hostility to the crown would never disappear completely, it was now considerably muted.

On his return to Clarence House, Affie was welcomed by the Stanleys, who were delighted to see the change in his expression. He confessed to being almost ashamed, wrote Lady Augusta to her sister, of ever having doubted that his brother would recover, but the sudden bad news of the previous week, and having seen one of the servants in tears, had completely unnerved him.

After a mild relapse at the end of the month, Bertie's recovery was steady if slow, and within months he and Affie had resumed their intermittent life of merry-making around London. Lord Rosebery, then an undergraduate whose interest in politics still took second place to the pursuit of pleasure, was asked by the Prince of Wales's private secretary, Francis Knollys, if he could see his way to making his London residence where Their Royal Highnesses could meet their 'actress friends'. Rosebery disliked Affie, and made the excuse that his house was too small, adding that he trusted the matter would not be raised again. Yet this did not prevent the future Prime Minister from being an occasional guest at all-night orgies of drinking, cock-fighting, and 'other amusements' at which the princes and their actress friends were regular guests of honour.

Affie's companion was a New York society lady, Fanny Ronalds. Her unhappy marriage to an alcoholic ne'er-do-well had driven her to find fulfilment in a theatrical career, and she had been attached for some time to an opera house run by Leonard Jerome, father of Jennie Jerome, the future Lady Randolph Churchill, in Madison Square Gardens. Later she moved to Paris, and during the Franco-Prussian war she settled in London, where her private income allowed her to entertain with lavish musical soirees. It was probably at one such event that she and Affie were introduced and became firm friends. There is nothing to suggest that she ever became his mistress, and her friendship would in time extend equally to the similarly musical Duchess of Edinburgh.

Early in 1872 *Galatea* paid off at the end of her commission, and Affie attended a two-month course in naval gunnery, after which he went on half-pay. It was noticed that he was being more than usually nervous and difficult. An undated and unidentified newspaper cutting, thought to have been published around this time, recorded that at a dinner on board ship he toasted the health of his 'wife' – the ship. This found its way into the Royal Archives, and the displeased Queen became more firmly convinced that a suitable wife should be found for him as soon as possible.

Little did she know that her son had made his choice already. Before setting sail on *Galatea* for his second cruise, he had visited Alice and Louis at Jugenheim in August 1868. Several of the Hessian ducal and Russian imperial family were there at the time, among them sixteen-year-old Princess Marie of Battenberg, eldest daughter of Prince Alexander of Hesse, and later Princess Marie of Erbach-Schönberg. She remembered this appearance of the Duke of Edinburgh, 'as brown as a mulatto, very quiet and grave'[9] for many a long year. So did the rest of the assembled company, for it resulted in Affie's first meeting with Grand Duchess Marie, the only surviving daughter of Tsar Alexander II. Affie was very taken with her, and needed little encouragement from his pro-Russian sister. Soon after returning from his cruise in 1871, he told the Queen that he intended to meet the Tsar shortly and ask for Marie's hand.

Her Imperial Highness the Grand Duchess Marie Alexandrovna was born on 17 October 1853, sixth child of Tsarevich Alexander and the former Princess Marie of Hesse and the Rhine. The family had consisted of six sons and two daughters; the eldest, Alexandra, died at the age of seven, and Marie thus became her parents' spoilt darling. When she was seventeen months old her father, a grey-haired giant with closely-cut whiskers and a habitually worried, rather forbidding expression, ascended the throne. He used to drive out in a small carriage drawn by a sleek black trotter, with Marie perched between his knees. The Tsarina suffered perpetually from ill-health, aggravated by the bitter Russian climate, and regularly took her daughter with her on visits to German relatives and health spas.

At St Petersburg the whole court idolised the child. Sailors on guard outside Peterhof Palace would prepare little surprises for her – a bunch of wild strawberries, a stick half-peeled as though a white ribbon had been wound around it, or a small wooden flute.

As the only girl among six brothers, her early years in nursery and schoolroom could account for her rather unfeminine demeanour and abrupt manner as an adult. The eldest boy, Grand Duke Nicholas, was slim and delicate like their mother. In 1864 he was engaged to Princess Dagmar of Denmark, but died of tuberculosis in Nice a year later aged twenty-two, after a deathbed ceremony in which he feebly joined her hand with that of his second brother Alexander. The latter, always known as Sasha and destined to be the last Tsar but one, was a large bear of a man whose great strength and chestnut beard belied his gentle nature. The third brother Vladimir was a patron of the arts, a lover of the ballet, and a renowned gourmet. He and his wife Princess Marie of Mecklenburg-Schwerin were to become the parents of Grand Duke Kyril, Affie's son-in-law, and a grandchild Marina would eventually become Duchess of Kent. The fourth, Alexis, was a massively-built 'perfect Lohengrin' and Grand Admiral in the Russian navy. After the destruction of the imperial fleet in the war with Japan of 1904-5, he reputedly died of a broken heart. Officially a bachelor, his youthful marriage having never been recognised by the Tsar, his life was said to be 'a case of fast women and slow ships'. Marie's favourite brother was Serge, who may have been pleasant enough in boyhood but grew up to be often obstinate, disagreeable, and arrogant, a much-hated governor of Moscow. Both he and his wife, Affie's niece Princess Ella of Hesse, met violent deaths; he was assassinated in the street in Moscow, and she was thrown down a mineshaft during the revolution thirteen years later. By contrast Paul, five years younger than Marie and the baby of them all, was the most pleasant and generally well-liked. Good-looking and an accomplished dancer, he married Princess Alexandra of Greece, who died in childbirth. He outlived his brothers, only to meet a violent death at the hands of the Bolsheviks in 1919.

The life of Their Imperial Highnesses could not be compared in any way with that of their royal cousins at Windsor. None of Queen Victoria's residences could match the magnificence or size of their Russian counterparts. While young Affie was painfully coming to grips with the rough-and-tumble of a midshipman's life, Marie and her brothers dwelt in a veritable paradise. There were several Romanov palaces and country estates both in St Petersburg and bordering the Gulf of Finland, to which the whole family would move at pre-ordained times of the year. St Petersburg, where

Marie was born, was the city of wonderful parks, fountains and gardens; huge family gatherings, military displays on parade grounds large enough for four hundred thousand men; religious services in churches that glittered with gold and the bejewelled copes of the priests; and, towering above all, the imperial palaces. There was the Marble Palace of clean stone, as opposed to the classic Italianate colour-washed townhouses of the gentry; the Yusoupov Palace, the scene of Rasputin's murder many years later; the Michael Palace, yellow and white; and the Imperial Winter Palace of light green stucco with its thousand rooms, one hundred staircases, seventeen hundred rooms and two thousand windows. The country residences varied from the grand and spacious to the small and intimate.

As the Romanov family grew, so separate establishments were built or acquired. The largest complex was Imperial Village, Tsarskoe Selo; here stood the Ekaterinsky Palace with its three hundred-yard façade of vivid blue, and eight hundred huge French windows separated by gold-painted caryatids. In the grounds stood the Hermitage, with its English garden and informal areas of trees and water. After breakfasting on green tea and toast Marie's grandfather had fed the birds here every morning at seven o'clock. But the grandest of all was Peterhof, a few miles down the coast, opposite the island of the naval base and fort of Kronstadt. Known as the 'challenge to Versailles' because of its fountains, but not nearly so large, Marie knew it well as a child and returned there every year after her marriage. Two miles the other side of Tsarskoe was Pavlovsk, distinguished by a dome over the great hall, while forty miles south of St Petersburg was Gatchina, traditional home of the Dowager Empresses. Marie's sister-in-law Dagmar later lived there, surrounded by stables full of silky borzoi dogs and quick little Siberian ponies kept for coursing. On each of these estates ample provision was made for the children, with a playhouse, the Russian equivalent of Osborne's Swiss Cottage, containing a kitchen and dining room with real plates, silver and saucepans. In the garden was a toy railway with tunnels, and a fortress which she and her brothers built with little bricks, complete with a small bridge over a stream. She even had a cow and played at farming.

All these memories Marie Alexandrovna cherished throughout her life, and countless others: horses, quick trotters with manes flying, flanks shining like mirrors; regiments of Cossacks in long red cloaks and heel-less boots, armed to the teeth; long corridors, echoing halls and the scent of Russian leather, perfume, cigarettes; the golden city of St Petersburg standing like a gas-lit jewel at the edge of the snowy Asian wastes beside a frozen Gulf of Finland, the snow, squeaking under gliding sledges and troikas beneath the curious eggshell blue sky of the northern winter; women in crinolines, wrapped up to the eyes in furs of sable, bear and scarce silver fox; wearing jewels at balls no other court could rival.

The young Grand Duchess whom Affie met was by no stretch of the imagination a particularly pretty young woman, but she was pleasant, ordinary and unsophisticated, even something of a tomboy. Altogether she breathed a freshness and energy which was so delightfully different from so many of the European princesses of her age. She had good skin, healthy teeth, and in short was very 'acceptable'. To her parents she was shy and affectionate, two characteristics which would find favour with Queen Victoria, and she was not too clever; bright women were anathema in Victorian Britain. Here was a girl, he knew, that even his demanding mother would approve of, and the endless lists she encouraged Vicky to compile could now be thrown away.

The Duke whom Marie met was a handsome, sunburnt, bearded, rather stocky young gentleman, in smart naval uniform, who had commanded fine ships and travelled throughout the world. He had deep blue expressive eyes, good features, and a hearty laugh, and when he told her of his adventures, he appeared more fascinating still.

Yet as far as the Queen was concerned, a Romanov daughter-in-law would be a very mixed blessing. Ever since the Crimean war Russian had been an enemy of England, who in turn was suspicious of her intentions over the Black Sea and central Asia, and regarded her ruling dynasty as 'false and arrogant'. Moreover, if Affie married a princess or Grand Duchess belonging to the Greek Orthodox Church, there would doubtless be a constant procession of priests in and out of Clarence House. But the Queen had long since accepted that finding him a wife would be difficult; as long as he could choose someone 'to suit and please him I would not mind who she was. The choice is becoming so narrow that I think we must get over the difficulties concerning religion.'[10] She was assured that the Greek Church, unlike the Roman Catholic faith, did not refuse to acknowledge any creed other than their own, and the foreign secretary Lord Granville advised her that a Russian Grand Duchess would be more suitable than an English subject, a Catholic, or a daughter of the dispossessed King of Hanover.

As promised, Affie met Tsar Alexander in Germany in July 1871, and the latter wrote to Queen Victoria that while he was not opposed to any union between their families, he could not impose his will in any way on Marie, and they would have to wait a year for 'any definitive decision' which however would not be binding. Alice added her opinion that Marie's tender age was the main obstacle and she was too young to think of marriage yet, a rather hollow excuse in view of the fact that Marie's mother had been married before her seventeenth birthday. Andrew Buchanan, British Ambassador at St Petersburg, reported that the Duke of Edinburgh had made a good impression on the Tsar and Tsarina but seemingly none on their daughter, who still appeared very childish for her seventeen years and dreaded the idea of marriage as it would separate her from her happy childhood home. His frustration at such indecisive answers did nothing to bolster up his naturally reserved disposition, and doubts assailed him. Would the Grand Duchess make him happier than Alix might have done? Would he have found more joy with the commoner, his 'secret love', presumably on Malta, about whom he had once confessed to his sister Helena? The Tsarina's haughty and non-committal letters that winter, and a report from Alice in February 1872 that Marie was too fond of her home and her freedom, did nothing to allay his fears.

By May, Affie and the Queen were so mortified at the Russian court's evasiveness that they insisted on being given a firm answer. A letter from the Tsarina in June proved to be the very opposite of this, and merely reiterated the old excuse that Marie must be left free to choose for herself. By August the Queen was convinced that the 'Russian project' was well and truly over. She blamed Alice for pushing them into it, without the slightest real ground for hoping that they would be successful, and concluded that the Tsar and Tsarina were so against parting with Marie that they would only let her marry another Russian.

Affie was determined not to be humiliated, but there was nothing to do at present but resign himself to the situation with what grace he could muster. However he felt some resentment against everyone involved, and offended both his mother and his eldest sister when he went to Alsace a few weeks before Christmas with Uncle Ernest. Officially both men were going shooting, but inevitably they had their fair share of wine and women. Vicky was saddened that Affie could give 'amusing ladies plenty of his time' but had none for her. The Queen was more irritated than shocked, but feared that he would never be really happy or contented, and that he might be condemned to spend an aimless life at the centre of fashionable society.

After Christmas, prospects suddenly improved. Marie realised that she would have to marry before long, and her rank severely limited potential suitors. If she did not choose someone from Russia she would have to content herself with a prince from one of the German courts like her mother before her, or else from England, and the latter seemed preferable. In any case, her home life was no longer as blissful as Affie and the Queen had been led to believe. The Tsar had openly acknowledged his mistress Princess Catherine Dolgoryuka, who had given birth to his son in 1872 and would bear him several further children. Although the Tsarina had long accepted mild infidelity as part of the Romanov tradition, she was shocked at her husband's mistress and child being paraded so openly, and the thought that her ill-health, which necessitated her spending more and more time at the Crimea, was partly responsible for the situation, made her blame herself. At about the same time as the birth of the Tsar's illegitimate son, she was told by doctors that her chronic complaint was advanced tuberculosis, and she had only a few years to live. Her sons adored her, strongly resented the presence of Princess Dolgoryuka, and as a result were barely on speaking terms with their father. On the other hand Marie adored him so much that she found it hard to censure him for his infidelity, much as she loved her mother as well. But this cannot have made her home life happy, and as she approached the age of twenty she knew that sooner or later she would have to reconcile herself to the thought of marriage.

In January 1873 Count Peter Shuvalov, Tsar Alexander's confidant and head of the Russian police, arrived in London. His official purpose was to report to Lord Granville with assurances of the Russian Empire's peaceful intentions concerning central Asia, but soon it became apparent that he was also charged with reopening the marriage question. He spoke separately to Affie and the Queen, explaining that the Tsar's only objection was that he did not want his daughter to live too far away from him; an assurance that Affie and Marie would pay visits to Russia during their first years of marriage would be sufficient. On behalf of the royal family, Granville told Shuvalov that the Queen had already considered the project as finished the previous year. If not, what was the meaning behind the Tsarina's vague letter of last June? The ambassador replied that the Tsarina had only thought it fair not to let Prince Alfred feel committed, and in any case she was inclined to procrastinate when asked to make decisions. (Three months later at home, Shuvalov realised it had been unwise of him to bring the Tsarina's personal failings into official conversation, and begged Lord Loftus, London's Ambassador at St Petersburg, to revise his memorandum describing the January talks for the Tsar accordingly, omitting any tactless references to her).

Affie was delighted at this turn of events, and everyone could see how much more contented he suddenly appeared to be. The Queen was displeased, considering that the Russians had treated them shabbily, and she was having renewed doubts on the political desirability of such an alliance. Only her son's 'very strong desire for it' persuaded her to accept the situation. She told Vicky in the strictest confidence – Alice, whom she considered too pro-Russian and did not altogether trust, was not to be informed – that Affie 'still seems to wish it so much – I can't, of course, after what has passed, entirely refuse these (to me somewhat suspicious) *avances*'.[11]

These suspicions were soon justified. Shuvalov left England on 14 January and promised to write again within ten days, sending Affie some new photographs of Marie. The next Russian communication came not from Shuvalov, but from Lord Loftus – a telegram requesting that arrangements for the betrothal be suspended until Granville received a secret letter detailing 'extraordinary rumours' about Marie which were circulating around the city. This letter duly appeared a couple of days later; she had had *'une affaire de coeur'* with a Russian officer, it said, and 'regular correspondence' with another.

Affie sternly refused to believe it, but he was not encouraged by a message from the Queen warning him that his intended had other affections, 'the existence of which may account for various phases in this strange affair'. Ponsonby wryly wrote to Granville that Prince Alfred's valentine was not a pleasant one. Although the Queen was somewhat sweeping in her judgment that the Tsar's sons as well as his sisters and brothers were notorious for their loose morals, it was hardly surprising that she thought the marriage question had been reopened merely so that an impatient father could get rid of his flighty daughter. Affie's first reaction was to visit St Petersburg and try to find out for himself, but he thought better of it after being advised of the risk of humiliation.

Then Loftus wrote again to say that according to further rumour Marie had taken 'a violent *engouement*' for the Tsar's aide-de-camp, Prince Galitzin, and she was willing to give up her royal position and rights for him. The Tsar was prepared to let her do so if it would ensure her future happiness, but the Tsarina would not hear of it, and on her insistence Galitzin was sent abroad on indefinite leave. By the time the Ambassador wrote to say that such rumours had died away so completely that they could have had no genuine substance, Queen Victoria was sufficiently angry to contemplate preventing the marriage altogether. If the young Grand Duchess had been indiscreet or merely enjoyed a momentary fling with her army officer, why had Shuvalov appeared so keen to press her claims?

All this put Affie in an unenviable position, but in spite of his mother's misgivings he eagerly accepted an invitation to meet Marie and the Tsarina in April at Sorrento in Italy. He had the support of Granville, who pointed out that the British court could not withdraw as they had accepted Marie in principle at the time of Shuvalov's visit. The Queen conceded defeat – she could no longer veto the match outright – but she insisted that there must be 'mutual attachment' between Affie and Marie, and they must marry within the year 'or else it must finally be put an end to'.

Encouraged by a letter from the Tsarina, Affie left for Italy in mid-April. His optimism was shortlived as Marie went down with a fever, and he was only allowed to spend a little time with her before being asked to leave. Moreover the Tsarina refused to agree to any possibility of a marriage between them. The Queen put this down to 'the apparent anti-English movement in Russia' and was astonished when Vicky wrote to say that she had heard in a roundabout way from a diplomat friend of Shuvalov that in St Petersburg the court considered the marriage as 'quite a settled thing'.

The two young people themselves also refused to be put off. Affie was prepared to bear with the Tsarina's dithering as long as all ended well, much to his mother's disgust. She deplored the insolent conduct of the imperial family, which he did not feel as he ought; 'he has no pride…or dignity though he has plenty of false pride when it ought not to be there.'[12]

For her part, Marie had made up her mind to marry him, and asked her uncle Prince Alexander of Hesse for his support. Under his persuasion the Tsar reluctantly conceded. How much substance there was in the rumours of her affairs, or in the protestations that she did not wish to leave her country or family, must be left to idle speculation. In June the Tsar joined his wife and daughter at Ems, and invited Affie to meet them later that summer.

But first Affie had a new round of royal duties to perform. As a prelude to closer acquaintance with the Romanovs, Bertie invited the Tsarevich Alexander, Tsarevna Marie and their children to stay for several weeks at Marlborough House. Affie struck up a lifelong friendship with them, and the eldest child, five-year-old Nicky, later Tsar Nicholas II, positively worshipped England and his uncles Bertie and Affie.

Later in June Affie and Arthur went to Dover to welcome one of the most remarkable royal guests of all – Nasr-ed-Din, Shah of Persia. Despite his primitive eating habits and unpunctuality, he fulfilled the fascinated public's highest expectations by dressing in an astrakhan cap, long coat embroidered with gold, and a dazzling array of jewellery. On his tour of Europe he had disliked Russia, perhaps because the court compelled him to send his three wives home, and the intense formality of Berlin had inspired in him no love for Germany either.

Yet the Shah found the English far more hospitable. Despite her initial reservations, Queen Victoria found him more dignified and better mannered than she had been led to believe, and she graciously gave him the Order of the Garter in exchange for two Persian orders. However Bertie and Affie had to provide most of the Shah's entertainment. They spent a night at Trentham with the Duke of Sutherland, and it was there that the Shah made his immortal comment that the ducal estates were far too grand to belong to a subject. When the Prince of Wales came to the throne, he said, he must have their host beheaded.

When Affie left for Jugenheim he was blissfully unaware that the Queen had drafted a letter to Alice detailing the problems, personal and political, that a Duchess of Edinburgh would have to face. Queen Victoria intended

Alice to show it to the Tsar and Tsarina, but mercifully second thoughts –
and perhaps the wise counsels of Ponsonby as well – prevailed, and it was
never sent. It would not have been a good time to add to Alice's problems,
for she had recently been stunned by the sudden loss of her two-year-old
haemophiliac son Frittie, who bled to death after falling from a window
in May.

Whatever the Queen's misgivings, it was too late to prevent the
inevitable. On 11 July Affie asked for Marie's hand and she accepted him.
He was nearly twenty-nine; she was nineteen.

The Queen and Beatrice were taking tea under the pines in the garden
at Osborne House when they received his telegram: 'Marie and I engaged
this morning. Cannot say how happy I am. Hope your blessings rest on
us.' Her initial reaction was to be 'greatly astonished at the great rapidity
with which the matter had been settled and announced.'[13] If only Marie
could alter her future husband's 'hard, selfish, uncertain character.'[14] Vicky
was thrilled, but her delight was not shared by the German royal family.
Fritz gloomily considered it a poor prospect for Germany if northern
Europe became 'populated with anti-German marriages', while his mother
Empress Augusta's acid acknowledgement of the news to Queen Victoria
drew a face-saving defence from the latter:

> You know I did not desire this alliance on various quite serious grounds.
> Principally on account of religion and politics, for these always seem to
> me precarious and undependable in Russia. But in spite of all difficulties,
> in spite of doubts and representations on both sides, it has nonetheless
> come to pass, and that through the decision of the young lady herself,
> hence I must believe that it is a dispensation of God.[15]

To Vicky she confided her anxiety in accepting a bride from another
church into the family as being the first instance since the revolution of
1688 – 'we must be very firm – or else we may pack up – and call back the
descendants of the Stuarts.'[16]

Affie received many letters of congratulation from family and friends
alike; he took great pleasure in showing them to Marie and her parents
and in replying to them. Typical of his answers was a note to the Duchess
of Sutherland:

> Accept my warmest thanks for your kind letter of congratulation. I felt
> quite sure that Stafford and yourself would take part in my happiness.
> I shall look forward to presenting you to the Grand Duchess when she
> comes to England which will not be however I think till the spring.[17]

Yet Affie was hurt by his mother's persistently ungracious attitude. He complained to Granville that her telegram expressed such surprise at the engagement that he could not possibly show it to his betrothed's family.

Part of the Queen's irritation stemmed from the fact that she had never seen Marie. Nevertheless she was going to insist on seeing her new daughter-in-law before the marriage, which would of course (she expected) take place in October or November. Little did she realise that on both accounts she would be thwarted. As she would not travel to the continent for anything resembling official business, either the Tsar or the Tsarina would have to bring her to England. The Tsar considered this an affront to his dignity, privately dismissing his fellow-monarch as a 'silly old fool'. The Tsarina's ill-health prevented her from making such a journey but she offered to meet the Queen at Cologne, only to be met with a retort that this was 'simply impertinent'. Alice bravely tried to persuade her mother to concede, but this brought forth one of Queen Victoria's most withering refusals:

> I do not think, dear Child, that you should tell *me* who have been nearly 20 years longer on the throne than the Emperor of Russia & am the Doyenne of Sovereigns & who am a Reigning Sovereign which the Empress is not – what I ought to do.[18]

The Tsar would not give way, and the Queen had to wait until after the wedding before she would see Marie for the first time. The ceremony could not be held until the new year, and she had to abandon one 'irrevocable condition' after another.

Reaction to the engagement throughout the country was less than favourable. In some areas, there was indifference if not downright hostility to the spending of more public money on another royal wedding, and the chartist weekly, *Reynolds's Newspaper*, reported several vocal objections under a long article with the heading 'Another rattle of the royal begging-box'. At a meeting of Birmingham ratepayers on 29 July, a resolution was passed protesting against any additional grant to the Duke of Edinburgh. The Nottingham Republican Club unanimously (if not surprisingly) carried a motion condemning any additional grants to royal personages, while the town itself was placarded with handbills headed 'Royal plunder' and 'Stop thief!', calling a meeting of inhabitants whose incomes were less than £20,000 per annum to protest.[19] It had not helped the bridegroom's cause that he had chosen his bride from a nation with whom the country had been at war so recently. Nevertheless such attacks were not entirely unexpected, and the royal family were relieved that this bachelor prince would soon be a bachelor no longer.

CHAPTER 7

Wedding in St Petersburg 1873–75

Affie returned to England at the end of July. Queen Victoria judged him to be 'very well satisfied so far – but...there is the same ungracious, reserved manner which makes him so little liked.'[1] It was perhaps strange that she failed to appreciate that her own attitude throughout the trouble-ridden courtship was hardly calculated to make him feel any different. Yet she was gratified that over Christmas he appeared suitably nervous about the 'very solemn and serious step he was about to take', though rather tactlessly she told him that Marie alone must have his love and he was to give up all his old habits. To this he wisely said nothing.

The engagement was announced to Parliament by Gladstone, who described the grant as 'avoiding parsimony and excess'. The Duke was allocated an additional £10,000 a year, bringing his appanage to a total of £2,000, and the future Duchess was to receive £6,000 a year if she survived her husband. Eighteen members voted against the motion.

One of the immediate problems which arose was the question of where the wedding was to take place. Queen Victoria had shown her 'vein of iron' seventeen years earlier when insisting that Prince Frederick William of Prussia would have to be married in London, as it was 'not every day that one marries the eldest daughter of the Queen of England'. Yet in this case the Duke of Edinburgh was only the groom, and the Tsar and Tsarina stood their ground as firmly as she had done. As doting parents, it was inconceivable that they would have allowed their only daughter out of their sight for a moment before the ring was on her finger and she was duty-bound to follow her husband wherever he went. The wedding was therefore arranged to take place at St Petersburg on 23 January 1874, and on the Queen's insistence it would have to be a double ceremony, with one in the Anglican faith, the other Russian Orthodox. She 'commanded and desired' right up to the steps of the Anglican altar in the Winter Palace. If she could not be present in person Arthur Stanley, Dean of Westminster, would perform the English service, and her great friend Lady Augusta must report back to her in the fullest detail.

The wedding of the Duke and Duchess of Edinburgh was unique among those of Queen Victoria's children in that it was the only one to take place outside England, and also the only one at which she was not present.

Accompanied by Colonel William Colville, controller of his Household, and two equerries, Affie spent a few days in Berlin with Vicky and Fritz on the way to the wedding. Although the news of the engagement had been received coldly there, especially as Bismarck was fearful of an anti-German alliance between Britain and Russia, the imperial family proved most welcoming. Vicky had assured her brother that even if Fritz felt he was unable to come to the ceremony in Russia, she would come alone, although in the end husband and wife were among the guests. The Empress Augusta, who was not always noted for her graciousness towards guests in her advancing years, put herself out to be particularly kind and affable.

Affie and his suite arrived by train at St Petersburg on 4 January 1874. The Tsar and his suite were waiting for them on the platform, where flags fluttered in the cold wind, as bands played and crowds cheered. Also representing the British royal family and court were Bertie, Alix, Affie's former governor Cowell, who had recently been appointed Master of the Queen's Household in recognition of his services, Arthur, and his governor Sir Howard Elphinstone. Despite his misgivings about 'anti-German marriages', Fritz, Vicky and Duke Ernest were present as well.

Though this Anglo-Russian alliance had caused some apprehension in England and Europe, nobody wished for any 'collisions', and it was generally hoped that the wedding would allay any hostile feeling. In any case, as the Russian press had stated, Tsar Alexander would not lightly give his only daughter's hand in marriage to a sworn enemy.

Lady Augusta took her 'reporting duty' seriously, as befitting such a royal command, and it is to her that one is indebted for a wealth of information about all the preparations leading up to the great day. With her went two parcels from the Queen which she guarded with her life. One contained two sprigs of myrtle from Windsor or Osborne which were to be placed in the middle of Marie's bouquet of white flowers to be ordered and presented to her on behalf of her mother-in-law just before the English service. The other held two prayer books, one bound in white with illuminated verses specially painted for Marie, and a plain one for Affie. At the station not only royal guests but also the Stanleys were given the full red carpet treatment, with a delegation in uniform and white gloves, lined up in a double row. Tongue in cheek, Lady Augusta wrote:

> I saw that the moment was come for me to ape the manners of my betters
> and graciously and condescendingly, to bow from side to side in regal

style – dazzling salons opened to receive us thro' which we only passed, however, into the Vestibule, where stood ranged, endless giant foot men in scarlet and gold great coats, lined with white fur…I was bowed on – a delicious little Brougham opened before me; I was stumbled into a pile of furs and before I recovered was being whirled along the white streets as fast as two horses could carry me.[2]

Soon came the inevitable summons from The Imperial Majesties:

The Empress was quite alone, dressed in dark green with a sort of fluffy trimming, and black lace in her hair. She received us most warmly and I was quite absorbed by Her grace and charm and sweetness and pleasantness, and by so much more of looks than I expected. She is not in the least like any of the Hesse family, so much more distinguished and good-looking…and then the Grand Duchess (Marie) came, looking most dear and bright. I did not think her perhaps quite so pretty as her photo; but just as nice and frank as described, and so happy looking. The Duke (Alfred) came in, and he also looked quite one of them and quite happy and at ease – There was nothing private – the Empress evidently did not trust Herself to talk much of what is nearest to Her heart, and I believe had never allowed Herself to break down – Poor thing, I believe she is as much comforted and upheld as possible by the sight of Her Daughter's happiness, but it is simply *agony* to Her, - to them both.[3]

Meanwhile Dean Stanley had been ushered into the Tsar's room. The latter

stood quite alone, in full uniform by a desk 'exceedingly gracious', and the Dean said that he hoped the benedictions of both the Churches might descend on an event so happy for both countries. 'The only sufferers,' he added, 'are the parents.' The Emperor's eyes filled with tears, and he said, 'Yes, it is true – she has been the joy of our lives, but it must be'.[4]

To Lady Augusta, the Winter Palace was rather a trial. She had to make what she called 'a four mile journey to the other end' which made her nearly cry with fatigue. At dinner she was placed between Marie's brothers, the Grand Dukes Alexis and Alexander. The former was 'a pickle, but intelligent, good-looking and sensible.' The Tsarevich she found 'a bit rough but honest and kind.' The bridal pair beamed at everyone, Affie a little shyly, and suffering from a cold, but on her home ground Marie was bright and smart in a 'white silk gown and a few rosebuds in her hair'.[5]

As the only daughter of the Tsar, Marie had inherited the most sumptuous jewels, including some magnificent sapphires which had been collected for her since she was born. Alexander II was one of the world's richest monarchs, and between 1856 and 1881 over £20,000,000 was carefully invested in London merchant banks, but even without these his fortune was immense. His annual income from the government was over £1,000,000, and his estates added considerably to this figure. There were also frozen assets in the form of the Romanov crown jewels, accumulated over the previous three hundred years and said to be worth sixteen million. Among these were the unique 195-carat Orlov diamond; the 120-carat 'Moon of the Mountain'; the 85-carat Shah; and the 40-carat pale red ruby, the Polar Star. The income at birth of a Grand Duke or Duchess was £28,000, to which had been added Marie's dowry of £100,000.

Her trousseau was lavish, as was to be expected. The trunks were enormous brassbound leather affairs, with three or four men needed to lift each one. They were full of clothes for all occasions; morning, sports, afternoon, evening and grand *soirées*. Her coats would follow the four seasons, furs being chosen from ermine, chinchilla, beaver, mink, seal and astrakhan, with several pairs of gloves, hats and umbrellas to match. To all this was added sets of linens, silver-plate, glass, porcelain, even a gold toilette set of over a hundred pieces which was a family heirloom. She would of course take a selection of her own furniture. The complete collection filled the whole of the White Hall of the Winter Palace, and was said to equal in quantity a season's stock-in-trade of any major Parisian emporium.

However, once she had arrived on English soil, Marie more or less lost all interest in her appearance. She became shabby, dowdy and fat, and did not seem to care. Only when she returned to St Petersburg and Peterhof would she shine again in her imperial court gown of Gentian blue trimmed with sable and wear her rubies and sapphires with pride.

The morning of 23 January at St Petersburg was cold and still, in the characteristic blackness of the northern climate, snow gleaming faintly under the pale blue orange hue of street lamps. At six o'clock the large bell of St Isaac's Cathedral boomed out sonorously, and lights began to twinkle in palaces and houses along the Neva. Soon all the city bells would peal out in honour of the Tsar's daughter and her husband-to-be. As daylight appeared a thaw set in, the streets and quays becoming mushy and dirty underfoot, and cannon salvos sounding hollowly in the oppressive still air. Flags and decorations had brought a vivid touch of colour to the streets for days beforehand, while inside the palace imperial organisation was at its best. With thousands of guests expected to arrive throughout the day, everything had to run smoothly.

The official wedding programme was in the internationally-recognised language of French, announcing with a flourish the titles of Bride and Groom: *Son Altesse Imperial Madame la Grande Duchesse Marie Alexandrovna, avec Son Altesse Royale Monseigneur le Prince Alfred Ernest Albert de Grande Bretagne, Duc d'Edinbourg.* Guests began arriving in a steady stream throughout the morning, and before long the palace reception room was packed with people whose gowns, jewels, uniforms and orders formed a dazzling kaleidoscope of all the colours of the rainbow, with the occasional gleam of drawn swords of the lancers in their dark green and silver uniforms, standing stiff and aloof on guard. Ladies in their shimmering gowns of silks, satins, velvets and lace, and dignitaries, whose padded breasts shone like jewellers' cushions, vied with each other like birds of paradise.

At the concert room, the Grande Maitresse and ladies on duty waited in exquisite court gowns – red, green or blue according to rank, their velvet trains and hanging sleeves like wings, heavily embroidered with gold.

At midday the imperial procession appeared. A sudden hush fell on the throng just before the first wedding service in the Greek Chapel of the palace. Sixty chamberlains in gold led the way walking two by two. The Tsar was in the dark blue uniform of a Russian general, his arm supporting that of the Tsarina, resplendent in her imperial gown and long train of white satin and a small 'Marie Stuart' cap. Affie wore Russian naval uniform and the Order of St Andrew. Among his presents and honours from the Tsar were those of honorary rank of Captain in the Russian Navy, and Chief of the 2nd Division of the Russian Black Sea Fleet. Affie and Bertie both loved uniforms, and the latter was very disappointed that Queen Victoria would not allow him to accept an honorary colonelcy offered by the Tsar, on the grounds that there was no precedent for such an appointment. The groom led Marie 'looking very pale but sweet, and calmly happy in her silver embroidered gown. Six gentlemen I think carried the long white cloth-of-silver train, and the Mantel trimmed with ermine'. Affie gave her his hand 'in a most touching and tender way.'[6] Contrary to the English custom there were no bridesmaids, just groomsmen – Affie's brother Arthur, and Marie's brothers. After the bride in procession came the Princes of Wales in pale grey silk with a long train of green velvet edged with ermine, and her sister, the Tsarevich's wife, in a gown of gold-embroidered satin and train of sky-blue velvet emblazoned with imperial insigniae, both of them blazing with diamonds.

During the Russian service Marie looked 'upward with such a confiding appealing look...most affecting and pathetic'. The couple stood on a crimson carpet before a small lectern with jewelled cover. The golden-robed Metropolitans (in the Russian hierarchy of the Orthodox Church, in rank above an Archbishop but below a Patriarch) of Moscow, Novgorod and

Kiev added more splendour to the scene. Bertie in his general's uniform of scarlet stood near Affie, and beside him Fritz in a German uniform of dark blue. Arthur and one of the Grand Dukes held the gold filigree marriage crowns over their heads, but Arthur soon tired of his position and had to be relieved by Grand Duke Alexis. As the ceremony reached its climax, it was observed, a ray of sunshine lit up the chapel, 'appearing as a ray of heavenly light betokening a divine benediction on the happy couple'.[7]

After the Orthodox service, everyone went to the *Salle d'Alexandre* for the English ceremony. Affie felt more at home when he saw Dean Stanley's familiar face, waiting with the chaplain at the improvised altar covered with crimson velvet. The *Salle* was lit by 'ten thousand candles and through the tall windows, long sunbeams from the weak wintry sun again added to the dazzle of the light'. According to *The Times* correspondent, Marie carried herself as 'a bride and a Romanov' while Affie 'bore himself throughout with that unconscious air of dignity, simplicity and high breeding which belongs to our Princes'. Lady Augusta thought that by this time Marie looked terribly tired and quite crushed in her heavy double dress:

> the small graceful head still so childlike, must have ached with the immense weight of jewels, the necklace of diamonds…the most beautiful I ever saw, and the gown was studded with them, round the body and the sleeves and down the front of the body and skirt. (She had) a most lovely neck and shoulders. The Duke looked very happy and all were cheerful and looked well.[8]

Like the groom, Dean Stanley had a heavy cold which rather dampened his spiritual enthusiasm. One of the Danish correspondents caught a warning glance from Affie who obviously wanted the Dean to hurry up with it. The bride stood with downcast eyes but answered the, 'Wilt thou have…' in clear unaccented English, while Affie leaned towards the Tsar when Stanley asked 'Who giveth this woman…'

The ring caused something of a contretemps. Arthur gave it to Affie, who passed it to the Dean, who gave it back to Affie after examining it with a puzzled eye. Encumbered with Mama's prayer book, he tried to pass it on to a page who refused it in obvious misapprehension. Waiting for her ring, Marie tried to relieve Affie of the book, but astutely he managed to hold both and slipped the ring on to her finger. The Dean then held both their hands in his – 'longer than was necessary' – but kindly, so that Marie could compose herself after 'the shiver that went through her whole body' on being at last well and truly wed.

After this second ceremony the happy couple received the blessings of an exhausted Tsarina, who embraced her daughter with a long loving embrace. Then Affie led his bride down the long gleaming corridors and salons till they reached the comparative privacy of their own apartments. At last they could relax for a couple of hours before appearing at the wedding breakfast.

For this next stage of the festivities, musical entertainment was provided by two of the world's most renowned operatic sopranos, Adelina Patti from Italy and the Canadian Emma Albani. During her performance the latter had to contend with the booming of guns from the fortress, but her voice still soared above the thunder. Each toast was drunk to the crash of music from a band; 'heavy guns booming through the lighted room were the most marked feature of the wedding breakfast, and spoke like the sullen voice of the military powers which fences round the wealth and greatness of the dynasty and Emperor of All the Russias', wrote *The Times* correspondent poetically.

The banquet began at 4.30 in the *Salle de Nicholas*, hung with enormous chandeliers, the candles of which automatically lit up one after another 'in a dance of fire' by the simple expedient of an inflammable cotton thread connecting each one. The imperial family appeared half an hour later, when everyone fell silent until they were seated. English and Russian coats-of-arms and the monograms 'M' and 'A' adorned the menu, which listed such delicacies as *Potage de Gibier à l'Indienne, Colettes de Perdreaux à la Maréchale*, and *Garni de Gelée Muscovite à l'Ananas*.

To conclude the day's celebrations there was dancing, at which the bride and groom were present though they did not stay until the end. At eleven o'clock that night, close to exhaustion, they boarded a train to Tsarskoe-Selo accompanied by a suite of five. The square in front of the Winter Palace had been thick with people braving the icy cold to see them depart for their two-day honeymoon. On both days the Tsar telegraphed to say how much he was thinking of Marie, and their walks and rides together.

At St Petersburg another round of receptions awaited them. According to Lady Augusta, Marie often looked very fine in a tulle gown and Russian-shaped tiara of pink diamonds which with her 'soft curly hair and the lovely rose bud complexion was exceedingly becoming'.[9] Affie, reported Vicky enthusiastically, looked 'so radiant and beaming and really another creature – his satisfaction makes him so amiable to everybody!'[10] After another week the whole party left by train for Moscow, where they stayed in the Kremlin. By this time, Marie was quite pale with fatigue. Nevertheless she could hold her own when faced with pertinent questions. Colonel Colville dared to enquire, '*A quand le premier enfant?*' ('When will the first baby appear?') She replied, '*Je ne suis pas pressée. Mais Alfred est très impatient!*' ('I'm in no hurry. But Alfred is very impatient!'

Affie and the English guests took back with them several lasting impressions of life in Russia. Sir Howard Elphinstone voiced the views of those who found the excessive heating at court functions too much of a good thing, and thought the room temperature at banquet and ball 'almost unbearable, and several ladies left the ballroom almost in a fainting state'. Hardly less extraordinary was the blend of magnificence and squalor in which the Romanovs lived. Superficially the atmosphere was very grand, with miles of corridors hung with 'frowning old Tsars', and scores of servants, augmented by soldiers called in to help when necessary. The supper rooms were beautifully decorated, with palms and other tropical plants arranged to create the effect of a conservatory – no mean feat when fifty tables were laid for five hundred people to sit down at once. Only on probing deeper did guests discover just how filthy the rooms were. One lady's bedroom smelt so dreadful that she feared a dead *moujik* was concealed beneath the floorboards.

On their journey home, the newly married couple and their suite stopped at Berlin, arriving on 3 March. Although Marie was noticeably very tired, they had to attend a series of visits around the capital, notably a reception at the British Embassy, followed by a state dinner and gala opera performance of Wagner's *Lohengrin* afterwards. At the opera house, which was packed with royalties and dignitaries including the English and Russian Ambassadors and the American minister, Empress Augusta escorted Marie into a state box, followed by Affie leading the Countess of Flanders, while the Count accompanied Vicky and Fritz. One British journalist remarked on the selection of such an opera being 'a mystery' as the Duke of Edinburgh was not a Wagnerian, 'and he did not seem to be much interested in the interminable duets between Elsa and Lohengrin. It is just to say, however, that the artistes hardly did themselves credit.' One had in younger days been 'a tolerable operatic singer', but her voice was losing power, while the tenor 'failed to equal himself'.[11]

The newly-weds landed at Gravesend and came to Windsor on the morning of 7 March. Lined with troops, the town was gaily festooned with flags, flowers and banners with messages of welcome in English and Russian, and a triumphal arch. Queen Victoria greeted them at the station and embraced the daughter-in-law whom she was meeting for the first time. She found her pleasantly unaffected and civil, but not in the least pretty or graceful. The Duchess, it was noted, did not hold herself well, and walked poorly, her neck and waist seeming to be too long for her face. Perhaps the Queen unconsciously betrayed more than she meant to in a letter to Vicky, noting that it had been eleven years to the week since Alix's arrival from Denmark. A plain and ungainly Grand Duchess from Russia could hardly be compared with one of Europe's loveliest princesses. All the same, Marie had recognisably good qualities; she was quite at ease with her mother-in-law without appearing too self-assured, spoke excellent English, and above all was not 'a bit afraid of Affie'. The Queen fervently hoped and prayed that she would have a good influence on him.[12]

The Stanleys had preceded them home to London, Lady Augusta more dead than alive. She took to her bed with exhaustion, but bravely got up to welcome them and dine with them on their first evening back. However her health had never been particularly strong, and from this time onwards rapidly worsened until her death two years later.

As a final flourish to the wedding festivities, the Peek Freans bakery and confectionery business did the new Duchess the honour of naming one of their products after her, the Marie biscuit. The company had made a feature of naming their wares after titled heads and other distinguished people of the day. There were Alexandra, Albert, Eugenie, Leopold, and naturally Victoria biscuits; but the humble Marie and the Garibaldi biscuit, which in view of its revolutionary associations was unlikely to have been served to Queen Victoria with her afternoon tea, have outlived them all.

Clarence House had been Affie's London residence since he attained his majority, and this would be the Edinburgh *pied à terre* for the rest of his days. It had originally built between 1825 and 1827 for the then Duke of Clarence, later William IV. Shortly before the wedding, the Duke of Edinburgh had had it refaced and heightened, with a new wing added, and a new entrance facing St James's Park. Most of the collections which adorned the walls or filled glass cases came from his world travels. Over the staircase hung the head of an elephant he had shot, and in the hall a stuffed bear stood on hind legs, holding a tray for visitors' cards. The corridors were filled with trophies from various other shooting expeditions, often rather badly stuffed, and a lifesize figure in Japanese armour with a grotesque grinning mask. One drawing room was arranged with Chinese antiques and curios, namely old weapons, bronzes, ivories, embroideries and precious jades.

When Marie moved in she decorated the other drawing-room with her Russian keepsakes – *objets d'art* carved from semi-precious stones from the Urals, dishes, vases and Fabergé Easter eggs. Her bedroom contained jewelled ikons, twinkling in the light of a sanctuary lamp, surrounded by fragrance of Russian incense, leather and cedar wood. At Clarence House, and every other home in which she lived, Marie kept a small Orthodox chapel, the walls of which were covered with religious pictures, and later, photographs of her mother and father on their deathbeds with an ever-burning lamp in front of them. Her retinue always included a Russian priest and two chanters.

Within a few months the forebodings of Queen Victoria, and perhaps her second son too, were to be proved. The Romanov connection brought with it no end of difficulties about Marie's precedence and style. Her father made it clear that he intended her to be styled Imperial, not Royal, 'as in all civilised countries' to which the (not yet Imperial) Queen indignantly retorted that she did not mind whether her daughter-in-law was called Imperial or not, as long as Royal came first. Then it was debated which of her titles should come first – Grand Duchess of Russia, or Duchess of Edinburgh? The Queen felt out of her depth a she was not yet an Empress herself, and referred the matter to Ponsonby, who was amused by the fuss and quoted Dr Johnson to his wife: 'Who comes first, a louse or a flea?'[13]

Alexander II's state visit to England in May 1874 coincided with another argument about Marie's position at court. It irked her that as an Emperor's daughter she was not granted right of precedence over the Princess of Wales, daughter of the King of a comparatively humble country like Denmark. The Tsar agreed gallantly with Queen Victoria that Princess Alexandra should indeed precede her, as she was the wife of the heir to the throne, but asked for his daughter to take precedence over her other sisters-in-law. This the Queen would not countenance, but Marie exacted her own subtle revenge. At her first drawing-room she took malicious pleasure in showing off her splendid jewellery. The English princesses could not hide their jealousy, while the Queen looked at the pearls and diamonds disdainfully 'shrugging her shoulders like a bird whose plumage has been ruffled, her mouth drawn down at the corners in an expression which those who knew her had learned to dread.'[14]

A few months later Ponsonby related one small but amusing anecdote about the Duke and Duchess, as one of the rare occasions when the flattery of Prime Minister, Benjamin Disraeli, failed to work. At Balmoral one evening in September 1874, they were discussing the edible properties or otherwise of toadstools. Marie said they were generally good, and Affie made some remark which Ponsonby did not hear. Disraeli answered, 'His Royal Highness must with his great knowledge of men and things gained in all the countries of the world through which he has travelled know the real state of the case better than any one.' Marie retorted that he knew 'nothing at all about it.' The Prime Minister looked at her with the 'comic face' which he generally assumed when he knew he had failed, and simply said 'Hum!'[15]

Although Marie had said that she was in no hurry to start a family, her husband's intentions prevailed. Barely nine months after the wedding, on 15 October, she gave birth to a son at Buckingham Palace. He was christened Alfred Alexander William Ernest Albert on 28 November in the chapel at Windsor Castle, where his father had been baptised. The Queen wrote to the German Emperor William, who stood as one of the godparents and was represented by Affie, that the baby was 'a very strong, beautiful child, who will some day, I think, be like his very big Russian uncles'.[16]

At the christening, Marie breastfed the baby, much to Queen Victoria's disgust. When he threw up over his mother's dress, she was not in the least embarrassed. She merely stood up, handed the child over to the Tsarina and, reported the astonished Princess of Wales to her sister, the Tsarevna, 'ran about with her *big breast* hanging down in front of everyone and wiped the dress clean!!!'[17]

Their eldest daughter Marie, always known as Missy, was born on 29 October 1875 at Eastwell Park, the Edinburghs' country residence, near Ashford in Kent. Rented from the Earl of Winchelsea, it was a massive pretentious grey bulk of mock-Tudor, with grounds of 2,500 acres overlooking Romney Marsh, which faded into the English Channel on one side, and the Medway Valley on the other. The grounds included rich woodland and rolling parks, where Highland cattle and deer grazed contentedly. Clarence House was too formal and lacking in privacy, and it was at Eastwell that they could relax and live as far as possible like any other well-to-do family in a country house. Every autumn Affie invited a houseful of guests for large shooting-parties to make full use of the facilities. Marie dreaded these occasions, complaining that after a day with their guns the men returned sleepy and in no mood for mentally stimulating conversation. A cultured woman, she once remarked that she preferred the company of politicians, diplomats and artists to that of soldiers, sailors and sportsmen. This must have been rather ironic in view of the fact that, notwithstanding his artistic and scientific interests, her husband was both sailor and sportsman.

Some years later she would write to her eldest daughter that 'Papa considers sport sacred above all.' She herself 'suffered so much from the selfishness of hunters in the first years in England'.[18]

Nevertheless she shared his love of music and friendship with the talented Fanny Ronalds, even though her performances on the piano appear to have been received by captive audiences with the same feeling of tolerance at best as her husband's violin recitals. Lady Ponsonby recorded an evening at Frogmore in January 1875 with the Edinburghs and others. After dinner Marie played the piano so badly that nobody pretended to listen, but turned their backs and talked. As soon as a more gifted guest began performing, they all stopped talking and listened attentively. According to Lady Randolph Churchill, who sometimes played duets with her, the pianist Artur Rubinstein later told the Duchess that she 'did not play so badly for a princess.'[19] Either her playing had improved considerably in later years, or else Rubinstein was more gallant than the plain-spoken Ponsonbys.

Meanwhile, at the same gathering Affie was surprised when another musician told him he would never play the fiddle if he only practiced once a month. To yet another he showed his instrument and accessories, saying that he used one rosin for his bow when playing in an orchestra and another for solo work. The lady in question said afterwards that she nearly remarked what a pity it was that he did not have a rosin for playing in time.[20]

Shortly before his marriage Affie had met Arthur Sullivan, the composer who was about to become a household name through the Savoy Operas with William Schwenk Gilbert. According to his biographers, 'Sullivan's friendship with the Duke of Edinburgh, a friendship woven in a common bondage to music, had been a friendship without royal condescension, the intimacy of two kindred souls.'[21] The Duke had attended the first public performance of Sullivan's oratorio *The Light of the World* at Birmingham, and he was one of the first to compliment him on it afterwards. Both men went from the hall together to hail a cab, Affie declaring repeatedly that it was 'a triumph'.

In November 1874 Arthur Sullivan paid the first of several visits to Eastwell as a guest. As it was a freezing cold afternoon, on his arrival 'the Duke immediately plied me with a sherry and bitters,' before taking him up to his room.[22] During this stay and on several subsequent occasions, the composer played piano duets with Marie, as well as accompanying Affie on the violin. The latter would often call on Sullivan at his London home for a similar purpose.

In spite of her initial reservations, by September 1874 Queen Victoria had formed a favourable opinion of Marie, and 'her wonderfully even, cheerful satisfied temper – her kind and indulgent disposition, free from bigotry and intolerance, and her serious, intelligent mind – so entirely free from everything fast – and so full of occupation and interest in everything makes her a most agreeable companion.'[23] Everyone, added the Queen, must like her. Unfortunately, not many others did.

Though her mother was a Hessian, Marie was essentially Russian by nature and upbringing. To her dying day she possessed the imperial traits of arrogance, quick wit, pugnacity, impatience, and a hint of irresponsibility. Deeply religious, she was also autocratic, proud, and like her mother-in-law very conservative in her outlook. For all her faults she had great tact, an almost masculine intelligence (as Affie had noticed on their first meetings), and a heart of gold, if this was not always immediately apparent.

Shortly after her first Christmas in England, the Queen was distressed that Marie was too wrapped up in motherhood to enquire after her brother-in-law Prince Leopold, who had been gravely ill; but this time Affie touched his mama with his heartfelt sympathy and concern. Yet Marie meant Leopold no ill will, and he was to become her favourite of the family. Being a haemophiliac denied him the opportunity to lead an active life or join the army or navy, and perhaps by way of compensation he had developed an all-consuming interest in education and the arts – a man after her own heart. Although his thirty years were rarely free from physical suffering, he had a mischievous sense of humour which proved almost too much for her on one occasion. When staying at Clarence House, he came down to breakfast one morning with a handkerchief over his mouth, explaining that he had lost a tooth. This could have had severe consequences, and Marie was alarmed. At her request he took the garment away to reveal a large hole in his gums. Having elicited her most tender sympathies, he roared with laughter. The cavity, he confessed, was black sticking plaster and the stains on his handkerchief were red paint.[24]

Another of Marie's most enduring friendships in England was that which she formed with Lady Randolph Churchill. Her elder son Winston was a mere six weeks younger than Prince Alfred of Edinburgh, and the two boys were regular playmates. Evidently Winston had other reasons for visiting the family, for he developed a boyish passion for Missy. She always remembered him as a red-haired lad with freckles, 'impudent, with a fine disdain for authority', who declared before witnesses one day that when he grew up he was going to marry her.[25] Thus might a Roumanian King have been denied a British consort, and a British Prime Minister have gained a princess of the blood royal as his wife.

A letter written in February 1875 to her friend in Russia, the poet and novelist Prince Vladimir Meschersky, reveals both Marie's intense homesickness and her delight in such cultured friendships:

Yet once more I hear your voice and every time I recall times past and the happy carefree days of my youth.

What has happened to them? when we so often met and passed such pleasant hours. Since then everything has changed; circumstances, people, commerce and we are all pulled in different directions.

Many have fallen by the wayside – maybe they are the lucky ones. Others are left to their fate maybe far away at the ends of the earth, far from the dear beloved Fatherland – take pity on them – and finally some have found the meaning and purpose of life through work – they are indeed the favoured ones.

I cannot express to you, dear Prince, how much you have moved my heart with the poem 'The Man'; and especially by your last letter in which you say that when I think of you I must not say to myself 'See – there is a man who does not love me.'

One thing, though, astonishes me. That you are in possession of such insight that with your intense verses you are able to peep into a secret world. You don't even know me well and I am now lost out of sight – how can you then, by your poetry, write so? Be that as it may, I beg you to believe that a grateful Russian heart beats in me and that every sympathetic voice from the Fatherland is sacred and dear to me. I listen with tears in my eyes...[26]

There can be little doubt that the Duchess of Edinburgh had deeply regretted leaving Russia and 'the carefree days' of her youth behind her. Maybe it had not taken her long to realise that she would never be really happy in England.

CHAPTER 8

A Life on Land and Sea
1876–85

In February 1876 the Duke of Edinburgh was appointed to the command of HMS *Sultan*. Built at Chatham and launched in 1870, she was a broadside ship with a complement of 600, she displaced 9,290 tons, was capable of a speed of fourteen knots, and was fitted with an engine and screw propeller. He spent several months on her in home waters as a unit of the Channel Fleet, and then transferred to the Mediterranean Fleet, based on Malta.

Already he had left some mark, albeit small, on the naval service – the uniform, to be precise. When he was issued with his Russian outfit, he found that it included a greatcoat, and as a result he had a similar garment added to the Royal Navy kit.

'The Duke would be in a singular position if war suddenly broke out,' *The Times* had written, a little smugly, on his appointment in the Russian navy. Within two or three years the prospect came uncomfortably close.

After Bismarck's unification of Germany in 1871, a large section of Russian opinion blossomed into Panslavism. Following the Prussian example, it was said, Russia should create an even larger, more powerful empire incorporating a Slavic federation, with the Slavs from European Turkey and the Balkans, with their capital in Constantinople. Panslavism found no favour with Tsar Alexander II, who had ascended his throne during the ignominious Crimean war, and dreaded the possibility of a small localised conflict that threatened the interests of other European powers (notably Britain) and could engulf the whole continent in war, but it was popular with the ruling classes and the army. The devout Tsarina saw it as a religious crusade, as it would surely prevent persecution of the Balkan Christians, and re-establish Constantinople as the greatest city in Christendom, while the Tsarevich was inspired by the prospect of opening the Dardanelles to Russian ships.

Such matters had seemed insignificant at the time of Affie's marriage, but Queen Victoria's continued worries about 'this Russian relationship' were not unfounded. Russia's expansionist ambitions ran directly against Britain's interests in seeing Turkey as a barrier between Russia and the Mediterranean.

In 1875 the Ottoman provinces of Bosnia and Herzegovina rose in revolt against the oppressive rule of Turkey. Unrest spread, and in May 1876 Bulgaria also rebelled. Determined to make an example of the Bulgars, the Turks met this threat with great severity; whole villages were destroyed and their inhabitants tortured and put to death, regardless of age or sex. The activities of these 'Bashi-Bazouks' horrified European opinion in general, and British Liberal leader Gladstone in particular. His fury roused him to pen a seething pamphlet, *The Bulgarian Horrors and the Question of the East*. 'Let the Turks now carry away their abuses in the only possible way,' he wrote, 'namely by carrying off themselves…from the province they have desolated and profaned.' At this time Gladstone was leader of the opposition; Disraeli, who had led the Conservatives to electoral victory in 1874, regarded his rival's intervention as unpatriotic, fearing that it could give Russia an excuse for declaring war on Turkey and seizing the Straits, believing that British opinion was behind her. Of all the Bulgarian horrors, he commented wryly to Lord Derby, Gladstone's vindictive and ill-written pamphlet was perhaps the greatest.

Most of the royal family thought the responsibility lay with Russia for driving the Turks to such desperate measures, by fomenting discord among other Balkan territories for her own ends. Queen Victoria was so angry with her *bête noire* Gladstone that she championed oppressed Turkey, and the Prince of Wales was inclined to agree. Complaints would soon be uttered by less partisan politicians about the anti-Russian sympathies of the Marlborough House set, in particular the heir to the throne and the Duke of Sutherland. On the other hand the Princess of Wales naturally took the side of Russia, not only on account of her family connections but also as Turkey was the hereditary enemy of Greece, and therefore of her brother King George as well.

As Affie sailed to join the fleet at Besika Bay, at the entrance to the Dardanelles, his sympathies could hardly lie with any nation other than Russia. A letter to Queen Victoria, written on 31 July 1876 on board HMS *Sultan*, moored at Thasos Island off the Greek coast, reveals not only much about his naval routine but also his views on the international situation:

> I should have written to you again much sooner, but I have been in the utter impossibility of either writing or sending a letter. Since my inspection, which occupied two whole days, we have been cruising at sea with the fleet, and I have had to be on deck the whole of the day from early morning, and a great part of the night, and when I do come below I am so exhausted with the fatigue and heat that letters are quite out of the question…

1. Prince Alfred as a midshipman on HMS *Euryalus*, 1860, after F. R. Say. (*South African Library, Cape Town*)

2. First page of letter from Prince Alfred to Alexandrine, Duchess of Saxe-Coburg Gotha, 8 October 1858. (*Bayerisches Staatsarchiv, Coburg*)

3. HMS *Euryalus* at Cape Town, 1860. (*Elliott Collection, Cape Archives, Cape Town*)

4. Prince Alfred (on right) on hunting expedition, South Africa, 1860. Note royal arms on side of wagon. (*Elliott Collection, Cape Archives, Cape Town*)

5. Cape Town breakwater under construction. (*Cape Archives, Cape Town*)

6. Cape Town breakwater under construction. (*Cape Archives, Cape Town*)

Above left: 7. Silver trigger used in breakwater ceremony, handed afterwards to Sir George Grey and then presented to Prince Alfred. (*Cape Archives, Cape Town*)

Above right: 8. Queen Victoria and Albert, Prince Consort, at Osborne House, 1860

Above left: 9. Albert, Prince Consort, 1861.

Above right: 10. Ernest of Saxe-Coburg Gotha, later Duke Ernest II..

Above left: 11. Queen Victoria, 1862.

Above right: 12. The Prince and Princess of Wales, with Prince Albert Victor, 1864.

13. The Duke of Edinburgh (in centre) on elephant hunting expedition, 1867. The group includes his host George Rex II (far left) and personal attendant John Smith (third from left). (*Cape Archives, Cape Town*)

14. The Duke of Edinburgh, 1867. (*Cape Archives, Cape Town*)

15. Visit of the Duke of Edinburgh to Cape Town – procession at Triumphal Arch, Alderley Street, 19 August 1867. (*Cape Archives, Cape Town*)

16. 'The Duke of Edinburgh's welcome by natives', from an Australian satirical cartoon.

17. The Duke of Edinburgh, February 1869, from a signed print. (*Frank Bradlow, Cape Town*)

18. HMS *Galatea* arriving in Hobson's Bay, Melbourne, 1869.

19. The Duke and Duchess of Edinburgh, from a print commemorating their wedding published by Messrs Stuttaford, Cape Town, 1874

Right: 20. The wedding of the Duke and Duchess of Edinburgh, Russian Orthodox ceremony, 23 January 1874. (*Det Kongelige Bibliotek, Copenhagen*)

Below left: 21. The Duchess of Edinburgh, 1875. (*Det Kongelige Bibliotek, Copenhagen*)

Below right: 22. The Duke of Edinburgh, 1880. (*Cape Archives, Cape Town*)

23. Meeting at St James's Palace called to establish the Royal College of Music, 1882. Group includes (from left): the Duke of Cambridge, the Duke of Edinburgh, the Archbishop of Canterbury, the Prince of Wales (standing), Sir Stafford Northcote, the Lord Mayor of London, Prince Leopold, Lord Rosebery, W. E. Gladstone. (*Det Kongelige Bibliotek, Copenhagen*)

24. Queen Victoria's sons as adults in Highland dress. The Prince of Wales, the Duke of Connaught (both standing), with the Duke of Edinburgh and the Duke of Albany (both seated), at Abergeldie Castle, 1881.

25. Palais Edinburg, Coburg.

26. Schloss Ehrenburg, Coburg.

Above left: 27. Crown Prince Frederick William, later Frederick III, German Emperor, 1883.

Above right: 28. William II, German Emperor.

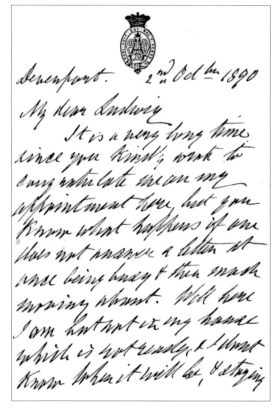

29. First page of letter from the Duke of Edinburgh to Prince Louis of Battenberg, 2 October 1890. (*Broadlands Archives, Romsey*)

Above: 30. The family at Coburg for the wedding of Princess Victoria Melita of Saxe-Coburg Gotha and Ernest, Grand Duke of Hesse, 19 April 1894. Seated, left to right: William II, German Emperor; Queen Victoria; the Empress Frederick; at front, Princess Beatrice of Saxe-Coburg Gotha; Princess Feodora of Saxe-Meiningen. First standing row, left to right: Prince Alfred of Saxe-Coburg Gotha; Nicholas, Tsarevich of Russia; Princess Alix of Hesse; Princess Louis of Battenberg; Princess Henry of Prussia; Grand Duchess Vladimir of Russia; Marie, Duchess of Saxe-Coburg Gotha. Second standing row, left to right: Albert Edward, Prince of Wales; Princess Henry of Battenberg; Princess Philip of Saxe-Coburg Kohary (facing left); Charlotte, Princess of Saxe-Meiningen; Princess Aribert of Anhalt; Louise, Duchess of Connaught. Two standing rows at back, left to right: Prince Louis of Battenberg; Grand Duke Paul of Russia; Prince Henry of Battenberg; Prince Philip of Saxe-Coburg Kohary; Count Mensdorff; Grand Duke Serge of Russia; Roumania; Grand Duchess Serge of Russia; Grand Duke Vladimir of Russia; Alfred, Duke of Saxe-Coburg Gotha.

Below left: 31. The Duke of Saxe-Coburg Gotha (seated) and Prince Alfred, 1895. (*Bayerisches Staatsarchiv, Coburg*)

Below right: 32. Shooting expedition at Coburg *c.* 1896. From left: Prince Alfred; Nicholas II, Tsar of Russia; Ernest, Grand Duke of Hesse; the Duke of Saxe-Coburg Gotha. (*Bayerisches Staatsarchiv, Coburg*)

Above left: 33. The Duke of Saxe-Coburg Gotha in full dress uniform as Admiral of the Fleet, 1897. (*Bayerisches Staatsarchiv, Coburg*)

Above right: 34. The Duke of Saxe-Coburg Gotha, 1900, the last known photograph before his death. (*His Imperial Highness Grand Duke Vladimir of Russia*)

Above right: 35. The Duchess of Saxe-Coburg Gotha (far left) and her three elder daughters, 1898. From left: Marie, Crown Princess of Roumania; Victoria Melita, Grand Duchess of Hesse; Princess Ernest of Hohenlohe-Langenburg. (*Bayerisches Staatsarchiv, Coburg*)

36. The Rosenau Guard House, where the Duke died. (*Bayerisches Staatsarchiv, Coburg*)

37. The Duke lying in state, Church of St Moritz, Coburg. (*Bayerisches Staatsarchiv, Coburg*)

38. The funeral procession, Coburg, with statue of Prince Consort (unveiled in 1865) on right. (*Bayerisches Staatsarchiv, Coburg*)

39. The funeral
procession,
Coburg.
(*Bayerisches
Staatsarchiv,
Coburg*)

40. The Duke's
tomb, inscribed
in German.
(*Bayerisches
Staatsarchiv,
Coburg*)

You need not fear that I should say anything to anyone of what I wrote to you only about the difficulties out here, that was entirely between myself and you. But I assure you that you frightened me with Leopold of Belgium's proposal [that the Duke should be appointed Governor of Constantinople]. I had no idea, although I had often heard it mentioned, that there was anybody who seriously thought of it. I am sure I would sooner end the remainder of my days in China, to such a fearful prospect, and with the exception of China, I am sure Marie would share my feelings...

I believe that the Emperor [Tsar Alexander II], who is a man of the most sensitive feelings, is deeply hurt at all the unpleasant (to say the least of them) and untrue things said of him in the British press. You will have received the letter from him which at your wish I got Marie to ask him to write to you...

Tomorrow I have unfortunately to prosecute one of my men at a court-martial for theft, which will be a very unpleasant task. One of my midshipmen...broke his leg last night skylarking, and I was up with him until half-past-one, and up again at half-past-four when we exercised manning and arming boats, so you see we don't let the grass grow under our feet, and we are not getting fat in consequence. I have one midshipman ill three weeks with fever, but he is the only person ill on board, but in a month's time, if we continue at Besika, ague and fever will set in on board all the ships, as the land winds begin now, and the ague comes fourteen days afterwards, and great care is necessary...[1]

Among Affie's officers in the Mediterranean was his cousin Prince Louis of Battenberg, whom he had engaged as an unofficial flag-lieutenant, a promotion his naval authority did not allow. Louis joined *Sultan* in July with high hopes of responsible duties, but to his disappointment found that he was expected to be the Captain's aide-de-camp and equerry, act as sub-lieutenant on deck and signal mate, relieve the duty officer at morning watch, keep first dog watch at sea, be permanent officer of the guard in harbor, and take the place of any lieutenant who was sick or on leave. He had to mess with Affie except at breakfast, and found him terribly touchy. Affie was barely on speaking terms with his commander, Richard Britten, who believed that as a prince he was incapable of managing the ship and needed help with every trifling little matter. Louis frequently had to act as peacemaker between them.

Louis's endless duties were not the least of his problems. The Mediterranean Fleet was popularly supposed to be the strongest in the Royal Navy, but he was shocked to find that it had fallen into a pitiful state of decay. It had become a collection of heterogeneous man-o'war ships, with a high proportion of dissolute or ageing senior officers who had scant regard for the fighting fitness of their vessels. Their quarters were riddled with rats, gunnery tactics had changed little since the turn of the century, and had it not been for the introduction of the high explosive shell, critics claimed that Nelson's fleet at Trafalgar could have defeated it before lunch. The Commander-in-Chief was Admiral Sir James Drummond, 'a dear old white-haired gentleman'. Deaf as a post, he distinguished himself and embarrassed everyone else at a concert on board by confusing *Rule Britannia* and *God Save The Queen,* scolding the company furiously for not standing to attention during the former and then sitting down grumpily when the latter struck up.

Nonetheless there were good times to be had during holidays at the Crimea for Affie, Louis, Marie, the careworn Tsar and the pitifully-ailing Tsarina. The ducal couple made San Antonio Palace on Malta their official residence, for the provision of nursemaids had enabled all officers' wives to live on the island. On 25 November 1876 Marie gave birth to a second daughter, named Victoria Melita, soon to be known *en famille* as Ducky. The name Melita was most appropriate, for as the local press observed, 'Malta now claims the honour of being the birthplace of a Royal child. No other colony in Her Majesty's broad possessions can claim the same.'[2]

San Antonio soon became the centre of society life on the island. Early in the new year Affie and Marie gave a ball at the palace, attended by nearly 500 guests. There was nothing but lavish praise for the hostess, who was certainly a very different Grand Duchess Marie from the one who had caused many a furrowed brow only months previously at drawing-rooms at the English court.

> There is a naturalness in her manner singularly attractive and taking. No one appears beneath her notice; and ash she passed through the crowd of her honoured guests, her eye, her manner, and her pleasant words put all at their ease.[3]

For the whole fleet there were sporting facilities on Malta, especially polo and horse racing. A pack of bugles had been sent out from England and was kenneled ashore off the Dardanelles, leaving Louis to refer scathingly to one of the more 'serious exercises'; disembarking beagles and ponies at speed from shore to ship and vice versa. When they required something a little less strenuous, Affie would play his violin to the piano accompaniment of Louis and one of his clerks. This time there was no member of the Ponsonby family to pass adverse comment on his technique. In the spring Affie and Louis accompanied Bertie on his regular holiday on the Riviera, where the highlight was an evening of *rouge et noir* at a new casino at Monte Carlo.

In January 1877 Drummond had been retired and replaced by Vice-Admiral Sir Geoffrey Phipps-Hornby. Recognising that his ships had to be turned into an efficient fighting force in the event of hostilities, he introduced a regular programme of steaming manoeuvres and gun drill. Gunnery practice was not without its dangers; one day a gun in the battleship *Thunderer* was accidentally double-loaded and burst on firing, wrecking the turret and killing nine officers and men.

In April Russia declared war on Turkey, and the Mediterranean Fleet sailed eastwards through the Dardanelles to the Sea of Marmora, dropping anchor within sight of Constantinople in order to be on hand to protect lives and property of British subjects in the area.

Both Affie and Louis were unhappy at being so close to the war, one which cut across family loyalties as bitterly as Prussia's campaigns had done in the previous decade. Louis had even closer relations on the battlefield, for his younger brother Alexander (Sandro) was aide-de-camp to the Russian Commander-in-Chief, the Tsar's brother Grand Duke Nicholas. Alone among ships in the fleet, the officers on *Sultan* did not raise their glasses to every Turkish victory in the first few months.

By February 1878 the tide was running in Russia's favour, and the fleet proceeded through the Dardanelles when a Russian victory placed them within striking distance of Constantinople. Within a few days the Turks were forced to surrender and sue for peace. The Treaty of San Stefano, signed on 3 March, justified Europe's worst fears in seeing considerable Russian gains. Foremost among these was the creation of a large Bulgarian state supposed to be independent but which would initially be garrisoned by Russian troops. Coincidentally the nomination for ruler of Bulgaria was none other than Prince Alexander of Battenberg. In Britain, votes of credit were passed through Parliament, troops were stationed at Malta in the event of war with Russia, and music halls rang with the refrain

> We don't want to fight,
> But by Jingo if we do,
> We've got the ships, we've got the men,
> We've got the money too!

Negotiations were begun between Russia and the Great Powers to persuade the former to moderate her demands. At this time the Mediterranean Fleet was in the Sea of Marmora, and a well-intentioned but tactless act by Affie brought home to them all the painful division of family allegiances.

When Louis heard that the German Ambassador and his wife that Sandro was in Constantinople, he was determined to see him, and Affie granted him permission to go ashore. The brothers were overjoyed to see each other safe and sound, and Louis invited Sandro on board *Sultan*. Later they went on to the flagship and then on to *Temeraire*, a modern battleship equipped with several new devices. Phipps-Hornby was embarrassed at having a foreign officer on board at such a delicate time, though Sandro had taken care to appear in German (not Russian) uniform; and he hesitated to interfere with what was really no more than a fraternal reunion. However, as Sandro was an officer he had to be accorded certain privileges, such as watching a demonstration of fleet exercises, and dined on board the flagship. The brothers later went ashore and visited Russian army headquarters, where they were received cordially by Grand Duke Nicholas and shown around the camp where several Turkish officers were imprisoned and captured armaments kept.

When he was informed of their activities the British Ambassador at Constantinople was aghast, fearing that peace negotiations would be jeopardised by the entertaining of a Russian officer on board a British ship and made party top confidential information. In order to prevent Queen and Admiralty from hearing vague rumours from unofficial sources, he cabled to London.

Queen Victoria's fury knew no bounds. When her eldest son had been named in the Mordaunt divorce case and appeared in court eight years earlier, she had almost despaired but still stood loyally by him, believing in his assurance that he was not guilty of adultery. Foolishness which verged on breaking the tenth commandment was one thing, but idiocy verging on treason was quite another. She wrote angrily to Affie that it was hard to believe even him capable of such indiscretion. The best that could be said in his defence was that he was guilty of extreme thoughtlessness, but as a Captain in command of a ship, and as son of the sovereign, at a time when the two nations might soon be at war, was much too serious to be passed over. He had undoubtedly injured the prospects of both Louis and himself. The Tsarevna wrote to her father King Christian IX of Denmark that Queen Victoria, who was 'completely mad', had called her son a traitor, considered him unworthy to command a frigate any longer, and told him that any possibility of him being appointed an Admiral was out of the question, now that he was married to a Russian wife.

Having administered her own stinging rebuke, she asked Disraeli to see that Admiral Phipps-Hornby should reprimand him on behalf of the Royal Navy. However the latter himself had also attended the dinner and could theoretically be considered as partly responsible. Disraeli complained to W. H. Smith, his First Lord of the Admiralty, that the 'Duke of Edinburgh business' was costing him more trouble than the Eastern question itself.

Only a few weeks earlier the question of the Duke of Edinburgh's promotion from Captain to Rear-Admiral had been discussed. Smith had consulted Disraeli, who replied, 'You can do what you like provided he does not come home.' This was at the Queen's insistence, for she regarded Affie as a bad influence on Arthur, her favourite and least troublesome son. As *Sultan* was due to come back to England to have her boilers replaced, her Captain was bound to return with her. In the light of this incident, it was doubly imperative that Affie should be posted elsewhere without delay, and perhaps even forfeit his leave. To have a prince whose behaviour was perilously close to treason arriving home was out of the question. At Darmstadt Alice had heard from various sources that the Duke of Edinburgh could not show his face there after such openly pro-Russian behaviour, and even his favourite sister Helena had written to say how ashamed she was of him.

Louis was promptly transferred to a depot ship at Malta. He and his parents were so upset by the storm that he seriously considered having to leave the Royal Navy altogether. The Tsarina, who was no admirer of Queen Victoria, wrote to Prince Alexander of Hesse to say that his son Sandro was beside himself that 'that crazy old hag' had made him the pretext for persecuting Affie and Louis. Distressed by the animosity between England and Russia, and on top of that this new incident, his father Alexander was resolute that Louis should resign from the service unless an apology was forthcoming.

At length the Queen was persuaded to believe that no harm had been done, and that the British Ambassador's telegram was exaggerated. Sandro had not been wearing Russian uniform, and he was not shown confidential equipment while on board *Temeraire*. A grudging apology was just sufficient to persuade Louis and his father that the former should go to London and gauge official opinion himself. Louis's welcome at Marlborough House by the Prince of Wales, who had done more than anyone else to calm the Queen's anger, showed that old friendships were as enduring as ever. Smith invited him to his office in London and assured him that his standing in the Navy was not affected, and the Queen invited him to lunch where he was 'received most graciously'.

Meanwhile the Duke of Edinburgh was transferred to the command of *Black Prince*, while *Sultan* proceeded back to Portsmouth for refitting. The Queen had warned him that he would shortly be receiving a letter of censure from the Admiral (despite his attendance at the fateful dinner), but by the end of May Disraeli was complaining to Smith that no letter had been sent, Her Majesty was 'left entirely unsupported', and Affie was demanding a court of enquiry to clear his name. Smith was able to assure the Prime Minister that Phipps-Hornby had in fact written a private friendly letter which any sensible man would thoroughly understand.

At last the whole business could be regarded as over. It was left to the

United Services Gazette to regret that 'a certain class of our contemporaries' should take liberties with the Duke's name, and treat him as though he was almost guilty of high treason. Far from being 'penally removed' to *Black Prince*, this was necessitated by his personal desire to retain a command in the Mediterranean.[4] Such a statement, while indicating that the matter was closed, did not quite convince everyone that there had never been any unpleasant undercurrents.

It was with some relief that Affie, his name cleared, went to Coburg for a few weeks that summer, partly for rest and partly to be with Marie during her fourth confinement. On 1 September she presented him with another daughter, Alexandra, who would always be called Sandra within the family.

By now the threat of war was long past, for Russia had bowed to pressure and taken part in the Berlin Congress in June. She held some small territorial gains, but the new principality of Bulgaria was much smaller than had originally been proposed at the Treaty of San Stefano. Turkey was preserved, and Britain was allowed to occupy the island of Cyprus.

As there was no prospect of active service Affie was anxious to return home, a wish which resulted in hated exchanges of correspondence between the Queen, her Prime Minister and the First Lord of the Admiralty. She was adamant that Affie should not return home until the following spring, for public and private reasons, and told them both. When she had a letter from Affie some days later saying that she had been mortified by Smith's secretary that the final decision as to *Black Prince*'s movements rested with her, she protested to Disraeli that the Admiralty was throwing the whole odium and responsibility on her shoulders. It was up to the department to make arrangements with the Duke. She was moved to complain to her Prime Minister twice at weekly intervals, and would doubtless have done so a third time had Affie not broken the stalemate by writing angrily to Bertie, threatening that he would resign his commission if not allowed home. Nonetheless she did not want him back yet; could he not be sent to some other Mediterranean station for a while? Smith and Disraeli, almost as weary of the problem as the Duke himself, were united in their opinion that *Black Prince* should return to port with her officers on board once peace was assured – and there was no reason to fear the threat of war any longer – but how could they tell their sovereign was sufficient dilemma in itself.

Just in time a solution presented itself. The Marquess of Lorne, Princess Louise's husband, had been appointed Governor-General of Canada. He suggested that in view of his wife's royal status it would be appropriate for them to land at Halifax from one of Her Majesty's ships. In giving her approval, it occurred to her that this would provide her second son with suitable employment that did not look too obviously like exile in disguise. The owners of a passenger ship *Sarmatian* placed their vessel at Lorne's disposal, Smith advised that it was the most comfortable for a long transatlantic voyage, and Lorne eagerly accepted. Neither of them informed the Queen, who told them that a ship of the Royal Navy was the only appropriate means of transport for the purpose. A further difficulty arose when Ponsonby was told that *Black Prince* was not fit to cross the Atlantic, particularly at that season of the year. To this Smith tactfully replied that she was a perfectly safe ship for the duty 'if properly handled, as she certainly would be by the Duke'.[5]

Louise and Lorne accordingly crossed the Atlantic in *Black Prince* on a ten-day voyage from Liverpool to Halifax, during which the new Governor-General was the only passenger not to be seasick. He paced the deck with a captured seagull which he intended to sketch.

In Canada the Duke was again to fall victim to the imagination of a foreign journalist. On 12 December *The Times* reported the details of an interview he had apparently granted to a reporter from the *New York World*, published the previous month. These alleged that he looked upon Disraeli, the author of England's 'peace with honour', with feelings of disgust; that the acquisition of Cyprus was in no sense a British gain; and when English people learnt about the fever-ridden island, they would 'be heard from most unpleasantly on the subject'. 'After finding this out, as they must, the people have to pay the piper, my belief is they will manifest a pretty general desire to pitch the piper overboard.' In conclusion the reporter gave his verdict that the Duke of Edinburgh was not a politician, but a gallant, outspoken sailor-like prince, by no means a Conservative but not necessarily a Liberal of the Gladstonian school. The correspondent suggested that the Duke was evidently 'not much amused with this Canadian trip', and was 'unfeignedly anxious to get home, whither he will doubtless sail as soon as he can'.[6] As the Duke of Edinburgh was known to be one who did not suffer fools gladly and was almost certainly quite capable of giving such an ungracious and indiscreet set of remarks to a journalist, this report probably did his reputation no good at all. Nevertheless, on 17 December the Admiralty firmly denied that any such interview had ever taken place.

The hoax was singularly ill-timed, for it added to the burden of a family suddenly plunged into deepest mourning. Affie was still on his way home across the Atlantic on 14 December, when an epidemic of diphtheria at the ducal palace in Darmstadt claimed his sister Alice's life. Though his arrival at Spithead two days later and subsequent return to London prevented him from being back in time to join his brothers at her funeral in Germany, Affie and Marie attended a memorial service held at Windsor on the same day as the ceremony.

However, at least the unhappy year of 1878 ended on a brighter note. Vice-Admiral Sir John Hay informed the Admiralty that he had nothing but praise for the Captain of *Black Prince* in his work during the disembarkation at Cyprus of Indian troops sent to Malta earlier that year in the event of war with Russia. On 30 December Affie was promoted from Captain to Rear-Admiral.

Christmas and the new year of 1879 saw Affie at Eastwell, and while there he wrote to his aunt Alexandrine on 4 January:

> You can imagine what a dreadful blow it was for me to come home and hear the dreadful news of dear Alice's death and the deep sorrow to the family and home which hung everywhere all over Xmas. Thank God my dear Marie and the children are very well and we are enjoying very much our life here in the country. Helena and Christian and their two sons are staying with us and Arthur goes tomorrow. Marie thanks you very much for your letter with the directions about the various Xmas presents. Perhaps you have heard that I am 'advanced' to Admiral.[7]

After having spent so long abroad, Affie was glad to be home in England again and have a chance to involve himself in the naval affairs of his country, as befitted the master of Trinity House. Of particular interest to him was the rebuilding of Eddystone Lighthouse off the south Devon coast. Smeaton's Tower had stood on Eddystone Rock, fourteen miles from Plymouth Hoe, since 1759. An inspection in 1877 revealed that despite the solid structure of the building itself, the rock was gradually eroding through sea action. Another lighthouse was therefore built on an adjacent part of the reef, but foundations could only be built at low water, and work had been delayed by the exceptionally wet weather of 1878-9. It was ready for the laying of a foundation stone by summer of 1879, and Affie was invited to perform the ceremony. He and Bertie travelled down to Plymouth for the purpose in June, but recent storms and heavy sea made a landing on the rock impossible, and it was postponed for a couple of months. It took place on 19 August, when both princes sailed out to the rock and declared the hand-lowered block 'well and truly laid'. They spent the night as guests of the Earl of Mount Edgcumbe, an equerry and later lord-in-waiting to the Prince of Wales, and enjoyed a shooting party on his estates the next day.

In June 1881 Affie returned to lay the final stone of the lighthouse, and in May 1882 he performed the inauguration ceremony. Little did he know that these were only preludes to a much closer association with Plymouth in the years ahead.

The Duke's appointment as Rear-Admiral was to bring curious echoes of the behavior of the previous sailor prince. The Duke of Clarence had declared on his appointment as Lord High Admiral in 1827 that he would be no mere idle royal figurehead. Now half a century later the Duke's great-nephew was similarly determined to have some say in matters within his province.

Affie's immediate objective was for some active office either at the Admiralty or some shore base. Smith suggested appointing him Admiral Superintendent of Naval Reserves. Before accepting he consulted several other officers as to the suitability of such a post, and as a result decided that it would be impossible for him 'to undertake these duties as they stand at present without risk of failure'. Smith's biographer calls this 'an extraordinary step',[8] but it is hard not to sympathise with his caution. After being attacked bitterly during the *Sultan* business, Affie knew that it would be all too easy for the Admiralty to make him as scapegoat if he did not make an unqualified success of the job. He proposed that he should be supported by a highly-qualified deputy whose efficiency would make the risk of failure more remote.

In spite of Disraeli's disapproval, Smith had no alternative but to seek the Queen's approval and find a Captain of sufficiently senior rank – to whom Affie originally objected. Later Affie accepted him, and then claimed a 'table allowance' of £200 per year which had been granted to his predecessor, or failing this an allowance for one year only. If he did not claim either of these, he argued, he would be prejudicing the interests of his brother officers who would succeed him. Smith gently but firmly refused this, saying that it was his duty to protect the Duke from 'the misapprehension which would arise', and it would place him in a difficult position if extra money was granted and he could not devote his whole time to the duties of Admiral Superintendent, owing to additional royal duties.

Affie accepted this caution with good race and the appointment was confirmed on 21 November. As it was, he could claim a small victory in having asked for and obtained his deputy, an extravagance for which Smith was reproached by Sir Ralph Lingen, Chairman of a Committee of Enquiry into Admiralty reorganisation, and Stafford Northcote, Chancellor of the Exchequer. The latter told him grudgingly that 'as regards HRH I suppose you could not help yourself'.

On his new appointment in November 1879 Affie hoisted his flag in HMS *Penelope*, an eleven-gun armour-plated iron corvette of 4,394 tons, flagship of the first reserve and coastguard and drill ship of the naval reserves, stationed at Harwich. Already he had earned a high reputation for his skill in the conduct of fleet manoeuvres, and he worked conscientiously at the task of bringing the reserves to a high state of efficiency. For each of the three years of his appointment he took ships to sea for exercises as far as the Baltic. He also visited all the major British fishing ports, and in 1883 he published a paper for the International Fisheries Exhibition in London on the national sea fisheries and fishing population, based on experience and information obtained on his travels.

Another duty allocated to Affie early in 1880 was organising the transport of stores for the relief of distress on the west coast of Ireland. There were already several different local relief committees, both British and American, and it was a task that called for considerable tact. As this was not a quality of which he had given much evidence in his previous dealings with the Admiralty, it says much for him that he handled it with success. The Viceroy of Ireland, John Winston Spencer, 7th Duke of Marlborough, wrote to Smith saying how much he wished to congratulate him on the Duke's work, and Affie wrote to Smith himself to say how he had gained great pleasure from the task. Considering that an Irishman had nearly sent him to an early grave in Australia, this was indeed a magnanimous comment, but no other member of the royal family had had the opportunity to see at first hand the sufferings and privations brought on the Irish by the great famine.

Later that summer, in the course of his duties, Affie renewed his acquaintance with the Duchess of Sutherland. On 6 July he wrote from on board HMS *Hercules* off Torbay:

I had no idea that you would be down here or I would have let you know that I was coming but I thank you very much for asking me to your pretty residence. I am only here for a few hours but will with pleasure avail myself of your invitation to visit you. I fear however that our early hours of on board ship may be inconvenient to you; moreover I must go to sea again at about midday. I will land at half past ten tomorrow morning with the intention of going out to Sutherland Villa & should that not be too early an hour I should be very much obliged to you if you would send a carriage to meet me.[9]

The reunion was a happy one, and five days later he wrote from Crookhaven off the Irish coast:

I must write you a line from the first place I have touched at since I left Tor Bay to thank you for your very kind invitation & the very pleasant reception you gave me. I regretted very much that my stay was so short & the weather so unfavourable that I could not ask you to visit some of the ships of my squadron. I was so charmed with your little house that

I hope I may soon be able to pay a longer visit to Torquay on one of my inspection tours.[10]

Eastwell was home to the Edinburghs every autumn, Christmas and new year, and usually at Easter as well. Affie generally spent every morning in his study reading and writing, while visitors would come in the afternoon and evening. A metropolitan police inspector and two constables were responsible for their security. While they might not go in daily fear of their lives like the Tsar and his family, the grounds would have been all too easy for the odd intruder to threaten them, and Affie may have been considered just as much at risk as the rest of them – in view of the attempt on his life in Australia, perhaps a little more so. A local reporter who was allowed to see the family at home in December 1879 was struck by the tranquillity of 'an interesting family, who find fair, quiet, and sweet rest among the Kentish woodlands,' even though he thought the house was 'one of the ugliest buildings in the prettiest part of Kent'.[11]

By 1880 the family was almost complete; Beatrice (Baby Bee), born at Eastwell on 20 April 1884, would be the last. With the exception of the delicate young Alfred, they were a healthy brood. It was ironic that Affie's lively, attractive daughters with their long golden tresses and high spirits should be almost everything that their elder cousins were not. Although the Grand Duchess Marie was plain and plump, the absolute despair of her girls, quite unlike the eternally youthful-looking and sylph-like Princess of Wales, unkindly if not inaccurately dubbed 'their royal shynesses' had little of their mother's beauty or zest for life. Even the Queen could not help comparing the puny Wales princesses unfavourably with her sturdy Edinburgh granddaughters.

Unlike his mother, young Alfred found himself in a nursery and later, briefly, in a schoolroom of girls. All five spent their summer holidays at Osborne running wild in the garden, though he was subjected to the time-honoured Coburg system in being expected to keep up his languages all the time. His French governor had a hard time looking for him on the lawns and up tall trees, where he climbed to try and avoid one of the hated *dictées*.

As second in succession to the duchy of Coburg, it was considered that young Alfred should be brought up in Germany as far as possible. He had no passion for the Royal Navy like his father nor, it just be said, his father's robust childhood health. When he was older he took up residence in the Palais Edinburg, a square, barrack-like building at Coburg with no pretensions or old-world charm. Here the boy became a sad lonely figure for several months of the year, relying on his mother's long letters, and frequently at the mercy of servants and tutors.

Because of his official commitments, particularly at sea, Affie was not often at home. Unlike his elder brother, he was always shy, and never managed to establish the good relationship with his children as youngsters that Bertie, and even their father, had done in the nursery. More at ease with his contemporaries, the role of playful father did not come naturally to one of his rather reserved nature. He had a habit of looking through them sometimes as if they were simply not there. This was a curious characteristic of all the Queen's children as adults; the younger Edinburghs found their uncles and aunts oddly absent-minded. The latter would occasionally become aware of a youngster in their presence, start a conversation with him or her and then wander off, leaving the child feeling rather hurt and dismayed. Moreover, with his uncertain temper and heavy drinking, Affie was possibly not cut out to be the best of fathers as well as the easiest of husbands. It was sometimes considered fortuitous for the survival of his marriage that he was away so much from Marie. Their daughter Missy later recalled that 'he was even a little bit of a stranger to us', and naturally their mother played a much greater role in the children's lives as well as having more say in their upbringing.

In spite of this, to his children Affie was a hero, exceedingly good-looking with his tanned skin and deep blue eyes. When he made the effort he could enjoy games with them, particularly one which was kept for winter evenings, and the memory of which never faded. All the lamps in the house were extinguished and he hid in a dark corner, pretending to be an ogre. They never knew which room he was in and they crawled around in the darkness trembling with excitement, until he caught them off their guard and suddenly sprang out, his growls and their hysterical shrieks and laughter ringing throughout the passages.

No less fun were the outsider sports of tobogganing down the slopes at Eastwell, and learning to skate on the lake as it lay beneath a glistening surface of ice. Father and children alike wore their best black velvet caps trimmed with Russian sable, as much a part of the skating expeditions as the hot cinnamon-flavoured red wine with which they refreshed themselves afterwards.

The children always left Clarence House and its smuts, smoke and gloomy walks in Green Park, with relief and eager anticipation for Christmas at Eastwell, synonymous with walks and games in the countryside. Like the Prince Consort, Affie keenly anticipated the hours of preparation that went into the festive magic each year. With the zest of a boy himself he supervised every little detail, and could become quite irritated if his plans were not minutely adhered to – setting up a tree in the library, putting out presents on white-covered tables placed against the walls, and getting everyone to take turns in stirring the servants' plum pudding. The climax came on Christmas Eve, when family and servants were called to watch the library doors thrown open to reveal the tree in a blaze of candlelight and fragrance of singed fir branches, everyone gasping with wonder as presents were distributed.

After Alice's tragic death, the bonds between Queen Victoria's elder children became stronger. There had always been something of a gulf between the first six, those who were adult or adolescent by the time of the Prince Consort's death, and the younger three who had still been too young and not independent enough in 1861 to regard their mother's grief as exaggerated and a shadow on their previously happy existence.

Affie welcomed his siblings to Eastwell whenever he could. Bertie was a frequent member of the shooting parties, and he returned the compliment by regular invitations to Sandringham. Another welcome visitor was his brother-in-law Christian, whose interests barely extended beyond sport and shooting. Though other members of the family thought him a bore, to Affie he was always congenial company. His good relations with Helena, interrupted only temporarily by the *Sultan* affair, had long since been restored. Brother and sister shared a down-to-earth commonsense outlook on life. Affie's blunt naval manners would have heartily approved of Helena's behavior one Sunday in the chapel at Windsor, when she scrutinised the Archbishop of Canterbury's special prayer to be said at the time of a dock strike, and put it down abruptly with the comment (in the penetrating royal whisper which carried much further than any average mortal's voice): 'That prayer won't settle any strike.'[12]

As a mother Marie tempered kindness with severity. She adored her children and encouraged them in their carefree garden activities, letting them rush around, skate, climb trees, and enjoy the healthy outdoor life essential to any youngster. But she also believed in a strict upbringing. They must always be ready to talk and entertain people, as nothing was more hopeless or rude than a prince or a princess who never opened his or her mouth. When they were invited out for meals, they must never insult their hosts by refusing what was put in front of them, or even leaving the slightest scrap on their plates. If the good made them feel sick, they would have to wait until they got home. As Marie was so healthy herself, they must never complain about minor ailments like colds or headaches. Because of her mania for punctuality, they must never be late for an appointment. She liked reading aloud to them the stories of Hans Christian Andersen and the Brothers Grimm, but her children must never sit idly listening, for they should be sewing or knitting at the same time. She would not teach them Russian, as she could not bear to hear it mutilated, and therefore English was always spoken at home. They grew up speaking it better than the

Prince of Wales, with his heavy guttural accent, and their father, who also spoke with a pronounced if less noticeable German inflexion.

Marie had her fair share of eccentricities. Her leather boots made to order in St Petersburg were designed to fit either foot, as she thought it irrational to have a left and a right. Despite her perfect command of English, she claimed that French was by far the most elegant language of all, and really beautiful letters could only be written in French – even though she disliked 'immoral republican France' as a nation. Indeed Marie could be remarkably hard to please. She detested the cold, damp, wet British climate, and once declared that she did not care to be blown to pieces in what the English called 'bracing' places where one could not keep a hat upon one's head. A letter to Lady Randolph Churchill, written from Stuttgart on 16 June 1886, expressed the pious hope that she had enjoyed Ascot, 'and that the hideous climate did not spoil, as usual, all the enjoyments'.[13] Moreover, she spurned the unwritten rule that in those ladies did not smoke cigarettes in public.

Inevitably such ways did not endear Marie to the British, and she was sometimes spoken of as 'the most unpopular princess in Europe'. Although she would not have condescended to recognise such a base distinction, a Grand Duchess being infinitely superior to a mere princess, she was oblivious to unpopularity in a land for which she was not afraid to show her contempt. Though she had arrived in England with the best of intentions, she could not forget how her father had spoken scornfully of Queen Victoria, and realised that relations between her country and that of her husband had never been easy. With the strong anti-Russian feeling of 1878 Marie's reserve hardened into lasting resentment. She had never been particularly attractive, and by the time she reached thirty she had lost whatever good looks she may have possessed, but she was under no illusions as to her appearance. In the summer of 1883 the German court painter Carl Rudolph Sohn was commissioned to paint a portrait of Affie, Marie and their eldest son, with a view of the Rosenau in the background. She wrote of the result that she disliked 'having my pig-like face reproduced on canvas and handed over to posterity'.[14]

To her intense bitterness was added constant fear and worry about her father. An attempt on Tsar Alexander's life in 1866 was the first of several. On a later occasion Marie too had a lucky escape. She was visiting him at the Winter Palace in February 1880, where one evening Sandro, Sovereign Prince of Bulgaria, was to be guest of honour at dinner. Though she was a stickler for punctuality, this time she had cause to be grateful that Sandro's train was half an hour late in arriving. Just as they were about to leave the drawing room and sit down to their food, a deafening roar shook the palace walls and resounded throughout the city. The dining room had been mined by terrorists and was completely demolished in the explosion. Ten soldiers and several domestic servants were left dead, and an even larger number seriously injured.

'Am I such a wild animal that I must be hounded to death?' the Tsar asked bitterly. In June 1880 the Tsarina died in her room at the Winter Palace, all alone without even the companionship of a nurse to ease her last hours. Grand Dukes, politicians and diplomats alike mourned the cruelly tried, disease-wasted woman who – they asserted – had died of a broken heart. They were disgusted then her widower lost no time in marrying Catherine Dolgorukya, whom he created a princess and attempted to have recognised as his Empress.

One morning in March 1881 the Edinburgh children were astonished to find their Mama kneeling in her room at Clarence House in floods of tears. The inevitable had happened. While returning from a military review in his capital, the Tsar had been assassinated by another terrorist bomb.

Affie and Marie immediately hurried to St Petersburg for the funeral, which turned out to be one of the grimmest family reunions imaginable. The new Tsar and Tsarina were perpetually haunted by the memory of their father's mutilated yet still semi-conscious body being brought back to the palace through snowy streets, already stained with the blood of soldiers who had perished from an earlier bomb which narrowly missed its imperial target. Stringent police precautions made the Romanovs and their guests virtual prisoners in the Winter Palace, and the only place where they could exercise was in a narrow courtyard which the English guests thought was even worse than a London slum.

Affie cabled to Bertie that they all wished for the presence of himself and Alix. Though Queen Victoria hesitated to risk the life of her heir and his wife on such a hazardous mission, her ministers believed that his presence could help to bring about a closer understanding between the two imperial powers, and Bertie and Alix knew that the least they could do was to share the danger with the new Tsar and Tsarina, Sasha and Alix's sister Minnie. From Germany came Fritz, sent by his unfeeling father and Bismarck who pooh-poohed the warning letters he and Vicky had received, telling him that he too would be killed if he went to Russia.

The obsequies passed off without incident, but several ingenious conspiracies and devices were discovered by the police while the guests were still in the country. Fear of mass assassination was paralleled by the grotesque custom that a memorial service had to be held beside the coffin of the Tsar every day until the funeral. His face was left exposed to be kissed by each relative in turn at these services, and as his features had been hideously distorted by the bomb and decay set in quickly, he was not a pleasant sight.

Alix stayed with her sister an extra week, but Affie and Bertie left at the end of March. The train in which they travelled to the frontier was heavily guarded, and their relief at leaving Russia safely was unbounded. Nonetheless it heralded a time of constant worry for them all, and in May Affie implored the Queen to invite him and Marie to Balmoral that autumn. She had not always looked kindly on them, but now she recognised that she was the only parent Marie had left, and she could not refuse.

In June 1881 Affie decided to combine business with pleasure, and took HMS *Hercules* on a cruise with the reserve fleet to the Baltic. With him came Arthur Sullivan, who was gratified when their first stop was Copenhagen. King Christian IX had long been an admirer of his work, and the Danish court orchestra possessed almost every page of music he had ever composed. They were invited to a sumptuous banquet in their honour, at which inevitably the music played was written by Sullivan, except for the National Anthem which was played after King and Duke had proposed each others' healths.

At Kronstadt they were greeted with a more formal welcome by Russian officers and diplomats in their uniformed bemedalled finery, crowding on board for a champagne reception. The Tsar's private yacht was in harbour waiting to take them to his palace at Peterhof. Here they were once again heavily guarded, but all possible comforts were laid on for them except baths. Sullivan was rather startled by the primitive sanitary arrangements. On leaving his bedroom at night to search for a lavatory, he was turned back by a Cossack guard at his door who revealed a secret convenience at the foot of his bed.

For Affie and the composer, the highlight of this Russian interlude was not to be found in state banquets, but in a concert given for them at the Winter Palace by the imperial chapel choir, all dressed in red and gold. Affie said it reminded him of a similar choral entertainment in the Chapel Royal at Windsor but even more striking, and in spite of his considerable musical experiences Sullivan himself confessed to a new feeling of exultation on hearing them sing.

Next stop on the cruise was Kiel, where the German Emperor William had asked his grandson William to welcome him. 'Willy' was also a devotee of the Savoy Operas, and when he bowed to Sullivan and sang, 'He polished up the handle of the big front door', everyone rocked with laughter. Affie invited him on a tour of *Hercules* before he steamed past the British ships, and after dinner that night introduced him to his commanders.

But Affie could not help noticing uneasily that the twenty-two-year-old prince was fast assuming the traditional Prussian airs and graces that were already estranging him from his parents, and which the Prince of

Wales had recently had reason to deplore. Affie also felt uncomfortable that Fritz had not been chosen to come to Kiel instead. As Crown Prince it should have been Fritz's privilege, if not his right, to welcome his brother-in-law, but he was held in such contempt by his doddering father and Bismarck, that they took every opportunity to insult him by refusing him the more pleasant representative duties. It was no accident that the future Emperor William II had come to meet his uncle Alfred, but was not ordered to risk his life by representing the Hohenzollerns at the St Petersburg funeral in March.

Under the influence of Sullivan and others, Affie became active in aiding the cause of contemporary British music. On 12 December 1881 he, his brother Leopold and brother-in-law Christian, were invited to address a soirée at the Manchester Athenaeum, attended by over 3,000 ladies and gentlemen, including members of the institution and their friends. Affie presided over the meeting, and in his opening speech he told the audience to loud cheers that his object was 'to enlist your sympathy on behalf of music, and more than that to obtain an expression of our opinion that the time has arrived when the advancement of music in England should be promoted by the establishment of a central public institution, ranking in importance with the national conservatoires on the Continent.'[15] After the other princes and dignitaries had spoken, there was a short singing recital by the Athenaeum Musical Society. The Royal Academy of Music had been founded in 1822 and granted a Royal Charter in 1880, but it offered so few musical scholarships that they firmly believed it was in the national interest to encourage the founding of a new school with a fundamental principle of more free tuition, so that all young people who had some knowledge of and aptitude for music should have a chance to compete. As a result the Royal College of Music was established at Kensington in 1882. It rapidly outgrew its inadequate premises, and the foundation stone for a new building next to Imperial College, London, was laid in July 1890 by the Prince of Wales.

In November 1882 Affie was promoted to the rank of Vice-Admiral, and the following December he was placed in command of the Channel squadron, hoisting his flag in the armour-plated ship HMS *Minotaur*. This vessel and her sister ships *Agincourt* and *Northumberland* were among a number of ironclads built about fifteen years earlier. Their hulls were protected throughout by thick armour, and they were fitted with steam-steering gear, a recent innovation. The squadron spent most of its time in manoeuvres and exercises, particularly the practice of defensive tactics against torpedo attack. When Affie relinquished command in December 1884 the Lords of the Admiralty expressed their complete satisfaction with the efficient performance of his duties.

Affie's extra-marital liaisons were conducted discreetly and, unlike those of his elder brother, never involved him in any serious difficulty with regard to public scandal. Very little for certain is known about any such relationships. However, it appears that even after his marriage he had a mistress, namely Bessie Cory (née Coulthard), who was eight years his junior. She married Richard Cory of Plymstock, who was thirty-four years older than her, in either 1881 or 1882, and had two daughters, Bessie, born in 1882, and Edith, or 'Diney', born two years later. Later generations of the family had their doubts as to whether Richard was in fact the biological father of both girls, and suspected that they were of royal blood. The Corys lived at Langdon Court, Wembury, near Plymouth, although they spent a few weeks every winter at 3, Elliot Terrace, Plymouth (later the home of Lord and Lady Astor, who successively sat as members of parliament for the Sutton division of Plymouth), and some time at London, generally during the spring. Affie remained a good friend of the family, and was a regular guest at Langdon Court as well as a visitor when they were in the capital.[16]

Not all of Affie's interests at this stage were connected with the Royal Navy or with music. At Michaelmas 1883, the lease of former tenants at Eastwell Farm expired, and he began to farm the 1,400 acres which were now free. Four hundred acres of this land consisted of brake and woodland, with no agricultural value. Three-quarters of the rest was pasture, the rest arable. Much of this was very light, with not much depth of soil on top of chalk, and as the whole had recently been impoverished by heavy use, some time would have to elapse before it would be in sufficiently good heart. With the aid of the Prince of Wales's steward from Sandringham, and later a young farmer as bailiff from the previous employment of Lord Sudeley, Affie began to improve the land by reducing the number of deer kept on it for grazing, and applying lime and other fertilisers to the soil. Some places were very wet because of the number of springs and wells, and extensive drainage schemes were undertaken. One was named Plantagenet's Well, as it was near the site of a cottage owned by Richard Plantagenet, natural son of Richard III, who fled to Eastwell from London after the battle of Bosworth in 1485, and worked as a bricklayer on the estate. According to an entry in the local registers, he was buried in a chapel in the parish church on 22 December 1550.[17]

As President of the Ashford and Canterbury Fat Stock Show for 1883, Affie took a keen interest in livestock on his farm. He began farming what he hoped to make one of the finest herds of Southdowns in the country, with an eventual strength of nine hundred. Scotch cattle were introduced into the park, with plans for bringing the number up to forty, ten of which were to be sold each Christmas. A herd of Jersey heifers and crossbred cows was maintained, the latter being good milkers. When the family was at Eastwell or Clarence House the dairy only supplied household requirements, but at other times butter was sold twice a week at Ashford. A new dairy was built, modelled on that at Sandringham. As well as cattle, eleven carthorses were kept in the stables. The most distinguished animal among them was Cossack, which had been a charger during the Russo-Turkish war. Affie used to ride him on Horse Guards' Parade on the Queen's official birthday ceremonies parade.

One family occasion in 1885 which gave Affie much pleasure was the marriage of Prince Louis of Battenberg's younger brother Henry (Liko) to his youngest sister Beatrice. At first the Queen had been so horrified at the thought of not having her 'Baby' as a spinster beside her for the rest of her days, that she refused to believe Beatrice was in love, and stopped speaking to her for several weeks. Communication was confined to written notes passed across the breakfast table. When at length she became reconciled to the prospect of not losing a daughter but gaining a son-in-law, she had to defend the engagement fiercely against the German court which looked down on the Battenbergs as parvenus not fit for the Queen of England's daughter. Their scorn was accentuated by political complications, for the position of Louis's and Liko's brother Sandro in Bulgaria was threatened by the Tsar's animosity. Tsar Alexander II had always been very fond of Sandro, but his son Alexander III never liked him. Political differences between both men after the latter's accession in 1881 worsened the relationship into mutual hatred. At the same time Sandro was seeking the hand in marriage of Vicky and Fritz's second daughter Victoria, a match which was bitterly opposed by Emperor William and Bismarck, and which soured relations between the Battenberg-admiring Queen Victoria and the German royal family.

Affie and Marie were among family guests at the wedding at St Mildred's Church, Whippingham, on 23 July 1885. A reporter, admittedly from the radical and hardly pro-royal journal *Truth,* was not impressed by their appearance, noting afterwards that the Duke 'looked even more supercilious than usual', and the Duchess's 'sullen expression which [had] become habitual…appeared to be accentuated for the occasion.' As for Queen Victoria, she looked 'exceedingly cross', tapping her foot 'in a very ominous way' during the Archbishop of Canterbury's lengthy address.[18]

Unfortunately Liko would soon prove that he did not care much for the company of his naval brother-in-law. He overcame the Queen's abhorrence of smoking at Windsor Castle sufficiently to persuade her to provide a room where the men could indulge without fear of censure. He not only smoked there but also talked incessantly about himself, reducing everyone else to virtual exhaustion. As a result Liko gave up smoking for a while. In a later age when health hazards of tobacco were more fully appreciated, the family might have been grateful to Affie, but medical science was not on his side in the 1880s.

Inevitably Affie had become rather a bore in certain quarters by middle age, but it was hardly surprising. He had been in the Navy since the age of fourteen and frequently in the company of fellow-officers and naval ratings. While they might have found him congenial enough in the officers' mess, as long as they granted him the deference appropriate to his lineage, Affie was not imaginative enough to realise that small-talk about oneself was acceptable to his professional colleagues, but not in the family. Moreover, because of lengthy absences on board ship, he had missed several important family events, being several hundred miles away from home when his father and sister died, and when his eldest brother was married. Therefore Affie was always something of a stranger not only to his children but also to his brothers and sisters. Maybe he tried too hard to make up for his absences when he was at home, with endless conversation, more often than not aided to some degree by drink which loosened his tongue.

Royal biographers are agreed that Affie was a heavy drinker in an age of heavy drinking.[19] It should be noted that his comparatively abstemious nephew Prince George of Wales, later Duke of York and King George V, was sometimes accused of being too fond of the bottle because of his blotchy complexion (due to the after-effects of typhoid) and a loud voice (only to be expected in a former naval officer). That heavy drinking was characteristic of the Victorian era is demonstrated in part by the Queen's liberal attitude. The best wine was always served at her table, and Prince Albert had been shocked when he first came to England and experienced the imbibing that went on at her dinner parties. Her toleration of tipsy servants, not least John Brown, is legendary. Yet she expected better of the upper classes, and disapproved of her second son who did little to set a good example.

CHAPTER 9

Malta and Coburg 1886–89

In January 1886 the Duke was appointed Commander-in-Chief of the Mediterranean Squadron in succession to Admiral Sir John Hay, who was now First Sea Lord. After paying a brief visit to Coburg, he hoisted his flag in HMS *Tamar* on 20 February and sailed for the Mediterranean. On 5 March he transferred his flag to HMS *Alexandra* and formally assumed complete command of the station, based on Malta.

One of his first priorities was to become acquainted with all the ships of his fleet, a varied collection. They included the broadside ships *Sultan* and *Superb*, the barbette ship *Temeraire*, the turret ships *Dreadnought* and *Agamemnon*, the armour-plated twin-screw ironclads Neptune and Thunderer, the armoured broadside corvettes *Orion* and *Carysfort*, the torpedo depot ship *Hecla*, the torpedo ram *Polyphemus*, the sloops *Gannet* and *Dolphin*, the gun-vessels *Condor* and *Falcon*, the gunboats *Grappler*, *Albacore, Coquette, Cygnet* and *Starling*, the steam vessels *Imogene* and *Cockatrice*, and the sailing sloop *Cruizer*.

However the new Commander's routine was temporarily overshadowed by another crisis which inflamed family loyalties and brought Europe to the brink of armed conflict. The new state of Bulgaria had just been augmented with the province of Eastern Roumelia, and the suspicious Greeks, fearful of this enlarged enemy territory on their border, demanded compensatory territorial acquisition. Alix's brother King George of the Hellenes identified himself with this patriotic cause, but when his statesmen and commanders threatened to attack Turkey in order to achieve their aims he was horrified. His objections infuriated the nation, which almost to a man clamoured for general mobilisation. The King appealed to his brother-in-law the Prince of Wales, saying that there was no peaceful solution to the problem but the addition, by the Powers, of some Turkish territory to Greece. Notwithstanding his wife's desperate entreaties, the Prince replied that this was impossible. The British Foreign Secretary, Lord Rosebery, stipulated that Greece must withdraw her demands. This was ignored by the angry Greeks, who mobilised in preparation for hostilities on the Turkish border.

The Powers, Great Britain in particular, were left with no alternative but a naval blockade, followed if necessary by bombardment of Athens and an armed landing.

As Commander-in-Chief of the Mediterranean of the Mediterranean Fleet, Affie was responsible for the blockade. On 8 March he wrote to the Marquis of Ripon, First Lord of the Admiralty:

> As there is a mail going direct to Naples by Italian Gunboat I take advantage of it to send you a few lines with regard to the telegram I received late last night to a contemplated blockade of the Greek Squadron. I at once asked my foreign Colleagues to come to me which they did immediately & we talked the question over at considerable length and were quite unanimous that a blockade as proposed without carrying out at once aggressive measures would be out of the question. The risk to the ships of the Combined Squadron would be too great to be compensated for by a completely inefficient measure.
>
> Had I with me a certain number of 1st class torpedo boats which could keep the sea in moderately bad weather (which the 3 boats I have cannot) an efficient blockade might be maintained without exceptional risk. In that case the entrances would be guarded by these boats during the night whilst the squadron would retire into the offing (?) returning within sight of the port at daylight when the boats return to their respective ships to be replenished and crews changed. This service could be kept up for any length of time on the plan I here describe. It seems a great pity that one should have allowed, within the last week or two, six very efficient torpedo boats to pass through Malta for the Greek Government; they would exactly have suited my requirements whilst at the same time not permitting such an important addition to the Greek Naval Force.
>
> In the case of a blockade being ordered it would be necessary for H.M. Government to intimate at once to the reek Government that the port of Piraeus would be closed to all trade also, otherwise the service could not be carried out.
>
> I have made very good friends with my foreign colleagues and they all seem most anxious to assist and maintain good relations with us.[1]

On 30 March Affie wrote to Ripon again:

> As you will have seen by my telegrams the second proposal i.e. to blockade the whole coast of Greece against the Greek ships of war and commerce is considered by my foreign colleagues and myself in being easy to carry out. They immediately accepted my plan...the districts mentioned will effectually stop reek commerce as regards their own

ships but we cannot stop their supplies without overhauling neutral ships which was not mentioned in the reference to me. All my colleagues have received answers from their Govts. To take part with us in this service, if it is decided upon, with the exception of the Russian Admiral who had telegraphed home for fresh instructions and who will telegraph to me the result, he having left yesterday under orders to fill up with provisions of which he has not more than ten days on board. Personally he is very anxious to take part as he thinks with me that pressure of this sort would very quickly make the Greek Government listen to the expressed wishes of the Powers...

I am doing what I can to prevent the landing of men and arms in this island [Crete] but it is not much I can do beyond showing our flag in as many places as possible for whatever is next comes in small fishing boats from creek to creek during the night which it would be impossible to stop from sea especially in the very bad weather we have had lately.[2]

On 2 May he found it necessary to write again:

The period of a week accorded to Greece in which to comply with the demands of the Powers is rapidly drawing to a close but beyond the last communicated to me by Sir Horace Rumbold that the Greek Government had given an answer which had been referred home, I have heard nothing.

We should all be ready to start for the carrying out of the blockade within 24 hours for the return of the small Squadron from the Pyraeus. The *Polyphemus* arrived ten days ago and the 21 and 22 torpedo boats on Thursday. The latter I am sorry to say are without their torpedos and many of their fittings which have not arrived from England. I think there must have been some unnecessary delay in their transmission. The boats will however be most useful as picket boats running to their high speed...

The appearance so early in the year of cholera of so severe a type on the Italian coast is I fear a sign that we shall have a bad year as regards this disease; very many of the ports of the Mediterranean will thus be closed to us and our communications with England much interfered with.

I am obliged to you for your expression of confidence in me in case the delicate duty of carrying out the blockade falls upon me, and you may depend upon my sparing no pains to justify your opinion.[3]

On 7 May the diplomatic representatives of Britain, Austria, Germany and Italy left Athens, leaving behind those of Russia and France. Nonetheless an allied fleet sailed into the Piraeus. For three weeks the continent held its collective breath, until early in June the Greek army decided to mobilise. Affie was thus spared from playing a major part in a war against the kingdom over which he had been elected to reign some twenty years before, a war for which the Princess of Wales might not have forgiven him had the Greeks been defeated and her favourite brother punished.

In October 1886 the royal yacht *Osborne* steamed into the Grand Harbour at Valletta with Affie's family on board. It was not every day that the Mediterranean command was filled by a prince, and bluejackets stood on the yards as they arrived, one above the other, cheering until they were hoarse. The yacht slowly passed down the double row of battleships and each band aboard struck up the National Anthem.

San Antonio was to be their winter home for the next three years, Marie and her children thus avoiding the cold of Europe. It was the Governor's summer palace, where the young found excitements by the score – the house with its huge stone-paved rooms and rocky garden containing a walled-in oasis, eastern and secret-looking, with a maze of trees; jasmine, knee-high geraniums, verbena, masses of roses, large clumps of feathery white chrysanthemums tumbling in snowy cascades; violets, narcissi and anemones in great quantity. Whenever the fleet was in Malta Affie lived ashore with them, travelling between ship and shore in a ten-oared galley he had had specially built.

The island, 122 square miles in area surrounded by seas of azure blue, provided them with a rich and active life with swimming, hunting, shooting, fishing and riding for all. With the Edinburghs in residence, any visiting prince or princess could be sure of a warm welcome.

At last Marie could be mistress of all she surveyed for a while. She alone had been glad to leave Eastwell Park for the last time, and with it the eagle eye and all-pervading presence of her mother-in-law. The damp British climate was another aspect of life she put behind her with relief, though Affie disliked the hot dry Maltese weather, complaining to Louis of Battenberg in a letter of feeling 'rather seedy' due to 'the great heat and Sirocco winds of the last week'.[4] As a hostess Marie entertained as only a Romanov knew how – lavishly and with no respect for the rigid castes of the Royal Navy. A midshipman and an Admiral were one and the same to her; she treated them exactly alike, secretly preferring the former. Many a shy young man was comforted by her warm hospitality and excellent food. By slipping a few pounds to the hungry sailors, she was the favourite of many a visitor.

However, even Mediterranean life palled after a while. A letter from Marie to Lady Randolph Churchill of 13 January ran:

It is quite unpardonable for me not to have written to you before, but somehow, cruising about as we did the whole autumn and living on board ship, being very hot and lazy, all this did not dispose one to active correspondence. And now it is the slight boredom of the Malta life, its uninteresting course and *milles autres excuses...*[5]

The Edinburgh princesses used to tear around the island in their small Barbary Arab ponies given them by their mother. Their short sturdy legs adapted well to the rocky scenery with only a few places of terraced fields edged by stone walls and hard roads; a menace to the islanders, but a charming sight all the same. Missy later admitted that their noisy canterings were highly uncivilised, and many a poor governess was led a fine dance keeping up with them.

Serving in the Mediterranean Fleet on board *Thunderer* as Fifth Lieutenant was a royal sailor from the next generation, Prince George of Wales. At first he was very homesick and missed the companionship of his family at Sandringham. It was partly due to the tact of his equerry Hugh Stephenson, *Thunderer*'s Captain, who had known him since boyhood, and partly the friendship of the Edinburghs, that helped to make him feel more at home. Both uncle and nephew visited Sultan Abdul Hamid of Turkey in October 1886, in a meeting that symbolised solidarity with Turkey whose independent existence had so recently been threatened by Greek belligerence. In recognition of Britain's support, a grateful Sultan duly showered the Duke of Edinburgh and his nephew with gifts, including lavishly-jewelled cigarette cases and two Arab chargers.

Affie was delighted to have George with him as part of the family at Christmas that year. He was more than happy to encourage the young man's interest in his lifelong hobby of philately, something which would be marked some three years later by the formation of the Philatelic (later Royal Philatelic) Society, with Affie was first Honorary President. He attended the inaugural ceremony in London and opened the first exhibition in May 1890, where he displayed part of his own collection. Shortly before his death he sold his collection to the Prince of Wales, who presented it to Prince George. It included the sheet of 6d stamps which had been printed for Affie in 1856.

Affie was also pleased to notice George's close relationship with his eldest daughter Missy. Although he was ten years older than her, his sheltered family life had made him a very young twenty-one, and 'not a bit too grand and grown up' to be the best of friends with her. She merely regarded him as a 'beloved chum', but on his side at least the relationship looked at one stage as if it might become something rather deeper.

In June 1887 the Edinburghs returned briefly to London for a triumphant celebration, the like of which had not been seen for decades – Queen Victoria's Jubilee. The fiftieth anniversary of Her Majesty's accession to the throne was well-timed, for in June there was an outbreak of cholera on Malta, and Affie later gave £200 to the relief fund. Marie and young Alfred were among those seated in the coaches on that never-to-be-forgotten procession on 21 June from Buckingham Palace to a service of thanksgiving at Westminster Abbey. Affie proudly rode on horseback in Rear-Admiral's uniform among the escort of his brothers and brothers-in-law accompanying the landau carrying Queen Victoria, a small, plump figure in black dress and white bonnet, homely but indomitably regal.

At the state banquet at Buckingham Palace that evening, Affie led Princess Liliuokalani, the future Queen of Hawaii, in the supper procession. She had initially been assigned to Leopold II, King of the Belgians, but with his enslavement of the native population of the Congo in Africa, courtiers realised at the last moment that this was an insensitive choice. The Duke of Saxony had indignantly refused to escort a 'coloured' person. Like his elder brother, Affie was mercifully free from such prejudices, and willingly accepted a request from his mother and eldest brother to step into the breach instead.

Affie would surely have agreed with the general verdict that, of all those honouring Her Majesty in that stately procession, nobody was braver than the magnificent Crown Prince Frederick William. He had looked forward to the day when this kindly brother-in-law who had so often entertained him in Berlin would reign over the German Empire, while he himself would be Duke of Coburg, but now he realised that this was almost certainly little more than a dream. Though Fritz in his gleaming white Cuirassier uniform towered splendidly above those riding next to him, only the family were aware that by now he could barely speak above a hoarse whisper. Since the spring he had suffered from a throat complaint that was eventually diagnosed as cancer of the larynx. After leaving Britain later that summer he sought the milder Mediterranean climate over autumn and winter, and on medical advice he eventually rented a villa at San Remo on the Riviera. Affie, who returned to his naval duties at the end of June, visited Fritz that winter during his last pitiful weeks as Crown Prince. In March 1888 the latter succeeded his ninety-year-old father as German Emperor and returned to Berlin, an incurably sick man who was destined to reign for ninety-nine days of mental and physical torment.

Soon after returning to his naval duties overseas, in October 1887 Affie was promoted to the rank of Admiral. With this superior rank, he felt more free to speak out against the backward state of the Navy, and the

Mediterranean Fleet in particular. Britain's naval supremacy had not been seriously challenged since the Napoleonic wars, and the apparent lack of any threat had induced a dangerous mood of complacency. Admirals Phipps-Hornby and Hay had each made some contribution to tightening up the fleet, but Affie recognised that there was still much to be done.

In April 1888 he was asked by Ponsonby to report on its suitability in the event of hostilities. He answered that

> ...the normal strength of the Squadron in the Mediterranean is insufficient in case of a sudden attack or outbreak of war; and that in the event of war becoming imminent it should be strengthened to enable it to take the initiative. The deficient strength of the Squadron is still further accentuated at the present moment by the fact that France, the principal Naval Power with which we could be brought into conflict, has recently concentrated almost the whole of her ironclad fleet in the Mediterranean. To me it appears obvious that, where the main body is, there it should be attacked.
>
> Supports would certainly be expected from home in the event of war, but hitherto I have not been able to obtain any definite information as to the additional strength I am to expect, or as to the time which would elapse before the whole or any portion would join me from England.
>
> Some of the ships, I regret to say, are at the present time not efficient; one ironclad is worn out and waiting to be relieved, other ships are non-effective pending completion of their necessary repairs and alterations.
>
> The resources of the dockyard are equal to the rapid and efficient repair of the Squadron; but, under ordinary circumstances, there are great delays in carrying out the repairs, arising from financial considerations, and the length of time and amount of correspondence required to get the necessary sanction from the authorities at home before the work can be proceeded with.[6]

As Affie had only one more year in command of the Mediterranean, there was little time to do more that sound such warnings about the squadron's shortcomings, but these and the efforts of his naval contemporaries all played their part in making good such deficiencies. Unlike them Affie did not live to witness the Anglo-German naval race that contributed to the outbreak of war in 1914.

For all his criticisms, Affie discharged his duties with a zeal and efficiency which was second to none. Several of his captains in the Mediterranean agreed that he was the most capable Admiral under whom they had ever served. His exceptionally high intellectual gifts, they said, enabled him to get through large amounts of paperwork quickly in his office, yet these were never carelessly perused. An eminent naval instructor visiting the fleet heard him say that he knew the constructional details of every ship in his squadron, and was astonished later, on testing him and talking to the captains, to find that his claim was no idle boast. With his capacity for inventing things, Affie devised an ingenious system for securing boats' davits in bad weather, and had he not been a Prince he would have probably patented the scheme. Had the Prince Consort and Stockmar lived another thirty years, they would have been very proud of him, but hardly surprised by his gifts in such fields.

Affie's chief quality as a flag officer in the Mediterranean was his ability as a fleet leader, and his mastery of naval evolutions under steam. A new signal-book was issued early in 1888, and by that winter he had put his ships through every new evolution, but without neglecting exercises in the older book. He tried to anchor his fleet in a different formation every time, and enjoyed changing the pattern just before they reached the anchorage. After a series of manoeuvres at Marmarice Bay, off Turkey, just after the ships had arrived, a Russian captain was so impressed with the way the British force was brought in that he sat down at once and wrote an official report on it to his government.

Affie often surprised his officers by his varied knowledge. If ever they found an unusual stone, shell or plant, it was unanimously agreed that 'We'll ask the Duke what it is.' As a master of Trinity House he always took a well-informed interest in the scientific aspects of lighthouse arrangements. A lecture he gave on the different classes of lights and lenses, 'without any ostentatious parade of superior knowledge', was much talked about for a long time afterwards.

As with any commanding officer, Affie's temper could be short, and subordinates might occur his wrath in no uncertain manner. Yet on reflection, when he realised he was tactfully shown by others that he had been too harsh, he would never hesitate to make amends for his impatience. He often took pains to help his men when they were in difficulties, and make them small presents, but preferred such matters to be handled with the utmost discretion.

During the summer of 1888 Affie and his officers paid another visit to the Sultan of Turkey. They travelled as members of a large party on board the yacht *Surprise*, giving passage not only to those who wanted to see Constantinople but also to a team of cricketers going to play with the English community.

For details of the Sultan's hospitality one is indebted to a letter from the Captain of *Surprise*, Maurice Bourke, beloved of the entire Edinburgh family and known as 'Captain Dear', who wrote to Missy of the delights in store for them. Their journey to a regatta was delayed because nobody had thought to oil the engines of their ships, which overheated after a few miles. At the regatta itself, for four solid hours they were 'refreshed by the sight of bobbing and struggling humanity in whose personality we could have no interest'. The Duke was pounced on by a proud regatta committee, as a result of which his officers found that looking at the races was 'better than having to make conversation with the natives of the islands who were doing the honours'. They were served with pineapple and strawberries in champagne, which might have tasted better had one fruit not come straight out of a tin pot and the other crushed and carried in a dirty basket.

Though the Turks may have been unable to teach their guests anything about seamanship or the culinary arts, a conjuring display in the Sultan's bijou theatre was more instructive. Affie and his party were placed in the gallery above the conjurer, a Frenchman, 'so that it was not quite fair, and (we) saw nearly everything he did.'[7]

The next day Affie presented his congratulations to the Sultan on the twelfth anniversary of his accession. In turn the latter congratulated his guest on completing thirty years in the Navy. That evening they attended 'an awfully long dinner and reception of all the Constantinople beauty and fashion. Fashion, yes, but very little beauty'. The festivities were to conclude later that week with a garden party and another full dress dinner, but 'one of the first cousins of the Sultan took it into his head to die, and so we escaped'. However the cricketers won their match, and the Sultan decorated his guests and showered them with numerous gifts of jewellery, vegetables and livestock.

The last few months of Affie's appointment were dogged by attacks of what the *British Medical Journal* called 'Maltese remittent fever'. In March 1889 he had a mild touch, but recovered after a few days at sea. After visits to Sicily, Genoa and Berlin he returned to Malta at the beginning of April, but he was still far from well. He stayed long enough to hand over the reins of office to his successor, Vice-Admiral Sir Anthony Hopkins, on 16 April, before leaving for home. By the time he sailed into Spithead on board HMS *Alexandra*, eleven days later, he was suffering so badly – with a temperature of 100.2°F – that the usual exchange of salutes between his ship and the Commander-in-Chief's flagship was omitted.

Attended by his surgeon-in-ordinary, Dr Oscar Clayton, Affie was taken back to Clarence House for a complete rest. At first there was anxiety lest he might have had a recurrence of typhoid, and for some weeks he was not allowed to work or to receive any visitors from outside the family. Queen Victoria came to see him on 2 May and found him 'looking very ill and very thin, and seemed very feeble and his voice very weak'. A week later he was well enough for daily bulletins on his condition to be considered no longer necessary, and he had fully recovered by 23 May when he and Marie attended a farewell luncheon with the officers and crew of HMS *Alexandra* at Chatham dockyard.

It was just as well that Affie's health had improved, for he had a demanding programme throughout the next few months. In June he and Marie left London for Germany. While she travelled via Kissingen to St Petersburg for the wedding of her brother Grand Duke Paul to Princess Alexandra of Greece, Affie and young Alfred went to pay a courtesy visit to the young German Emperor William at Potsdam.

William II, who celebrated the first anniversary of his accession that month, had several fences to mend with his British relations. During his father's unhappy reign of three months the previous year, as Crown Prince William he had appalled them all with his thoughtless if not downright disloyal behaviour, and after his father's death he sided with Bismarck and the German political establishment in the systematic persecution of his mother, younger sisters and the Scottish doctor Sir Morell Mackenzie, who had attended the late Emperor during his fatal illness, and was now accused by unsavoury Prussian elements of having killed him by gross mismanagement of the case. Queen Victoria had often been more ready than most to make allowances for the impulsive actions of her eldest grandchild, and the only one the Prince Consort had ever known, but before long her patience gave way as well. Willy complained that the Prince of Wales treated him like an uncle treated a nephew, in spite of the fact he was an Emperor, and he persuaded the embarrassed Emperor Francis Joseph of Austria to cancel with some misgivings an invitation for the English heir to come to Vienna as he (William) wished to come instead. Such 'misunderstandings' were hastily smoothed over in the interests of Anglo-German relations, and a reluctant Affie was asked to play his part in humouring the self-proclaimed All-Highest.

Dressed in naval uniform, William welcomed his uncle and young Alfred, on whom he conferred the Red Eagle 1st Class, the first Order the fourteen-year-old prince had received, to the Neue Palais with a grand review of Prussian soldiers from the Lehr infantry battalion. Affie left Potsdam less impressed with the military splendour of Germany than with his nephew's insufferable airs and graces, and he felt more at home on subsequent visits to Coburg and to Tsar Alexander III at Peterhof the following month.

After Malta, the Palais Edinburg at Coburg became the Edinburghs' home. Young Alfred, now training in the German army, was thrilled that at last his parents and sisters were joining him. In due course they would move into Schloss Ehrenburg, the Duke's official residence. Originally a monastery, it had been modernised by Duke Ernest I for his young bride some seventy years earlier. Above it was the Hofgarten, and beyond on the hill, the twelfth-century fortress of the Feste where Martin Luther sought asylum and wrote his hymn *Ein feste burg*.

The best loved home was Schloss Rosenau, the Prince Consort's birthplace, four miles outside Coburg. It was a gingerbread-yellow villa *orné* with gothic windows, stained glass, and a squat tower with battlements. On one side it commanded views of the soft blue mountains, and on the other the massive Feste. In the garden were stone seats, a romantic fountain, splendid vistas, a mock-waterfall and a grotto. The Schloss itself had a grand entrance hall with gilt and marble pillars, black and white tiled floor and an enormous fireplace. Above it, a large balcony gave marvelous views across the countryside, and the panelled library filled with allegorical paintings and tapestries had changed little since the days of Prince Albert's boyhood. Affie was deeply moved to find himself often in this house, the place Papa had loved more than anywhere else in the world.

Marie held court at the Palais Edinburg. There were no pretentious marble halls or armies of servants, as she had known in her homeland, but the simple life suited her in a small social circle where *Gemutlichkeit* (cosiness) was more important than elegance. She had apparently give up all hope of being smart and fashionable, except on great occasions when once again she could dazzle in her jewels, brooches, silks and satins. Above all, the autocratic Romanov in her preferred the freedom of a German state to a country house in England where she was never far from Queen Victoria. At Coburg, as Missy put it, she 'was her own mistress; it was a small kingdom perhaps, but her will was undiscussed, she took her orders from no one, and could live as she wished'. The years in which she had been at Malta, travelling to every corner of Europe and Russia as she pleased, had given her a sweet taste of independence which she would not relinquish by returning to her husband's country. She supervised her daughters' education with an eagle eye. They all had German governesses and tutors, who were under orders to turn them into thorough Germans. This they secretly hated, as they had been born princesses of Great Britain and Ireland, and wished to remain that way.

For the unambitious or lazy, Coburg was a pleasant enough, undemanding place to live. Affie did not care for its dreary day-to-day existence, and although he enjoyed being at Rosenau, he was heartily grateful that his naval and representative duties allowed him to spend no more than a few weeks at a time there.

There is a most entertaining letter (undated, but probably written in the mid- or late eighties) from Affie's equerry, Lieutenant-Colonel Arthur

Haig, who had the thankless task of escorting the imperious Marie *en famille* on her many journeys:

> ...as no one else has had the grace to thank me for the arduous duties, which in that character I performed, I must take this opportunity of expressing to Haig our extreme gratitude for the untiring energy and unparalleled skill with which he conducted Her Royal and Imperial Highness to her journey's end. It is true that there was a slight mishap at Brussels. We got there at six in the morning. I put the Duchess and Miss Corry into one carriage and the children into another. Then I ran back to the platform, where I was instantly transfixed with horror. Hutchins, our page, was seated on a silver night-stool, the *only* article of all our luggage that he had succeeded in securing. The rest of the luggage, the nurses and nursery-maids, the dressers, footmen and valets were scattered to the four winds. Some of the luggage was at the Gare du Nord, some at the Gare du Midi, some had gone on to Cologne, the rest in a fit of disgust had gone back to London. And all our money in my dispatch box amounting to nearly £3,000 had gone off in an excursion train towards Antwerp. It was a general débâcle. The manservants were stupefied and the women 'stood crying and wringing their hands'.
>
> My first idea was to send in my resignation on the spot – and to return by the next train to Scotland, but I overcame that temptation, and by dint of superhuman efforts I actually succeeded in rallying our beaten forces and in recovering all our lost luggage at Cologne in the evening.
>
> The next time I travel on the Continent in charge of
>
> A Royal and Imperial Highness,
> 3 Royal and Imperial Children,
> A Lady-in-Waiting,
> An Equerry,
> 4 Nurses,
> 3 Ladies' Maids,
> A Page,
> and 4 Footmen,
>
> *without* a courier – may I be – never mind. I will *not* do it again. And am I not to be rewarded for all this? What! No decoration? Oh try and procure me the Cross of Ernest the Second-Rate.[4]

As Haig's letter makes clear, the Duke of Coburg's indiscretions had long been public knowledge:

Coburg is in a state of intense fermentation. It is moved, I may say, to the very dregs. On the 1st June will take place, with great pomp, the celebration of the 50th Anniversary of the Foundation of the Ducal-Saxe-Coburg-Gotha Opera! There will be a performance of unequalled brilliance in the Great Theatre! Where also the most distinguished artistes of the Thuringian theatre will be crowned with laurels, Ernest – the Great, the Good, the Chaste, The Second, The Father, nay the grandfather now of many of his subjects, will appear in state. His Consort and all his other Consorts will be there – all, those that have been – that are – and that are going to be – all. Imagine! – but I have not paper enough to imagine it upon. Send out a Hogarth quick to paint the picture '*La Famille Ducale et demi-Ducale*'.

After the theatre there is to be a grand ball in the Giant's Hall of the Great Palace. There all are invited, the First, the Second, the Third Societies and the Great Actors and Actresses. How fortunate a man I am, to be sure! I am wild with excitement, and I would not have missed this sight for anything.

Ah! But there is something much more important than this to tell you. Hush! '*She*' is no longer here. She has gone. Those little dinners '*à trois*' are a thing of the past. A Burgher of Leipsic has made her an honest woman and taken her to his own home. It seems that after the last visit the Duke of Edinburgh paid to Coburg she saw that he had an invincible dislike to her – so she went to the other Duke one morning and said 'May it please your Highness! You are growing old, and you will probably die soon. Your successor hates me and will certainly drive me penniless away. Therefore, my August Master, you must purchase a house and a husband elsewhere for me and I will go—' She is coming to the ball though, so I may see her once again...[10]

Well might Affie, Queen Victoria and others endorse the maxim that those whom the gods love die young, for already Ernest's younger and more hard-working brother Albert had been dead almost thirty years. Not the least of the Prince Consort's fortunes in having been called to an early grave was to be spared the sight of seeing Ernest descend unrepentantly into a lecherous and infuriating old age.

To his sad, dutiful wife Alexandrine, Duke Ernest was a lord and master whose brazen infidelity and unconcealed rudeness must be borne weekly as the will of the Almighty. To his nephew-heir and his wife he was a tiresome relic of the previous generation, to be humoured from time to time but otherwise avoided as much as possible. To his great-nieces he was an elderly ponderous beau, an ogre-like figure with a rosebud always in the buttonhole of a frock coat far too tight for his formidable bulk. To his sister-in-law he was such a threat to the female of the species that only bachelor diplomats and ambassadors from England were safe at his court.

In younger days Ernest had been renowned for his support for a united Germany, and at the declaration of the empire in January 1871 at Versailles the newly-created Emperor William I had acknowledged his role with the words, 'This I owe partly to you.' He had shared Albert's fascination with science and natural history, composed songs and operas, and instituted a competition for operas among German composers at Gotha. Of late, however, his interest in the theatre had been confined to ogling young and pretty actresses. Maintenance of his mistresses and illegitimate offspring had made him heavily dependent on disreputable financiers, and plunged the duchy into difficulties that made Affie dread the day when such responsibilities would be his.

Ernest's insatiable passion for causing mischief and his admiration for Bismarck, the architect of German unity, led him into a thoroughly despicable episode which finally succeeded in alienating him once and for all from his brother's family. After the tragic death of Emperor Frederick III, his widow and his memory were vilified and misrepresented throughout the empire as having tried hard to subvert the interests of Germany to those of Britain. Even William II, who it was impossible for his relatives at Windsor to forget was at heart the same naughty boy Willy who had bitten his uncles' kilted legs in a moment of childish defiance at the Prince of Wales's wedding, did nothing to dispel the official Berlin attitude that Fritz's reign had been an unfortunate but meaningless interlude. The novelist Gustav Freytag had been a friend of both Ernest and Fritz. In 1889 he published a volume of reminiscences in which he had quoted and misquoted the then Crown Prince Frederick William's confidential conversations, and inferred that he and his wife's relations at Windsor had betrayed military secrets to French commanders during the Franco-Prussian war. This new attack had been instigated by Bismarck, who paid the temporarily financially-embarrassed Freytag handsomely for his dirty work. All this had been bad enough, but Ernest chose to make things worse by publicly congratulating Freytag on the book and ostentatiously inviting him to dinner by way of celebration. Not content with this he proceeded to dismiss Dr Aldenhoven, Director of the Gotha Museum and regarded as one of the few respectable honest men in his service, on the grounds that he was a liberal and well-known for his admiration of the late Emperor Frederick. Thus Ernest would be compromised in the eyes of Emperor William II if he retained such a man in an official position.

Next Ernest published a pamphlet anonymously (which he later boated was his own work) accusing Fritz of treachery and saying how dangerous it would have been for the Fatherland if he had lived longer. A Dr Harmening joined the pamphlet war; his contribution defended the late Emperor from the insinuations of his detractors, notably the Duke of Saxe-Coburg. The latter now swore that he had not written the pamphlet after all, engaged unscrupulous lawyers (probably financed, like Freytag's diatribe, by Bismarck) and issued a writ for libel. Harmening was found guilty, imprisoned for six months and ordered to pay his own costs. Only lack of proof of Ernest's own authorship, and the shame of adding further to the scandal for Affie's sake, prevented Vicky from bringing a court action herself in Harmening's defence.

Affie, Marie and the children all pitied Aunt Alexandrine. She was a perfectly harmless, colourless old lady, whose drooping stayless form was always dressed in black and draped with a cashmere shawl. A weak, grisly beard covered her chin, and two kind yet bleary eyes peered out at the world. 'Dearest Aunt secludes herself more and more,' Queen Victoria had written censoriously to Vicky some sixteen years earlier, 'and it is so bad for them both.'[11] Her life was as dull as that of the average Coburg labourer, with little joy except the letters and solicitude of the kind-hearted nephew who would in due course succeed her husband as Duke.

CHAPTER 10

The Devonport Command 1890-93

Naval matters were again foremost in occupying the Duke of Edinburgh's thoughts during 1890. Early that year he was appointed Chairman of a committee on naval officers' uniforms, and their findings resulted in new regulations being issued the next year. The main changes comprised a reduction in the number of buttons on a full dress coat from ten to eight, and gold lace on the skirts formerly worn by flag officers being removed. Alterations were made to the cocked hat and frock coat, and the device used on epaulettes of Admirals of the Fleet was changed to a crown above crossed batons surrounded by laurel leaves.

A recommendation put forward but not adopted was that Admirals of the Fleet should wear an aiguilette and receive a baton, in the same was that Field Marshals did in the army. Former Admirals of the Fleet had been accorded this honour, but it was not approved by the Admiralty. Thanks to the Queen's insistence, an exception was later to be made in the case of her distinguished second son.

In the summer the Prime Minister, Lord Salisbury, announced at a Trinity House banquet that the Duke of Edinburgh had accepted the appointment of Commander-in-Chief at Devonport, in succession to Admiral Sir William Dowell.

The Duke was introduced to his new command on 4 August, two days before his forty-sixth birthday. Dawn was breaking as he arrived in *Vivid* and anchored off Mount Wise; two hours later he hoisted his flag in HMS *Foudroyant* as Dowell received a seventeen-gun salute of departure. After landing he went to Admiralty House, the Commander-in-Chief's official residence, where Dowell presented to him the principal naval officers of Devonport. After lunching together, they took the dockyard train to Keyham for his reception at the Royal Navy Barracks. Affie then re-embarked in *Vivid* and watched the royal standard flying from the Devonport column as he sailed out of Plymouth Sound for Cowes on leave. While he was away, alterations were to be made to Admiralty House to accommodate a larger domestic staff.

Plymouth's history had been steeped in naval tradition since the Elizabethan age, but the origins of Devonport itself were comparatively recent. The Plymouth naval dockyard was established in 1689, and the town of Plymouth Dock which grew up around it was named Devonport in 1824. When the Royal Navy began to change from sail to steam Devonport Dockyard expanded considerably as a result, and the Royal Naval Engineering College opened in 1880. Affie was thus proud to be associated so closely with a naval town which was well-prepared to meet the challenges of a new age.

By the end of August he was in Coburg, paying visits to his brother-in-law Grand Duke Paul, and Duke Ernest. He left the continent on 10 September, returned to Devonport six days later, and initially stayed in the Royal Hotel. That Admiralty House was still not ready is clear from a letter to Louis of Battenberg:

> It is a very long time since you kindly wrote to congratulate me on my appointment here, but you know what happens if one does not answer a letter at once being busy & then much moving about. Well here I am but not in my house which is not ready, & I don't know when it will be, & staying in an hotel by myself, comfortable no doubt as far as hostelries go but more like a commercial traveller than a Commander-in-Chief. The work is very different from that in the Mediterranean consisting only in signing a few papers, which a clerk on 2/6 a day could do just as well, but I am led to the flattering hope that there is something to do at some time of the year. Marie & the children who are at Coburg are all in great form. Alfred's confirmation went of [sic] admirably at Easter... [1]

Yet Affie only had to wait a couple of weeks for something more interesting to do than signing papers. On 21 October, Trafalgar Day, he unveiled the National Armada Memorial, an imposing bronze figure of Britannia on a pedestal overlooking Plymouth Hoe. The foundation stone had been laid by the mayor during the Armada tercentenary celebrations of 1888. Although the occasion was not officially fêted with a holiday, 'it may safely be asserted that little business was done, the interest in the event being so great.'[2] It was estimated that crowds of some 50,000 watched the ceremony. Afterwards the Commander-in-Chief attended a celebration luncheon in the Guildhall together with local Members of Parliament, the Mayor, and other civic dignitaries, and in his speech Affie congratulated everyone responsible for the success of proceedings which commemorated 'one of the greatest events in our national history'. He took the opportunity to thank everyone for the welcome which had been extended to him, said he had been received with much cordiality, had found many old friends living in the neighbourhood, had made some new friends and was sure he would make many more.[3]

Only three weeks later there was a naval disaster which was to concern the whole of Plymouth from her Commander-in-Chief downwards. On 8 November HMS *Serpent,* a new cruiser carrying a local crew of 176 men, steamed out of the Sound on foreign service. Two nights later in pitch darkness she was wrecked off the north coast of Spain, with only three survivors.

The misery of bereaved parents, widows and orphans touched Affie to the heart. Within days he had formed a relief fund committee, of which he became President. The Soldiers' and Sailors' Rest at Devonport was declared a sanctuary to which the needy could go for assistance. As President, he helped to race every stricken family, and one of his first actions was to convene a public meeting in the Guildhall to call for public subscriptions. Donations that evening amounted to over £35, and over the next few weeks nearly everyone became involved in fund-raising activities. A benefit drama performance at the Theatre Royal was attended by the Commander and his fellow officers, and collected £40. The committee held their final meeting on 10 June 1891 at Admiralty House, and announced that £12,388 had been raised. The merits of every family affected were considered, widows and mothers were pensioned, and a sum of money invested at compound interest was set aside for each child. Throughout the weeks of hard work nobody did more to coordinate the administration of the fund than the royal President and Commander-in-Chief himself, often moved to tears by the sufferings of those whose menfolk had so recently been familiar faces around Devonport.

Affie spent Christmas 1890 with the family at Clarence House, and returned to Devonport on his own in the first week of January 1891. His first engagement of the new year was to attend a ceremony at the garrison chapel where he unveiled a tablet and brass eagle lectern which had been presented to the memory of Major-General Sir Howard Elphinstone. Formerly tutor and then comptroller to the Duke of Connaught, Elphinstone was also military commander of the western district. After a bout of influenza, he had sailed from Plymouth to Tenerife for a period of convalescence in March 1890, but while walking on deck his ship he was tragically washed overboard.

Marie joined her husband at Devonport later in January 1891, although if her letters are anything to go by, she did not enjoy the experience. In April 1890 she had written to her eldest daughter in disparaging terms of London, which she found bitterly cold and dark – admittedly during a time of heavy rain, and especially Clarence House, which was 'like going into a dark grotto, all yellow and smoky'.[4] However, only a few days after her first appearance in the west country, she noted that London seemed like 'a real paradise after Devonport and Clarence House a grand palace' after their comparatively humble lodgings at Admiralty House.[5] A special welcome was prepared for her in the form of an officers' ball at the Royal Naval Barracks, attended by over 1,200 guests. During the next two years her visits to Devonport were rare, for she did not relish the role of a Commander-in-Chief's wife in England. But for the sake of appearances she showed herself once in a while. She accepted an invitation to stand as godmother to Flag-Lieutenant Keppel's baby daughter who was christened at the dockyard chapel in February 1891, and she often accompanied Affie to performances at the theatre.

Nevertheless, she did nothing to give the people of Devonport and Plymouth the impression that she was at ease there. Some years later, a local woman who could remember life in the towns as a young child, recalled what it had been like to have royalty in their midst. While the Duke made little impression on her, she was aware of the superiority of the Duchess who

> obviously felt she had come down in the social scale, having married a mere Duke, and being obliged to come into contact with the likes of us. All their pretty daughters were at home and unmarried, and apparently found like in a Service town a very cheerful affair. The contrast between their gay young faces and Mama's glowering looks was quite remarkable.[6]

Young Alfred was commissioned in the 2nd Volunteer Battalion Devonshire Regiment, this being largely an honorary position accorded him by the Colonel, Lord Mount Edgcumbe, in view of his father's command. When he was in Devonport, which was seldom, as in his mother's case, he performed the duties of a subaltern with the battalion. A studio portrait of him in full dress uniform hung in the Officers' Mess at Millbay Drill Hall, but was destroyed in the Blitz of 1941.

Like their brother, the Edinburgh princesses only came to Devonport during vacations. Despite Marie's by now almost implacable dislike of England, Missy enjoyed the west country. In her eyes it was inferior to Malta's southern sun and mysterious eastern atmosphere, but still she treasured memories of 'that beautiful country of Devonshire, so enchanting with its hills and dales, its rivers and forests, its steep roads and high hedges, beautiful gardens and, in places, quite southern vegetation',[7] her last taste of England before she married. She cared less for Admiralty House, which was uninteresting and notable only for a minute garden at the back where they played quarrelsome games of croquet. Far more fascinating and mysterious were the house and garden opposite of the General-in-Command, Sir Richard Harrison, and his family. Their three daughters were contemporaries of the princesses, and all became firm friends, inseparable in their games and swimming expeditions.

As Commander-in-Chief, the Duke of Edinburgh threw himself wholeheartedly into the naval and cultural life of Plymouth and Devonport. He undertook quarterly inspections of the Royal Naval Barracks at Keyham, and of training ships and naval contingents in port. Sometimes there were visiting foreign vessels to be welcomed, such as a German squadron of four ironclads, and their officers were honoured with a banquet at Stonehouse Barracks at which the Commander was the host. At the end of the summer term in July 1891 he distributed prizes awarded to students at Plymouth College, and in doing so he remarked that he was sure nobody would contradict him when he said that English public schools were among the grandest institutions the country possessed; 'though intended directly for educational purposes, they brought out everything that was noble, honourable and manly in a lad.'[8]

Family criticism had not persuaded him to give up his treasured violin. He joined the Plymouth Orchestral Society and regularly performed in concerts at the Guildhall. He also procured the then unprecedented honour of a visit and two concerts by the Royal Orchestral Society, of which he was President. When the Choral Society conductor Samuel Weekes retired, Affie was one of the first to subscribe to the beautiful solid silver tea and coffee service presented to him and his wife, bought from funds largely contributed by contemporary and previous society members.After presiding over an annual meeting of the Devon and Cornwall Female Orphan Asylum, Affie organised a fund-raising concert at which he conducted the orchestra.

Another local charity in which he took a keen interest was the Royal British Female Asylum. At one of their annual meetings, he commented on its disappointing progress and said it was deeply to be deplored that the amount of annual subscriptions stood at such a low figure.

Like the people he served, Affie was not immune to everyday inconveniences which plagued royalty and commoner alike. In March 1891 there was a savage blizzard which affected the west country, resulting in the deaths of over two hundred people, mostly lost at sea; the loss of about half a million trees, and postal and railway communications being brought to a standstill for several days. At the beginning of the month he had travelled to Chelsea to visit a naval exhibition, but his return from London to Plymouth was delayed when the train was temporarily snowbound at Taunton.

Seven months later Affie was invited to pay a visit to Bristol. On 23 October he took part in a concert at Colston Hall, where he led the orchestra in a programme which included the first two parts of Haydn's *Creation*. He stayed overnight at the Mansion House, and on the following day he opened a new wing of the city hospital, after which he left a subscription of £5 towards hospital funds. Afterwards, a short ceremony was held at which the honorary freedom of Bristol was conferred on him. What he probably did not realise was that the decision to do so had been quite divisive. The town council's resolution to extend the honour to the Duke had only been passed by three votes, partly due to the presence of several radical members who were less than enthusiastic about the crown, and partly as the mayor had recently made himself very unpopular among the working population by telling them that they ought to be prepared to work longer hours for less pay. A committee of protest against the resolution was formed, proclaiming that 'to confer the honour upon any who have done nothing to merit it tends to bring it into contempt and make it meaningless'.[9] After the ceremony, a radical newspaper reported scathingly that one of the councillors had made 'a scramble for the blotting paper with which the Mayor had blotted the Duke's signature, and walked away with the trophy in laudable triumph'. It was, the correspondent said, the climax of 'flunkeyism and sickening absurdity'.[10]

Although Affie was frequently absent from Devonport for short periods, circumstances twice required his being away for several weeks at a time. The first was after family and nation were plunged into mourning for the death of the Prince of Wales's elder son Albert Victor (Eddy), Duke of Clarence, on 14 January 1892. The demise of 'poor dear Eddy' after a bout of influenza, and only six weeks after his betrothal to Princess May of Teck, was not altogether unfortunate for the monarchy. A chronically backward, listless and dissipated young man, 'as heedless and as aimless as a goldfish in a crystal bowl,' Eddy would not have made an impressive king. Only months previously, he had been the absolute despair of his father. History had repeated itself. The grief-stricken father and equally disconsolate mother retired from public life to mourn for a while, and it fell to Affie to take Bertie's place at a number of levees and functions as the Queen's representative.

Ironically, there was soon to be a temporary rift between the two brothers. Both Affie and Queen Victoria hoped that Prince George of Wales, created Duke of York in May 1892, might become engaged to Missy – to the Queen 'it was the dream of Affie's life'. The cousins were extremely fond of each other, and Affie could not have wished a better husband for his eldest daughter than the industrious, naval-minded, stamp-collecting nephew with whom he had so much in common. But Marie was determined that no daughter of hers would marry an English prince. She made Missy write Georgie a stiffly-worded note to the effect that he must not think there was anything definite in the friendship that had formed between them in Malta. Missy's Anglophobe German governess likewise helped to assert her malign influence over the sixteen-year-old princess. Almost before she realised what was happening. Her mother had taken her to be introduced and then engaged to a far less promising suitor, Prince Ferdinand, Crown Prince of Roumania.

Nando, as he was called, was the nephew and heir of King Carol. The King's marriage to Princess Elizabeth of Wied had produced only a sickly daughter who died in infancy. Carol and Elizabeth made a strangely ill-assorted couple, sharing nothing beyond a complete lack of sense of humour. He was a stern unbending pedant whose sole relaxation was a regular evening game of billiards. He had overworked his shy insecure nephew with the result that Nando had become very withdrawn, and had developed a nervous giggle. Elizabeth, who might have become Duchess of Edinburgh had it not been for her bizarre taste in woodland violin recitals, had become steadily more eccentric with age. She wrote poetry under the *non de plume* of Carmen Sylva, and declaimed her efforts to captive audiences of ladies-in-waiting. Her eyesight was poor, and on yachting excursions down the Danube she would wave a large white table napkin in greeting to herds of cows, fondly believing that they were peasants who had come to salute her royal progresses. When Nando fell in love with one of her ladies, Helene Vacarescu, she eagerly encouraged the romance. The furious King ordered him to choose at once between his loved one and the Roumanian throne. On the young man's penitent submission to the path of duty, he was dispatched to the courts of Germany in search of a more suitable wife, while Helene was banished to Paris. Queen Elizabeth herself was ordered back to her mother until granted permission to return home.

By the standards of the day this was an infinitely poorer match for Missy, not least because the comparatively new Balkan kingdom of Roumania was hardly a model of stability. It was significant that Affie's permission for the betrothal of his eldest daughter's until it was virtually a *fait accompli*. For some years the Duke and Duchess of Edinburgh had appeared together in public only for form's sake. Much as he adored the children, he had always found it difficult to show his feelings and communicate with them, something which became more pronounced as he became older, and he had allowed his wife to be the dominant parent in their upbringing.

Affie was displeased with his wife, and more angry still when Bertie accused him of snubbing Georgie, still in a fragile state from the after-effects of a near-fatal attack of typhoid, and the subsequent death of his beloved elder brother. For a while relations between Bertie and Affie were strained, but at length commonsense prevailed and Bertie appreciated how he had wronged him. Affie had as true a friend as ever in Alix, who was delighted at the turn of events. Her relationship with Marie had been difficult ever since the latter had fussed about court precedence; Alix thought Missy 'a perfect baby' and much too German, certainly no wife for her only surviving son. Hence both mothers were firmly against such a marriage, while both fathers were in favour.

Although reassured to some extent by the good-heartedness of the diffident Nando, Affie was too glum to say much to Missy after her return from Germany. She was nervous herself at the realisation that neither he nor 'Grandmama Queen' had been asked for their consent to the betrothal. Queen Victoria made her disapproval plain, and the Duchess wrote to King Carol of Roumania that her 'discontented and unhappy' mother-in-law had accused her of sacrificing her daughter's youth and happiness 'to an uncertain future with few causes for celebration'.[11] Four months later, her anger had not cooled, and she complained bitterly to the King that Queen Victoria 'behaves in this way about every marriage and every family event'. She herself refused to get involved in what she saw as the intrigues of the ladies in waiting and the servants at the court of Windsor, and she kept her own suite and servants away from such business, 'in spite of all the terrible blunders and the weakness of character of my husband.'[12] It is clear that she resented Affie's refusal to take the side of his wife against that of his mother.

Nevertheless he accepted that he would have to accept what he and his mother saw as a disappointing match. He threw himself wholeheartedly into making practical arrangements for the wedding, but for some time he deliberately avoided talking to Missy in private, much to her relief. Her last unmarried weeks at Devonport and Coburg sped by all too swiftly.

At length Affie could contain himself no longer. One day in late December he called her to his room. Putting his arms around her tenderly, he burst into tears. Brokenly he told her that this was not the future he had dreamed of for her. While he hoped Ferdinand was a good man and would make a model husband, it was hard for him to see her leave for such a distant country. After mentioning the dowry he and her mother would be providing, he made her promise never to forget that she was and always would be a British princess and a sailor's daughter. By now feeling equally emotional, she fled to her room and wept bitterly.

In January 1893 family and guests flocked to the castle of Sigmaringen in Württemberg, where Missy and Nando were married on the 10th. Queen Victoria was unable to travel there and, bitterly offended that King Carol had refused to allow the ceremony to take place in England, she sent the Duke and Duchess of Connaught to represent her. The wedding consisted of three ceremonies – one civil, one Catholic (in the Church of St John adjoining the castle), and the other Protestant (in one of the castle drawing rooms). At each it was noticed that Nando's responses were clear and confident, while those of Missy were almost inaudible.

On the day of the wedding, Emperor William, who was among the guests, conferred on Affie the rank of Admiral in the German navy. Affie remained in Germany for the next fortnight, as he was to represent Queen Victoria at the wedding of another of her granddaughters, that of Princess Margaret of Prussia, the Emperor's youngest sister, to Prince Frederick Charles of Hesse-Cassel. On 24 January, the day before the ceremony, the Emperor gave a luncheon in Berlin in honour of Affie, at which sixty higher officers of the German navy were present, as well as the Duke of Connaught and Prince Henry of Prussia, a naval officer who eventually rose to the rank of Grand Admiral himself. In his speech, the Emperor thanked the Duke for the honour of consenting to become one of the navy's admirals. The German fleet, he said, had always modeled itself on that of England, and 'though like a baby in arms compared to the mightiest navy in the world, was being built up like a house, brick by brick'. Though it was intended as a safeguard for the preservation of peace, it would not fail to do its duty in case it should be called upon to fight, and if it should happen that the English and German fleets should find themselves shoulder to shoulder against a common foe, the saying that England expected every man to do his duty 'would find an answering echo in the patriotism of the German navy'.[13]

In May 1893 Affie presided over an annual meeting of the Devonport Sailors' Rest. After commending the work of those responsible, he have what was in a sense a farewell speech to the profession which he had loved and sadly knew he was soon to leave. During the period in which he had been connected with the service, he said, a great change had taken place in the conduct of men in the Royal Navy. Their behaviour was remarkably good, offences of all kinds were less numerous, and this particularly applied to cases of insubordination, want of respect to senior officers, and disobedience of command. This, he believed, was owing to greater sobriety among the men, and improvement in their conduct was due to the fact that they entered the service as boys and were trained in habits of discipline on board the training institutions of the profession.

On 1 June he performed his last public duty as Commander-in-Chief, the opening of a bowling alley at Keyham Barracks, provided for the ratings after he had commented on the lack of recreational facilities available to them and suggested something of the kind. Once he had declared it open, he completed two rounds and achieved a high score. Recalling an even more famous game of bowls played at Plymouth three centuries earlier, it was a fitting end to his career at Devonport, but this time no Spanish Armada lay in wait. Instead, that evening the Duke sat down with the captains and commanders in port to a farewell dinner at the Royal Hotel. Afterwards he delivered a speech thanking them for having made the last three years such a success for them all.

Two days later, a large muster of naval and military officers and a large crowd of civilians gathered to see him off at the station. He arrived in his new uniform as Admiral of the Fleet, to which rank he had been promoted that morning. The train was fifteen minutes late, and he spent the extra time in conversation with his successor Admiral Sir Algernon Lyons. Affie's departure was accompanied by strains of the National Anthem, which were barely audible above prolonged cheering.

What his own feelings were about leaving the town, one can only guess. Marie was certainly glad that his appointment as Commander-in-Chief was now at an end. Only two months earlier, her eldest daughter had sent her condolences in a letter from Bucharest, saying how 'you must hate the idea of dragging yourself now again all the way to Devonport, really you never can remain quiet even for a month, no wonder you feel tired.'[14] However, the Duke of Edinburgh had now reached the zenith of his days in the Royal Navy. With the expiry of his land command and promotion to Admiral of the Fleet, he recognised with some sadness that his career in the service to which he had belonged for thirty-five years was over. There was nothing to look forward to – inappropriate as the phrase may sound – but to succeed to his birthright, the duchy of Coburg.

That week the *Naval & Military Record* referred enthusiastically, with perhaps an element of pardonable exaggeration, to 'the departure of a Royal Commander-in-Chief, who may justly be described as the most popular port admiral that has ever held the reins of power in this district'.[15]

This view was not universally shared. Later that summer, a small but vociferous band of radical members of Parliament attacked his record. Led by Hudson Kearley, one of two Liberal members for what was then the two-member seat of Devonport, they asserted that the Duke of Edinburgh had systematically neglected his duties at the town, and received leave of absence unduly and improperly. Within the two years and ten months of his command, noted Kearley, he had been absent for 369 days, just over the equivalent of a calendar year. While this was beyond dispute, Sir Ughtred Kay-Shuttleworth, Secretary to the Admiralty and National Liberal member for Clitheroe, answered that the Duke had been subject to and complied fully with regulations governing leave. It had been appreciated before he took up his appointment that he would have to be away from Devonport from time to time for the purpose of attending the Queen on occasions of state ceremonies, but he had never been unduly absent. His two prolonged absences had been unavoidable, and nobody could accuse him of discharging his duties inefficiently.

The press were quick to condemn such complaints. 'All but the dregs of the constituency, of which Messrs Kearley and Morton [Edward Morton, Liberal member for Devonport 1892-1902] have allowed themselves to be made the cat's paws, recognised the advantage of having one of the Queen's sons officially connected with the port, and probably even the dregs when brought face to face with royalty would be profoundly obsequious',[16] noted the *Naval & Military Record.* An attempt to pass a vote of censure on the Duke was soundly defeated, as was a petulant proposal by Kearley to reduce the salary of the Secretary to the Admiralty because of his allegedly evasive answers concerning the Duke's service in the town.

Affie returned from Devonport to a London which was making eager preparations for the wedding of the Duke of York. In true fairytale tradition, the previous year's tragedy had had a happy ending, for Queen Victoria's second cousin Princess May of Teck, who had been betrothed to the hapless Duke of Clarence, became engaged to his infinitely more satisfactory brother in May 1893. Affie and Marie were both present at the wedding on 6 July at the Chapel Royal, St James's.

Though Affie was sorry that Georgie had not become his son-in-law, perhaps the thought crossed his mind that Missy was just a shade too restless, too theatrical for the cousin who was her 'beloved chum'. Nevertheless the close bonds between uncle and nephew were never broken. Affie was deeply gratified a year later when Georgie asked him to attend as godfather to his eldest child, the future King Edward VIII and Duke of Windsor, born on 23 June 1894.

Shortly after the Duke and Duchess of York's wedding, Affie left for Coburg. There were signs that at long last the life and reign of Duke Ernest II, who had caught a chill while out shooting and then had a stroke, was drawing to a close. Affie spent his forty-ninth birthday at Schloss Rosenau, and that same day he wrote to Aunt Alexandrine:

> I was very upset when I heard about dear Uncle's health. I have just arrived here. Marie gave me the message about your letter the day before yesterday, and I am happy to understand that he has no pain.
>
> Meanwhile I pray you to receive me tomorrow at Rheinhardsbrunn as I have a lot of things to talk over with you. Uncle must not know that I have come and as I do not want to disturb him I will come on foot. I also pray you to receive me in a remote part of the castle...[17]

Although members of the ducal household were not enthusiastic about a visit from their next Duke, he and Marie thought it only right and proper that he 'should show his authority and insist on spending at least a day there to see himself the true state of things.' Yet Marie thought that it would be difficult for him as there could not be any shooting under the circumstances, and he was bound to be difficult and ill-tempered if deprived of the sport which meant so much to him. 'We know so well,' she wrote to her daughter Marie, 'how little he appreciates the quiet country life, how bored he gets of the Rosenau and how little we can ourselves enjoy the delightful stay here when he does nothing but grumble.'[18]

The Duke's condition stabilised, and the doctors told the family that there was no immediate danger. However he was unable to speak, was almost completely paralysed, and nobody expected him to recover. Sad though the circumstances were, Marie had to admit that his imminent death was 'a real God-send' for which she could not thank Providence enough. Just at a time when her husband did not know what to do himself, 'when he might have become discontented and displeased with everything, he sees before him a new activity, and a new, fine position, with plenty to do and at the head of a charming country and master of such beautiful possessions.'[19]

After lingering for several more days, Duke Ernest died shortly before midnight on 22 August, aged seventy-five.

CHAPTER 11

Duke of Saxe-Coburg Gotha
1893-96

One of the first duties of the new Duke on the day he came into his inheritance was to send telegrams to the Burgomasters of Coburg and Gotha announcing the death of his uncle and predecessor. That same morning Emperor William arrived at Rheinhardsbrunn and was present when his uncle took the oath to the constitution, witnessed by the duchy's ministers of state. These proceedings were notified to the next meeting of the Common Diet of the duchies.

After lying in state, Duke Ernest II was buried on 28 August at the Church of St Moritz in Coburg. The ceremony was attended by the Duke and Duchess, and also by the Prince of Wales, the Duke of Connaught, Prince Ferdinand of Bulgaria, King Albert of Saxony, the Dowager Duchess Alexandrine and her brother Frederick, Grand Duke of Baden.

For Affie, the long-awaited – and long-dreaded – succession to the duchy was not a happy one. Though he may have looked forward to it with childish innocence during boyhood, the gradual shift in Anglo-German relations during his lifetime had been markedly for the worse. A traditional love-hate relationship had veered closer to hate during the Franco-Prussian war. Queen Victoria was forced to admit by 1871 that the Germany of her angel Albert had changed most unpleasantly, and for Affie the Coburg inheritance steadily became a less attractive prospect in view of the many family tragedies and irritations in the new upstart Reich – and above all Uncle Ernest's scandalous behaviour and financial mismanagement, the untimely deaths of Alice and Fritz, and the bullying behaviour firstly of Bismarck and then of Emperor William II.

Above all Affie shared his elder brother's aversion to Emperor William, who never tired of reminding his uncles that they were merely an heir apparent and a hereditary duke respectively. To be a duke in the empire of which this breezily familiar, unfilial and brash relative nearly fifteen years his junior was the leader was a prospect that made Affie shudder. Well might Missy recall in later life that her father, who was considered by his contemporaries to possess something of the Prince Consort's teutonic temperament, 'as a real Englishman dreaded the change which stood ahead of him, for he was thoroughly British in taste and habit and bitter was the prospect of expatriation'.[1]

Most bitter of all was being made to abandon his 'passion for the Navy', the great love of Affie's life for so many years. On a visit to Windsor some months later he shared a railway carriage with Admiral John Fisher, who reported that the Duke looked all right, but talked of nothing but the Navy, saying morosely that he found Coburg 'deadly dull', and that he expected one day he would cut his own throat.

Not only had Anglo-German relations changed. Conversely, Russia was moving away towards her traditional adversary Britain and away from her old ally Germany. Dynastic connections between Hohenzollerns and Romanovs had long bound the courts of Berlin and St Petersburg, and Emperor William I's affection for his nephew Tsar Alexander II had been the last of several personal links that helped to keep their countries allied. In June 1887 Bismarck had concluded a Reinsurance Treaty with the Russian Ambassador Count Shuvalov, to last three years; although its existence was kept secret for a while and Frederick III died twelve months later without any knowledge of it, he would almost certainly have maintained the long-standing Russo-German bond of friendship. By the time of the treaty's expiry in 1890, Bismarck had quarrelled with William II and angrily resigned, and it was not renewed by his anti-Russian successor Count Leo von Caprivi. Slowly but surely old allegiances were altering, with alliances between Russia, France and Britain in the air. That Alfred, Duke of Saxe-Coburg Gotha, should be an English prince and married to a Russian Grand Duchess, went rather against the grain. Had Affie succeeded twenty years later, divided loyalties would have made his position well nigh untenable, but fortunately he did not live to see the day.

As he realised only too well, German opinion was less than pleased at the succession of an English prince and Duke to a German dukedom. Both conservative and radical journals were suspicious, not to say hostile. According to *Reichsbote*,

It was generally expected that so much consideration would be paid to German national sentiments as to cause the idea of the succession of an English Prince to a German Dukedom to be abandoned. We deplore what has taken place the more because public opinion has been led to believe that the young Prince who has been educated in Germany and who is not in the English service would succeed Duke Ernest. We confess openly that it offends our national sensibility that an English Duke and Admiral should be the Regent of a German state and, as such, one of the Federal princes...we should have thought that in the glorious era of the newly-founded Empire and of constitutional Governments a foreigner could not succeed to the sovereignty of the German people as one inherits a piece of land. The thought is intolerable for German sensibility, and, if it is imposed upon the nation, we fear that it can only conduce to diminishing the importance and prestige of the monarchy. The German people is accustomed to see in its Princes its leaders and to feel itself at one with its reigning houses. This is no longer possible if the tie of national union is wanting and a foreigner sits on the throne.[2]

Other journals took a less hostile view. While *Berliner Tageblatt* regretted that the new Duke had not been brought up entirely in German surroundings and stressed he would find many difficulties in his new position which called for prudence and personal tact, it complimented him on having had mature political experience and his acquaintance with the world in general. If he introduced English constitutional ideas regarding the duty of a prince in lieu of cabinet government, it continued, the people of the duchy would thank their good fortune. Moreover, as the German Emperor was the first to bring his condolences in person, it was surely because he wished to put an end to insinuations that Prince Alfred was not *persona grata* among federal princes because of his English birth.

In Paris, where public opinion of the day had long been smarting under the humiliation of 1871 and where certain nationalistic elements were biding their time to avenge the Franco-Prussian war, *Le Temps* referred to the new Duke's accession as 'a derogation of the fundamental principles of the German Empire', and reminded its readers of Bismarck's already legendary letter to his henchman General von Gerlach of April 1856 commenting with suspicion on the engagement of the Princess Royal and Prince Frederick William, that if the princess succeeded in leaving the Englishwoman at home and became a Prussian, she would be a blessing to the country, but if she remained even only partly English, the court would surely be surrounded by English influence. If applied to the new Duke of Saxe-Coburg Gotha, how much more relevant such thoughts were in 1893 than in 1856, now that Prussia and Saxe-Coburg were no longer merely states of a loosely-knit German confederation, but now at the forefront of an ambitious military empire born out of military victory, intent on challenging England's supremacy as the foremost world power.

In 1893 the duchy of Saxe-Coburg Gotha was renowned especially for its excellent hunting forests and picturesque castles. It comprised estates not only in Coburg and Gotha but also Upper Austria and Tyrol, with a total area of 765 square miles. Of the population of 216,624, 31,670 lived in Gotha, and 18,688 in Coburg; the majority belonged to the

Protestant faith. Since 1866 the Duke, like all other minor German kings, reigning princes and grand dukes, had wielded no effective political power. Government was left effectively to the ducal parliament of two chambers, one containing nineteen members and the other eleven. A representative from the duchy sat on the federal council of the German empire. Affie, who still held his titles of Duke of Edinburgh and Earl of Ulster and Kent, was not only Duke of Saxe-Coburg Gotha but also Duke of Julich, Cleve, and Berg, of Engern and of Westphalia, Landgrave in Thuringia, Margrave of Meissen, Count of the Principality of Henneberg, Count of Mark and of Ravensberg, and Lord of Ravenstein and of Tonna.

Although there had never been any doubt among the family that Affie would automatically succeed Duke Ernest and reign for the rest of his life, the press was less certain. Throughout Coburg it had been rumoured that he intended to abdicate in favour of young Alfred on the latter's twenty-first birthday, thus enjoying a reign of only two years, and then return to England. Just over a week after Ernest's death, Marie wrote to Missy that people seemed to have the idea that her husband was not becoming the next Duke after all; 'I think the world in general was astonished and taken by surprise.' They all thought that young Alfred would do so instead, 'which would have been a terrible drawback, as he is far too young and there is much serious work to do for which Papa has a great talent and he is occupied from morning till night.'[3]

Even at home, not everybody was convinced at first that Affie had indeed succeeded to his long-planned inheritance. *The Illustrated London News* of 26 August announced that eighteen-year-old Prince Alfred had succeeded his great-uncle. Not until Affie had taken the oath to the duchies' constitution was the true succession established beyond doubt.

In her Journal for 23 August, Queen Victoria commented on a 'kind telegram' from the German Emperor after her son took the oath, and who had been the first to congratulate him on his accession. This, she recognised, was important in putting an end to remarks about the doubts that still existed. Emperor William had made a point of being present at Rheinhardsbrunn immediately after the death of Duke Ernest, in order to help make it clear that his uncle Alfred was officially his successor and to quell rumours that Affie's son was being chosen as the new Duke and Affie was there only as his Regent. It was said by some that the Emperor was in fact there to give his uncle the choice of succeeding to the duchy, or else abandoning it altogether as far as he and his son were concerned.

Another report in the German press declared that, during the reign of William I, Bismarck had tried to buy off the Duke of Edinburgh's claims to the Duchy 'as he could not be expected to possess such a high degree of interest for the German national cause as to place himself unhesitatingly on the side of Germany' should her interests clash with those of England. This scheme (which would have been quite in keeping with Bismarck's character), it was said, had been frustrated by the intervention of the Duke's brother-in-law, Crown Prince Frederick William. From his retirement at Varzin Bismarck indignantly denied all, but throughout Germany it was felt that he had originally fed it to the press in order to satisfy his own Anglophobia.

As for the rumours concerning young Alfred's succession, once again Bismarck may have been responsible. It could alternatively have been the work of his friend and admirer Duke Ernest, who had long resented Queen Victoria's refusal to take him more closely into her confidence and regard him as an unofficial family adviser after the death of King Leopold I in 1865. If he ever had any regrets about initiating baseless stories that the Duke of Edinburgh was not going to succeed him after all, it was only because his (Ernest's) death would prevent him from witnessing the irritation and confusion such mischievous gossip would cause. Yet another rumour in the English and German papers suggested that in 1885 the then Duke of Edinburgh had agreed to waive his rights of succession to the duchy in favour of his son, on the grounds that he would as an English prince with a Russian wife never be popular or practicable as a German sovereign, and that his German-educated son would be far more suitable. Like the other stories, this apparently had no foundation in fact.

For the first few months of Affie's reign, politicians and lawyers on both side of the North Sea argued endlessly on his nationality and privilege as a subject or sovereign prince, and where his true allegiance would lie.

On 13 November, the ever-vocal member for Devonport, Hudson Kearley, asked in the House of Commons if it was 'legally competent' for the Duke of Coburg to continue holding the position and receiving the pay of an Admiral of the Fleet in Her Majesty's Navy, or to remain a member of the Privy Council. The attorney-general replied that the Admiralty had advised that the Duke, having assumed a position incompatible with rendering active service, should he be called upon, ought not to continue holding Admiral's rank or receive the salary. Indeed, he had not pressed his claims for such pay. As for his membership of the Privy Council, this raised 'a point of such nicety but of no practical importance' because the Council's executive and administrative work was now under cabinet control, as was the issuing of summonses to councillors to attend meetings. To Admiral Field's question if there was any legal objection to the retention of the Duke on the Navy List as an honorary member, the Prime Minister, Gladstone, answered that his name would indeed remain there, but without pay or the capacity for active service. To general cheering, he elaborated that the Duke would keep his place as a mark of honour in respect of his long and distinguished service. It was a matter of great regret to the Duke that, as his heart was always in the naval profession, any changes in his position might weaken his relations with the Navy. As for his Privy Councillorship, it was not the government's intention to offer the sovereign any advice with respect to a change.

Affie had a staunch defender in the Foreign Secretary, Lord Rosebery, who was shortly to be appointed Prime Minister on the retirement of Gladstone early in 1894. The previous week, the cabinet had decided to advise the Duke to renounce his annuity as he was now a sovereign prince over foreign territory. Rosebery was shocked at what he considered to be a heartless gesture, and even more so by the 'truculent and Jacobin' language of his colleagues. To Gladstone he wrote despairingly:

> We toss over the Queen's second son into bankruptcy or sheer dependence on his wife and without a word of care for him or for his aged mother to whom this cannot but be a cruel blow...It is deplorable to live under a monarchy and make a football out of it, and rejoice in starving it.[4]

By coincidence Affie was back in England that month, and Rosebery's passionate defence of a man he had once disliked may well have been prompted by the fact that both were among the guests at Sandringham who were celebrating the Prince of Wales's birthday on 9 November. It had always been understood that he would be free to continue to visit England on a regular basis, and he spent several weeks 'at home' that winter. After leaving his brother's house, his schedule of visits to family and friends included appearances at Windsor and Cumberland Lodge, shooting with Prince Christian, and a few days at Plymouth, where he lunched with Admiral Lyons and General Harrison at Keyham Barracks, played golf, and went shooting at Langdon Court and Mount Edgcumbe. Shortly after returning to Clarence House, he attended a concert of the Royal Amateur Orchestral Society in London with the Prince of Wales, and conferred the Grand Cross of the Saxe-Ernestine Order on Sir Sydney Webb, Deputy Master of Trinity House.

Most important of all, while at Clarence House Affie wrote Gladstone a lengthy letter on the legal issues very much at the forefront of his mind, which may usefully be quoted in full:

> My accession to the Dukedom of Saxe-Coburg and Gotha causes me to recognize that my position as the recipient of money granted to me by the British people is understandably affected.
>
> I read the words of the provisions contained in the Acts of 1866 & 1873 as intimating that Parliament reserved to itself the right if I

succeeded to the Sovereignty of the Duchy of Saxe-Coburg to re-adjust the provisions made for me under those Acts.

I recall the following explanation given by you when the Act of 1873 was discussed in the House of Commons –

Though in the course of time the Duke of Edinburgh might become a foreign sovereign he would not therefore cease to be an English Prince. He would still continue to have family relationships and household connections. His visits would be frequent if his stay was not long, and it would not be possible to treat him as entirely cut off from his own country. The grant might in that case be modified; but it could not be extinguished.

Accepting as I do the spirit of the views thus expressed by you I desire to be subject to their application – and it is in the hope that I may be able not only to meet but also to anticipate the wishes of Parliament that I now ask you to enter with me upon the consideration of how far the modification contemplated by the Acts of 1866 & 1873 should be carried into effect.

It is to me a matter of the highest satisfaction that although I now occupy a sovereign position over a foreign state I shall still remain, certainly in spirit, a British subject.

The affection for my family, the friendships and associations of my life, my interest in the public affairs of this country all bind me closely to it, and I strongly desire to maintain – to strengthen if I can – these ties so directly affecting my happiness.

I therefore wish to pass a substantial portion of every year in this country, and for that purpose to retain possession of Clarence House maintaining within in the establishment necessarily attending such an occupation.

I also feel that it is impossible for me with propriety to part from the members of my household or to discharge old servants without making some provision for them.

There are likewise many institutions in this country in which I have been deeply interested, and it would naturally be to me a cause of great regret if I were compelled to withdrawing my connection and support from them.

Under these circumstances I have to express to you my desire to renounce a certain portion of the income now enjoyed by me under the Statutes of 1866 & 1873, but to retain a sum sufficient to enable me to bear the expense of effecting the objects I have above referred to.

The annual sum to be received by me will be expended in this country – and solely with the object of only maintaining my position as a member of the Queen's family.

For the purpose of determining the amount that is necessary to be retained by me in order to carry out these objects I trust you will allow authentic figures and estimates to be placed before you. My representative will be happy to afford the fullest explanation of them.

I am unaware how far you may deem the income I derive from other sources other than the Parliamentary grants as a matter to be considered when forming your judgment upon the subject I now submit to you.

All information you may desire I will most willingly afford.

But I wish now emphatically to say that after meeting the many obligations I am under in consequence of having to make provision for my family, I shall not be enabled without the retention of a portion of the Parliamentary income to maintain any establishment in this country.[5]

Before his departure for the continent, an Order-in-Command officially recognised Affie's retention of rank of Admiral of the Fleet, but withdrew his right to sit or speak in the House of Lords. It was no loss to him, as he had hardly ever been there. The social life of Marlborough House was more his style. He resigned his membership of the Privy Council and relinquished the annuity of £15,000 granted him in 1866, but kept the £10,000 granted on his marriage as an annual allowance for the maintenance of Clarence House, and came into receipt of the Coburg crown revenue of £46,000.

On 26 December Affie wrote to thank Gladstone for his help, expressing his hopes that there would 'be no more trouble, but some of the German papers are publishing disagreeable articles'.[6] Nevertheless, by this time most of them had realised that there was nothing more to be said on the matter. It had however not made his first ducal Christmas any the happier, and he was doubtless well-prepared for – though nonetheless irritated by – renewed debates in February 1894.

Early in the new year the British press asked whether the Duke of Coburg was still a British subject or not. On 5 February Herr Friedburg, a lawyer and leading member of the Imperial Diet, asked in the *Reichstag* whether the British government considered it compatible with German interests for a federal prince to be the subject of a foreign state; and whether British ministers would take steps to remedy the defect in their constitution that made such a state of affairs possible. Though there was no doubt that the Duke was now a German, he should relinquish henceforth all claims to being a foreign subject. To this, Chancellor Caprivi replied that as the Duke was German and a legal sovereign duke, notwithstanding whatever learned jurists might say to the contrary, he could not simultaneously be the subject of a foreign power. Otherwise, in case of war between Germany and the other power, the latter could accuse him of high treason. The Duke had already sworn an oath to the constitution of the duchies, and it was not the Diet's business to decide what his obligations to England were. It was incumbent on him to regulate his former relations with the country of his birth so they did not come into collision with his German ties. The discussion was terminated by Herr von Bonin, plenipotentiary member of the Federal Council for Coburg, who declared on behalf of his government that it was self-evident the Duke was no longer in the position of a subject, and therefore had no obligation towards England which ran counter to his present status as a ruler.[7]

Later that week *The Times* pointed out that the case could not arise whereby the Duke could be indicted in England on high treason as a result of his acts as a German sovereign. By English law, he retained British nationality 'modified...as to some of its incidents, by his status as a German sovereign'.[8]

With this the tedious wrangling closed, much to the relief of all concerned. Affie had expected something of the sort, but he could not have anticipated that his succession would cause so much controversy. It only made his first six months in Coburg more wearisome, coming on top of his move from England and the personal adjustments this necessitated, and also trying to make some order out of Ernest's chaotic finances, such as cutting down on his personal expenditure at court, and paying off outstanding debts.

The late Duke Ernest had left his finances in a deplorable state, and Affie and Marie therefore had to embark on a course of retrenchment. Affie was his father's son in that he had acquired a reputation for being careful with money, but any intentions Marie had of watching their outgoings with care were probably shortlived. As a Romanov, she had never had to worry about finance. Now that she and her husband had come into their inheritance, she could not resist the chance to refurbish the duchies' castles as she wanted.

From her country residence of Friedrichshof, near Kronberg, the Empress Frederick wrote perceptively to her daughter Sophie, Crown Princess of the Hellenes, that her brother had had a difficult time ahead of him, 'but he will do it all so well, and Aunt Marie will love being No. 1, and reigning Duchess, I am sure.'[9] The move had made little difference to Marie's lifestyle, but her sister-in-law struck the right note. Now that she was not only a Grand Duchess of all the Russias but also the reigning Duchess of Saxe-Coburg Gotha, Marie could at last feel genuinely superior to the princesses in England to whom she had been made to give precedence so many years before. She savoured every moment of this to the full.

Her husband's reservations, if not exactly lack of enthusiasm, about becoming Duke, were not shared by the woman born a Grand Duchess only forty years earlier. It seemed providential to her, she wrote to her daughter, that he had this new role in life just at a moment when we all felt rather in despair about his want of work and the consequent 'grand ennui' that would have been the inevitable result. Now all is changed as if by magic and Papa hardly speaks of going to England. He is very contented and has entered most seriously into his new serious position.[10]

Vicky had been delighted by her brother's succession to the duchy. She was always devoted to her brothers and sisters, and in the last few years Duke Ernest's endorsement of Bismarck's underhand behaviour and denigration of the late Emperor Frederick, which she saw as nothing less than gross betrayal, had left a bitter after-taste. Affie, she wrote to Queen Victoria in September, would surely make an excellent duke. 'If only he will observe the constitution of his country, as an Englishman would, and not copy the tricks played at Berlin with the constitution, he will secure the respect and confidence of the best German elements and in due time become a support to the right-minded people and an example to William.'[11]

Marie's best friend in the German courts was the Emperor's eldest sister Charlotte (Charly), Hereditary Princess of Saxe-Meiningen. The vain and mischievous Charly had exasperated her parents by siding with Bismarck and his cronies in pouring scorn on their English sympathies. Soon after her marriage she established herself as uncrowned leader of the Berlin smart set, holding sway among the sophisticates who 'had their own joys, their own mannerisms, their special language, their loves, enthusiasms, and abhorrences'.[12] Charly had discreetly helped to bring about an engagement between Missy and Nando, when almost everybody else had expected the princess to become Duchess of York. Outside her own exclusive circle, Charly was actively disliked for her fickle nature and nauseating superiority. No love was lost between her and the German Empress Augusta Victoria ('Dona'), whose plain plump figure, abhorrence of frivolous society and lack of interest in anything outside her immediate family made her everything her sister-in-law was not. Charly delighted in teasing Dona behind her back. One morning in 1892 before the annual Hubertus hunt, Charly and her lady-in-waiting arrived at the royal stables, slightly drunk. To the shocked delight of other ladies present, she offered to ride *à la* Florence Dixie if somebody would lend her a pair of breeches. After being told that everyone knew she wore the trousers in her household, she demonstrated how the Empress mounted her horse – by raising herself on tiptoe into the stirrups and then falling into the saddle, 'like a majestic sack of flour'. Hours later came an imperial decree that all ladies-in-waiting and princesses were barred from attending the hunt that year.

Of far greater pleasure to Affie at the time were his children's activities. On 15 October 1893 he became a grandfather for the first time. Missy's first few months of married life at the oppressively dull court of Roumania had not been made any easier by immediate pregnancy, but Marie came to attend her confinement when her daughter gave birth to the prince who would one day ascend the throne as King Carol II.

In January 1894 Ducky was betrothed to her cousin Ernie, who had succeeded his widowed father as Grand Duke of Hesse nearly two years previously. This marriage between her grandchildren was one which Queen Victoria had ardently wanted. Since Alice's tragic death she always had a special place in her heart for the motherless children of Darmstadt, and she was sure that Ernie would find an excellent partner in his tall dark-haired cousin. Affie also believed that they would suit each other perfectly, and Marie did not raise any objection to marriages between first cousins as she had tried to in Missy's case.

The wedding on 19 April in Coburg was made the occasion of festivities such as the duchy had not seen for many years, with torchlight processions and an amnesty in which Affie pardoned prisoners convicted of *lesé-majesté* and other minor offences. Queen Victoria, who had initially tried to insist on the wedding being held at Windsor until she was overruled, came and paid her first visit to the duchy for eighteen years. She was welcomed by Oberburgermeister Muther, who addressed her on behalf of the municipality and graciously informed her that he had held the same office on her visit in 1865 when she had unveiled the Prince Consort's statue. Nearly every name in the *Almanach de Gotha* crowded into the normally sleepy little town. *The Times* correspondent faithfully reported the arrivals of Emperor William, the Prince of Wales, the Empress Frederick, Crown Prince and Princess Ferdinand of Roumania, Prince and Princess Henry of Prussia, Prince and Princess Philip of Coburg, Grand Duke and Duchess Serge of Russia, the Duke and Duchess of Connaught, Prince and Princess Henry of Battenberg, the Hereditary Prince and Princess of Saxe-Meiningen and their only child Princess Feodora. They attended the family dinner hosted by Affie and Marie, and a gala performance at the Riesensaal on the eve of the wedding.

At the ceremony itself, the bridegroom and the bride's mother were reported to be very calm, in contrast to Affie, Queen Victoria and Vicky, down whose cheeks tears flowed freely. Crowds thronged to see them drive off from the *Schlossplatz* amid showers of rice, in a phaeton decorated liberally with spring flowers. While the guests were waving them goodbye, four enterprising photographers ran into the courtyard square and frantically signaled to the assembled company not to move. Far from regarding this as an intrusion on their dignity, the most distinguished gathering to be seen anywhere in Europe that year, smiling good-naturedly, posed for several photographs. They were just in time, for only a few minutes later sunshine gave way to such violent thunderstorms that the town's evening illuminations had to be postponed.

The only major problem at the wedding was caused by the behaviour of the Munshi, Queen Victoria's Indian servant, whom Affie like most of the family and royal household bitterly loathed. John Brown had sometimes been arrogant and churlish to others, but he rarely took advantage of his position, and was unfailingly honest as well as personally generous. The Munshi was a shifty character, who was trusted by nobody apart from the Queen. He travelled with the royal suite to Coburg, and Affie told Ponsonby through Monson, his equerry, that nothing would induce him to allow the Munshi to come into the chapel with the Queen's suite for the wedding ceremony, and that he was to tell the Queen as much. Well aware that this would not go down with the Queen, Ponsonby informed her, and she was as indignant as was to be expected. She would not speak to Affie about it, and Ponsonby bore the brunt of trying to make arrangements to get round the situation. Affie stood his ground, and at length it was arranged that the Munshi was to be taken to a gallery in the church by the son of one of Affie's gentlemen, the Queen in particular stipulating that there must be no servants there. But on being conducted to his place, the Munshi recognised among his neighbours some of the grooms, and was so furious that after a few minutes he left without staying for the wedding. Instead he wrote an indignant letter to the Queen, which was not given to her until after the bride and groom had left. She wept on reading it. Word quickly spread round all the servants, who were delighted that the Munshi had had his come-uppance, but were still saddened that the Queen should have been so affected.

After this she took all decisions about the Munshi out of Ponsonby's hands and asked Sir Condie Stephen, Affie's private secretary, to deal with it. As a result the Munshi drove every day in a royal carriage with a footman on the box, and was invited to the state concerts, but everyone did their best to avoid him.[13]

Before the royal throng returned to their respective countries, Princess Alix of Hesse was betrothed to the Tsarevich Nicholas, who so resembled his cousin the Duke of York that they had been mistaken for each other at the latter's wedding in London the previous year. The possibility of such a match had provided European courts with much speculation for months beforehand. Not the least of Alix's reasons for taking the step of changing her faith and conforming to the Russian Orthodox Church in order to become the future Tsarina, it was rumoured, was her dislike of her new sister-in-law. Almost pathologically shy, she was the very opposite of boisterous Ducky, and resented the idea of having to give her precedence at Darmstadt.

Everyone expected that Nicky and Alix would have an apprenticeship of several years together as Tsarevich and Tsarevna, for Tsar Alexander III was not yet fifty and in apparently good health. He himself had done nothing to prepare his heir, whom he regarded as a 'mere boy', for the throne. However, in September Alexander suddenly fell ill, nephritis was diagnosed, and on medical advice he was sent to his summer palace in Livadia at the Crimea. Neither doctors nor a milder climate could save him, and he died on 1 November. Affie and Marie arrived just before he breathed his last, the latter distinguishing herself by a none-too-tactful greeting of 'Thank God I've arrived in time to see you once more.'[14] They stayed for the funeral at St Petersburg and the numerous masses that followed, and attended the wedding of the new Tsar and Tsarina at the Winter Palace three weeks later. It was a magnificent yet sad ceremony, with Nicholas still stunned by the suddenness with which he had succeeded to his inheritance.

After almost a month of funeral rites and marriage celebrations, an exhausted Affie broke his journey at Friedrichshof while on his way back to England for a while. Vicky was overjoyed to see her brother again, and not altogether sorry that Marie had gone straight back to Coburg without coming to visit her as well. On the first night of his stay Affie's presence of mind narrowly prevented disaster. He retired early to bed and woke up at about 4 a.m., almost stifled by smoke. After calling his servant to rouse everyone he poured several jugs of water over where the smoke was coming from, and turned on his bath to have some more ready. The local fire service was summoned, and found that two beams under the floor by the fireplace had been smouldering for a couple of days. Had Affie not been there, the whole building might have burnt down.[15]

On 15 October 1895, young Alfred celebrated his twenty-first birthday. This was marked by a ceremony at Schloss Ehrenburg in which Herr von Strenge and his ministers made a formal announcement of the Prince's majority, and Affie addressed a letter exhorting his son to be mindful of the duties of a German prince, to assist in advancing the prestige of the ducal house, and to help promote the welfare of both duchies and their inhabitants for the preservation and strengthening of the German empire. No more, however, was heard of Affie considering abdication in his favour. His son's health was not good, and evidently he felt that to abdicate would be a dereliction of duty. He also knew that the young man had been leading a dissolute life in the army and was almost certainly aware that he had contracted venereal disease.

Ironically, Affie's own health had already given increasing cause for concern. In October 1894 James Reid, the Queen's physician, received a note from Sir Henry Ponsonby, enclosing a letter from Sir Condie Stephen, warning them of the Duke's drinking habits and the effect they were having on him. Stephen asked that his letter should be shown to the Queen, but Ponsonby was disinclined to let anybody discuss such details with her. He probably knew better than anyone else that any words of warning from his mother would be a waste of her time. Nevertheless Stephen was adamant that unless Affie could 'moderate the quantity' of his drinking, 'his health will soon entirely break down, and unless he is frightened he will not change his mode of living – the kidneys are already slightly affected.' Although the Duke was 'very touchy just now about his health', he would probably consult a specialist in London if he was asked to by the Queen.[16]

Sir Arthur Sullivan, the composer and lifelong friend of Affie, was another one who had long been worried about his old friend's excessive love of the bottle. In an undated letter written to Princess Louise between 1894 and 1900, he poured out his heart about 'the evil tendency which was manifesting himself' even during the Duke's bachelor days. To keep him at home, and 'to prevent his going out into society injurious to his health and reputation', Sullivan made a point of visiting him late at night, taking little pieces of music he had specially written or arranged for him, 'and then having got him interested would remain playing accompaniments till two o'clock in the morning.' After his marriage Sullivan naturally saw less of him, and did not dare to resume the old bachelor relationship, as he saw 'there was a distinctly *hostile element* risen up against me, which made me feel very uncomfortable, and always embarrassed.' Much as she loved music, Marie did not see Sullivan as a friend of hers, only another crony of her husband's whose presence she resented. He had observed 'little scenes' and 'heard words' between husband and wife which 'pained him dreadfully'. In spite of this Affie remained as sweet, gentle and forbearing as he had always been; Sullivan 'could not help admiring and respecting him more than ever, and could hardly blame him if he sought a little 'soulagement' in a resource which was neither right nor healthy.'[17]

Marie was certainly finding her husband increasingly difficult. Only four months after their accession to the duchy, she was pouring her heart out to Missy about his bad humour, the fact that he was 'impossible at dinner', and his anger at such little details as the food. Evenings, she said, were 'hard at home, and he swears at the theatre.'[18]

On his visits to England, Affie obviously found the company far more congenial, and he continued to spend his time regularly with various old friends. He had kept in touch with Richard and Bessie Cory and their daughters, and in later years the girls would recall his visits to them at London and at Langdon Court. While they were in the capital in March

1896 he had tea with them at the Buckingham Palace Hotel, and particularly amused them by playing a game in which he would put a penny on his head, and invite them to creep up and take it. Only Diney, aged eleven at the time, would dare do it. Although Bessie, who was two years older, would stand tongue-tied with her finger in her mouth, they both thought he was 'a sweet old man'.[19] Richard Cory died in 1904, aged eighty-two, and his widow married Colonel; George Gore. The latter had also been an old friend of Affie; both men had served on board ship together, and while he was Commander-in-Chief at Devonport the latter had obtained him a job at the naval barracks so he would not have to return to sea.

By this time, there was another forthcoming marriage in the family. Affie's third daughter Sandra had become engaged to Prince Ernest of Hohenlohe-Langenburg. He was an attaché at the German Embassy in London, a grandson of Queen Victoria's half-sister Feodore, and was also related distantly to the German Chancellor Prince Clovis of Hohenlohe-Schillingsfürst. The betrothal had been first discussed in the early weeks of 1895, but Sandra was only sixteen at the time, fourteen years younger than her husband-to-be, and the family thought it best to wait for a few months. Marie was very enthusiastic about the match, but Affie less so. She regretted the fact that her husband 'so little tries to know people really well and therefore, hardly understands all the real worth of a man like Erni H.'[20]

However, before long he was equally impressed by the young man. When the betrothal took place at Rosenau in September 1895, he was delighted as he sat down to send telegrams to members of the family to tell them the happy news. They were therefore furious when they received a reply from Queen Victoria, which was, said Marie, 'even more nasty and rude than we could possibly have expected! Not one good wish, only surprise and anger and reproaches.' Affie answered stiffly to say how grieved and surprised he was at her want of sympathy, and the next morning Sandra received a much more conciliatory telegram from her grandmother, regretting her haste in replying and wishing her every happiness. Affie was prepared to forgive his mother, but Marie intended to 'be rather stiff' with her for some time, as she was so angry at the Queen treating them all like little children who could not be allowed to decide for themselves.[21]

Ernest was a guest of his fiancée's family in January 1896, but to their despair Affie insisted on taking him out shooting. The young man, who was not really interested in such activities, had no option but to resign himself and try to look grateful.[22]

In April 1896 Affie, attired in the uniform of the 9th Prussian Hussars, and Marie, welcomed family and guests to the wedding at Coburg. Queen

Victoria was not present this time, and she sent the Duke and Duchess of York to represent her. Among the others were the German Emperor and Empress, and Grand Duke Paul of Russia, uncle of Tsar Nicholas II. The Duchess of York noted that the civil and religious wedding ceremonies passed off pleasantly, but the second was rather emotional as both the bride and her younger sister Baby Bee, then only twelve, burst into tears during the rather lengthy sermon.[23] Piously May did not hazard a guess as to whether emotion or boredom was responsible.

One month later Affie, Marie and young Alfred were in Moscow for the coronation of Tsar Nicholas II and Empress Alexandra. The festivities were tragically marred when what was to have been a free open-air feast at Khodinsky Meadow turned into a mass stampede of impatient people, some probably drunk, fighting for their share of what was rumoured to be an insufficient supply of souvenir gifts and food. In the confusion an estimated two thousand people were crushed to death.

Ever since Missy's marriage, Affie had longed to pay her a visit in her new and far from happy home. King Carol did not spare his family from the rigid unbending rule which he presided over country and court. When Missy entreated him to give her back her youth before it was too late, he replied that only the frivolous considered youth the best part of life. Queen Elizabeth had only just returned from the exile imposed on her as a punishment for encouraging the romance between Ferdinand and Helene Vacarescu. As for Nando, he accepted his uncle's Spartan regime with a submissiveness that exasperated Missy. Well might she have regretted her mother's Anglophobia that had denied her a future as Queen of England.

When Affie announced that he wished to pay a visit to Roumania, Missy was thrilled. Emperor Francis Joseph of Austria was about to make an official state visit, and King Carol did not wish to offend his venerable ally by inviting a mere German Duke at the same time. He asked her to write gently to her father suggesting that perhaps he might prefer to delay his visit. With equal tact, and one imagines a twinkle in his eye, Affie wrote back to say he would be delighted to meet the Emperor whom he had not seen for many a year. The King therefore had no choice but to include both Emperor and Duke in his programme.

Fortunately for his hosts, Affie asked for little more than to be left to his own devices much of the time. He did not want an endless round of receptions and inspections, but would far rather stay at home with the newspapers and an ever-ready glass of beer beside him. Missy was much amused by the behavior of her small daughter Elizabeth, who watched him carefully, dragging a straw chair round with her while she waited for him to settle down. As soon as he had chosen his seat and made himself comfortable, she brought her chair next to him and sat absolutely silent but apparently content. The moment he moved, she repeated the performance. From time to time he peeped over his paper at her, but neither exchanged a word.[24]

Though his old shyness with children remained, Affie was secretly flattered at his granddaughter's silent attention. He prolonged his stay until after Francis Joseph's departure, which in retrospect turned out to be an unwise move. For Queen Elizabeth was still at heart the same extravagantly theatrical creature who had bidden the young bachelor Duke of Edinburgh to play her his violin in the woods. Naively she had told Missy beforehand that she expected to find him the same handsome youth, still imbued with an all-consuming love of music and perhaps even with his musical instrument tucked under his arm wherever he went.

Affie's protests at such sentimental nonsense were to no avail. His visit coincided with a time when the Queen was besotted with a mediocre singer and painter who had convinced both himself and her that he was a musical genius. She therefore organised a picnic in the mountains, where her protégé could inflict his vocal powers on her guests and others in an appropriately wild and romantic landscape. Believing in the more the merrier, she collected as large an audience as possible – people of any nationality, any class, any pretensions to be musical connoisseurs themselves, and anyone who secretly just wanted a good laugh.

Not realising that a Queen of Roumania could possibly make such an exhibition of herself, Affie did his duty as a good guest and trudged along unwillingly with this motley crowd, Missy escorting him up steep mountainous paths as she watched anxiously for the warning signs on his face, notably a habit of sticking out his lower lip in a pout, an expression which all the family had long since learnt was a sign of his patience wearing dangerously thin. Eventually they reached the picnic area, and he took his place with evident discomfort on the rocky seat allotted to him. In due course the so-called singer appeared suddenly from behind another rock, striking a supposedly heroic pose to match the landscape, and gave a theatrical performance notable more for effort than for any degree of musical competence.

The Queen and her band of intense sycophants watched and listened with clasped hands, while others with more sense tittered politely or not so politely, but Affie was furious. Turning to Missy, he exclaimed that it was outrageous and he had no wish to be part of this lunatic asylum. With knees trembling at his anger she made her excuses to the Queen to get away, as he muttered crossly all the way home.[25] It was no wonder that his first visit to Roumania also proved to be his last.

CHAPTER 12

Last years 1897-1900

Prince Alfred's role as Duke of Saxe-Coburg Gotha resembled nothing so much as that of a kind and sympathetic landlord, living the life of a country squire with few responsibilities. It was a painful, and boring, contrast to his life in the Navy. Fortunately the tedium was alleviated by regular visits abroad, to England, Russia, and most European countries in turn.

The last great family reunion of the nineteenth century was in London for Queen Victoria's Diamond Jubilee celebrations in June 1897. To everybody's relief Emperor William did not come, in spite of his intention (or, as others might have said, threat) to be there, but he was represented by his surviving brother Henry, who was married to his Hessian cousin Irene and much more acceptable to his English relations. Affie and Marie, together with most of the Queen's other children and children-in-law, contributed jointly to present her with a diamond sautoir chain, the St Andrew's Cross on a chain with diamonds, as a commemoration gift.

The Queen wished to give her second son a present as well, although this was easier said than done. At the end of May one of her private secretaries, Sir Fleetwood Edwards, wrote to the First Lord of the Admiralty, George Goschen, to say that Her Majesty intended to present a baton to the Duke of Saxe-Coburg Gotha, and asked if the whereabouts were known of one which was given to the Duke of Clarence in 1821. Goschen replied that a baton had indeed been given to Clarence and also to Admiral of the Fleet the Earl of St Vincent simultaneously, the latter being awarded to him as Colonel of the Marines and not in his capacity as Admiral of the Fleet. As Goschen did not mention what had happened to Clarence's baton, Edwards wrote to suggest that the Admiralty disapproved of batons being carried by Admirals of the Fleet. Moreover, as those previously awarded had been personal gifts, King George IV must have paid for them, and Her Majesty might perhaps do the same, otherwise the Treasury would be certain to object. The Garter King of Arms added his judgment that it was not necessary for an Admiral of the Fleet to receive a baton on account of his rank, despite this being the practice for Field Marshals in the army.

But the Queen insisted that her son should have one and ordered the court jewellers to make it. She paid for it herself, but got her own back on the Admiralty by having a notice inserted in the *London Gazette* on 22 June 1897 that she was presenting it to him by virtue of his rank as Admiral of the Fleet. For an officer who frequently recalled the happy days he had known since joining the Royal Navy nearly half a century earlier, there was perhaps no gift he could have appreciated more.

The Duke was among the guests present at the Buckingham Palace banquet on 21 June, and on the following day he rode in the procession to St Paul's Cathedral for the Service of Thanksgiving. On 3 July he was among those accompanying the Prince of Wales at a review of Indian and colonial troops, where nearly 1,000 jubilee memorial medals in bronze and silver were distributed.

If the Diamond Jubilee was the last great occasion of Queen Victoria's life, it was in a sense the same for her second son, for his remaining three years would be anything but happy.

The worst trouble was Affie's increasing boredom and deteriorating health. By now he lived mostly for his beloved sport, and there was little else that meant anything to him. He had very little in common with Marie regarding personal interests, and she lamented that he became irritable if not downright furious if she discussed anything to do with the theatre in his presence with anyone else. It made conversations ever more difficult, and she was often in despair to know what to talk about. While he hated literature, she thought politics were dull and anything to do with hunting ten times duller. It would be a tremendous rest for her, she admitted, the next time he went to England.[1]

As for his drinking, he would not think of reducing it, let alone give it up. Apart from his guns, this was one of the few pleasures still left to him, and he was apparently oblivious of the effect it was having on his liver. While he was staying at Windsor in November 1897 he consulted Reid, who was never afraid to give his royal patients the plain unvarnished truth about their personal health, unpalatable though it might be. Reid told him bluntly that he was taking far too much, and other people had noticed that he was the worse for wear. He had also seen Affie's personal servant Farquharson, who gave him 'a dreadful account' of his master's drinking habits, and was sufficiently alarmed to discuss the problem of his health with the Queen and the Prince of Wales. While Bertie's consumption of food was legendary and the corresponding effect on his girth noticeable, to say nothing of his heavy smoking, he had always been a relatively light drinker. Between them they agreed that, for his own good, the Duke must be removed from the pernicious social life of London and spend some time recuperating in Egypt.

That winter he was very unwell, and in the last week of January 1898 he sailed for Alexandria, Egypt, where he was to stay at the Helouan Hotel. It was hoped that a few relatively abstemious weeks in a mild climate would help him to regain his strength. *En route* from Alexandria to Malta, where he was going to renew old friendships, he was stung by a mosquito and the bite turned septic. Suffering from acute pustular eczema complicated by an abscess on the eyelid, or a 'developed rectal inflammation', he arrived at Villefranche, on board his yacht *Surprise* on 24 March. Fortuitously Queen Victoria and Dr Reid were at nearby Cimiez, where she was then taking her customary spring holiday on the Riviera. Reid was sent for, and found the Duke in agony from which required urgent surgery. On the next day he was operated on under anaesthetic, and when the Queen was informed she sent a telegram warning that her second son 'must be most careful, and after such an attack must not travel without a doctor.'[2]

Meanwhile Marie stayed at home where she and her daughters absorbed themselves in the theatre and amateur dramatics. Although she was a little hurt at the initial lack of letters from her husband, she was at length relieved to hear that he sounded well and comfortable, and did not want to hurry back, which was 'a good thing'. It was important that he did not return before the end of April. He could not stand the cold, would only spend his time grumbling, and never leave his room or take proper exercise. He no longer read anything except newspapers, letters no longer seemed to 'amuse him', and he had no conversation; as she admitted to Missy, 'if only you knew how easy and comfortable life is without him.'[3]

Over the few days following the operation Affie stayed to convalesce at the Château de Fabron, Rizza, and he was much cheered by visits from his sisters Helena and Beatrice. The Queen demanded to see his medical notes, which theoretically could have been regarded as a breach of privacy. Nevertheless Reid probably felt she had a right to know, and in any case it was not always easy to say no to Her Majesty Queen Victoria. He accordingly allowed her to see them out of curiosity, even though there was nothing more she could do. In fact there was no real solution, and though he apparently made a satisfactory recovery, Affie was never in good health again afterwards.

Another cause of unhappiness was his position as a passive spectator of contemporary naval affairs. With every succeeding year, he missed his close involvement in his former profession all the more. His honorary rank of Admiral of the Fleet and occasional invitations to naval ceremonies in England could be no more than mild compensation for the end of his active career. What made the matter worse was Emperor William II's determination to create a powerful German fleet. In 1897 William appointed Admiral Alfred von Tirpitz secretary of state for the navy, with special responsibility for naval propaganda, in which the German public was ceaselessly lectured on the necessity of becoming an invincible sea power. The following year the Reichstag passed a bill authorising the construction of nineteen battleships and forty cruisers within five years.

Affie did not live long enough to see the acceleration of the naval arms race, but during his nine-year reign, King Edward VII would be one of the first Englishmen to sense the threat of the German navy, and there can be no doubt that his brother was similarly filled with foreboding at the sight of his imperial nephew's naval ambitions. As a German federal prince whose heart remained with the British navy he had served so faithfully, and having been recently made a German admiral, Affie's position was awkward in the extreme. Mercifully such cruelly-divided loyalties would never be put to the ultimate test.

With sadness Affie had to acknowledge that all was not well with the marriages of two of his daughters. While Sandra and Ernest were happy enough together, the same could not be said for her elder sisters. Missy was still suffering under the strict Roumanian court regime. She had been unable to attend her grandmother's Diamond Jubilee celebrations as Nando was then at death's door with typhoid, complicated by double pneumonia. During his convalescence she was left to amuse herself with her aide-de-camp, Lieutenant Zizi Cantacuzino, and the result was an ill-concealed affair that probably resulted in the birth of a child which was either stillborn or placed in an orphanage. In later years Missy was to admit gracefully that prudence was not her strong point.

Yet at least Nando was a good if rather uninspiring husband. Far more disturbing to her father were Ducky's problems at the nearby court of Darmstadt. She and Ernie had never been really fond of each other, and she nursed a grudge against Queen Victoria for having helped to arrange the marriage. Temperamentally husband and wife were too far apart, much as they tried initially to make their life together work. Ernie was melancholy and sensitive, mentally scarred for life by the premature deaths of his only brother, sister and mother. He was afraid of horses, sometimes stayed in bed all day to write poetry, and although he attempted to conceal his brooding nature under a mask of gaiety, he was conscious above all of his responsibilities as a Grand Duke. Ducky also alternated between high spirits and depression, but as a fearless horsewoman she regarded his phobia as nothing less than physical cowardice. When one of her horses – admittedly the wildest – was let loose in the courtyard one day, it went straight for her husband and removed a piece of his trousers. She roared with laughter, but he was not in the least amused. As a Grand Duchess she would not accept her conventional duties, postponing visits to boring old relations, and talking to people who amused her at official receptions while she ignored everyone else. When Ernie attempted to remonstrate with her, Ducky would lose her temper, and on one occasion she knocked over a heavily laden tea table in her fury.

They had one daughter Elizabeth, born in 1895, and a stillborn premature son five years later. Exasperated by her husband's fondness for male stable-hands and kitchen servants, Ducky sought consolation in the company of another cousin, Grand Duke Kyril of Russia. This ill-starred marriage and 'the little spitfire' were the talk of every court from London to St Petersburg, and Affie was deeply worried by their behaviour. Whenever they went to stay at Gotha, it was evident that she 'simply cannot stand him sometimes' and he got on her nerves.[4]

Though Affie and Marie had not enjoyed the happiest of marriages themselves, their silver wedding in January 1899 was celebrated in the duchies. Deputations from Coburg and Gotha came to offer their congratulations at a ceremony in Schloss Friedenstein, and on 3 January several members of the family joined them at a grand dinner and gala theatre performance. At a reception the next morning Affie, deeply moved, thanked all those present for their signs of love and confidence that had been extended to the Duchess and himself. He would ever remain at one with his people, he added, and would know no higher law than the welfare of the duchies. A special silver wedding medal was struck and bestowed on all who took part in the festivities. Presents came from home and abroad, among them, four standard lamps with solid silver feet from Queen Victoria, and a clock made in the Imperial Porcelain Manufactory of Berlin sent by Emperor William II.

Yet one absence from the celebrations signalled Affie and Marie's greatest tragedy of all. While they did their best to make the occasion as welcoming as possible for their guests, young Alfred lay severely ill in a room on the lower floor of the Schloss.

Never very strong, the prince had been appointed to the 1st Regiment of Prussian Guards, where he led a very dissipated life. Totally at the mercy of others, he soon found himself getting into bad ways. A ghostly figure rarely seen except in photographs as a German officer in his *pickelhaube* helmet and Prussian uniform, looking very like his father at a similar age but clean-shaven and less handsome, it was believed that all young Alfred thought of was the set of his collars and the spit and polish of his uniform and boots.

Affie had not seen nearly as much of his son during adolescence as he would have liked, and Marie was the dominant influence during his brief life. As a mother, he must have found her impossible to please. According to Missy, he was always getting into trouble;

People were too impatient with him and Mamma, hoping to find perfection, was often disappointed in her son. Mamma had a supreme horror of the shady side of life and in every way tried to ignore it, and when for all that, it approached her through any member of her own circle, her grief and indignation were extreme. She was never able to talk with Alfred; she thought that severity and religious principles must keep him straight; he found no mercy when he sinned, so he lost confidence in those who might have helped him, and later...became secretive, led a double life, and made a mess of things.[5]

With a frequently absent father, an unsympathetic mother, a governor who took every opportunity to ridicule him in front of others, and a military aide who from all reports seems to have been a thoroughly evil influence on him, Alfred never had a chance. Like his similarly shortlived cousin Albert Victor, Duke of Clarence, his constitution was evidently unequal to the debauched life which he led while he was in the army. At the time of his parents' silver wedding, the press announced that he was suffering from 'nervous depression'.

On 28 January 1895, the Court Circular had announced that a marriage had been arranged between Prince Alfred and the eighteen-year-old Duchess Elsa Matilda Marie, elder twin daughter of the late Duke William Eugene of Württemberg and the Grand Duchess Vera of Russia. No marriage ever took place, and two years later the Duchess married Prince Albert of Schaumburg-Lippe.

Many years later, it was rumoured that the prince had married Mabel Fitzgerald, a young Irish woman, in Potsdam in 1898. She was a commoner and therefore no wife for a future Duke of Coburg, and under the Royal Marriages Act of 1772 the match would have been no more valid than that of the Prince Regent and Mrs Fitzherbert in 1785. Had this been the case, and had Prince Alfred been instructed by his angry parents to annul the union, there would have been ironic parallels with the tragedy of Mayerling, when Crown Prince Rudolf of Austria-Hungary shot his pregnant mistress and then himself in January 1889, exactly ten years earlier. There is however no record of such a marriage, let alone any firm evidence that Alfred and Mabel ever met. In 1898 she was only fourteen years old, and when she married William Clarke Hadoke in 1910, she was described as a spinster, not a widow. While some might say that there is no smoke without fire, it can safely be assumed that this was no more than a fabrication.

However, like Rudolf, young Alfred was in the grip of venereal disease. The previous year, he had been dismissed from his regiment on the grounds of ill health and excessive drinking. By January 1899 he was painfully thin, unable to walk properly, appeared disorientated, and his speech was becoming incoherent. When Missy arrived at Gotha for the anniversary celebrations, she was horrified at the state of him, noting that he hardly appeared to recognise anybody any more, 'and often does not know what he says'. According to rumour, he had had an argument with his mother, got hold of a gun, and shot himself. It was suggested that at the start of the new year his parents did not realise how critical his condition was, and they believed that he was still well enough to go to Meran for a period of convalescence. Marie was less sympathetic than furious, and ordered that he be sent away to recover and then ponder his fate. It would be embarrassing to have him in the Schloss with so many guests and delegations present. According to Marie Mallet, a lady-in-waiting to Queen Victoria, the doctors told the Duchess that her son must not be moved or he would surely be dead within a week, but their warnings were brushed aside. However Marie disliked the Duke and Duchess, and her version of events needs to be viewed with caution. The more likely truth of the matter was revealed by a letter from Queen Victoria to Vicky, in which she said that 'none of the doctors thought he was likely to die soon and they had hopes he would recover ultimately.'[6]

The physicians evidently did not appreciate the seriousness of the ailing prince's condition. He was sent off to Meran in the Tyrol, accompanied by his French tutor and by Rose, who had been his valet for several years, as well as Dr Bankart, a naval surgeon whom his father had long known. Plans were made for him to spend a few weeks recovering in Egypt in the company of Ducky and Ernie. In view of the couple's marital problems, the prospect can hardly have filled the invalid with joy. Ducky was not over-sympathetic herself, and had refused to have him to stay at Darmstadt with them the previous year, on the grounds that she found him 'so dull'.[7]

On 6 February Affie was about to leave for Meran to see his son when a telegram arrived. The doctors' dire warnings had been proved correct; Alfred was dead. Affie and Marie were shattered, their feelings exacerbated by guilt at the thought that they had not realised the gravity of his case, and that he had slipped away with none of the family beside him – only his faithful tutor and a medical attendant.

Alfred was temporarily interred on 10 February at Friedenstein Church, Gotha. As the funeral procession entered the castle courtyard, the church bells pealed their sad toll, and muffled tones of a funeral march added to the gloom of a winter's day. For once Marie was almost as demonstrative in her grief as her husband. She sank to her knees as the march began, crossing herself several times and sobbing brokenly while her daughters knelt down beside her, 'whilst the bells seemed to be ringing in our heads and our hearts'.[8]

For years the exact manner of Alfred's death was kept secret.

Contemporary obituaries discreetly gave the cause of death as phthisis or consumption, and in due course the obituary notices of his parents added nothing more to this.

A postscript to this affair emerged some eighty-two years later. On 30 September 1981, a Mrs Irene Victoria Alexandra Louise Isabel Bush died in Miami, Florida. In the local papers' obituaries, much was made of this woman who was supposed to have been a great-granddaughter of Queen Victoria. According to the *Miami Herald*, she was born Lady Irene Fitzgerald Coburg in Carton, County Kildare, Ireland, on 28 February 1899, a great-granddaughter of the Queen and the daughter of Prince Alfred of Saxe-Coburg Gotha.[9] As with the matter of a marriage between the latter and Mabel Fitzgerald, no corroborative evidence for this has been traced, and one must assume that the story is without foundation.

Affie was completely broken by his son's death. From this time he drank more heavily, and his relations with Marie, which had hardly been harmonious for the last few years, worsened even more. As she had been largely responsible for his upbringing, he felt that she had much to answer for in the manner of his death. It now seemed that he was determined to live out the rest of his days which, he probably realised, were numbered, as far away from her as possible. It was thought that he now took steps to arrange his routine so that they would never spend another night under the same roof, and were unofficially separated at the time of his death.[10]

Queen Victoria was naturally full of sympathy for her son and daughter-in-law. 'To lose their only son, in whom their hopes and life were bound up, is fearful,' she wrote to Vicky. She had heard from Ernie that the grief-stricken Affie was 'in a dreadful state' the first time he went to see his son's body. However she was reassured when he sent a telegram to say he had 'returned from praying near my dear boy who looks so peaceful.'[11]

As winter dissolved into spring Affie took his sorrows and his own declining health to the sunnier climate of Cimiez. At his first meeting with Queen Victoria after his arrival, she noted, 'he was very upset and could barely speak'.[12] After composing himself, he was ready to discuss the problem which faced the family, and mother and son in particular. As young Alfred had died without issue, who was going to be his successor as Duke of Saxe-Coburg?

The Prince of Wales had long since renounced the succession for himself and his children, and now it fell to the Duke of Connaught and his son to prepare themselves for the possibility. Initially the Queen's reaction was one of gladness that her favourite son should eventually rule the duchy where her husband was born and raised. Without consulting the German Emperor, she gave her immediate consent to Arthur taking up his position as heir presumptive. In spite of the local Diets' enthusiasm for such a choice, Willy was very angry at not being asked for his permission. He insisted that the Duke of Connaught and his son would have to live in Germany and enter the army there, or else the *Reichstag* might pass a law declaring foreign princes incapable of succeeding to a German throne. Such a measure would have added to the complications which soured Affie's first few months as Duke, or might perhaps have even prevented him from taking up the inheritance at all. Even though Affie had spent a great deal of time in Germany before succeeding, he had been well aware that people resented the fact that he had not been brought up there. He warned that if German wishes were not complied with, it could result in his 'being turned out altogether'.[13]

Endless discussions ensued, some of a stormy nature. The Queen's lady-in-waiting Marie Mallet, who seems to have nursed a violent grudge against Affie for some reason, remarked disdainfully that the Duke of Coburg's life was not one to be accepted at any insurance office, but he talked as if certain of outliving the Duke of Connaught who was 'as hard as nails'.[14] Affie appreciated his brother's reluctance, while warning at the same time that German wishes had to be respected. Because of his English education and naval service he had experienced no little hostility on his own accession.

On 10 April 1899 the Diet at Gotha read out a declaration that the Duke of Connaught and his house were prepared to fulfil their duties towards their ancestral duchies, but as the weeks passed so did demands that they must come and live in Germany, and his sixteen-year-old son Arthur be educated there. Steps were made to provide the latter with a set of apartments in the ducal castles.

But the Duke of Connaught made no secret of the fact that he disliked the prospect of uprooting himself and his family, and giving up his army career. *Punch* published a cartoon of him with a caption taken from the libretto of Gilbert and Sullivan's *HMS Pinafore*: 'But in spite of all temptations to belong to other nations, He remains an Englishman.' He was strongly supported by his Duchess, who had been born a Prussian princess, a cousin of the late Emperor Frederick III but who had led a very unhappy life in Berlin and now felt herself almost as English as her husband.

Arthur and Affie had an official meeting with the Emperor at Wartburg Castle, Thuringia, at the end of April. William denied threatening to introduce a bill which would prevent the accession of foreign princes to German thrones, but said he had merely emphasised that national feeling demanded the Coburg heir apparent should serve in the German army; have his principal residence in that country; and send his son to be educated there. The same view, he said, had been expressed to him by King Albert of Saxony. If the Duke of Connaught decided to remain a British prince and abrogate his claims in favour of his son or nephew Charles, Duke of Albany, everyone in Germany would consider it a natural decision, but it was impossible that the heir to the duchy could still hold a commission in the British army.

After due consideration and further consultation with the Queen, who deprecated her grandson's tiresome interference, the Duke of Connaught renounced the succession, as he would not give up his British army career, and in any case Her Majesty would not allow it. Young Arthur, she added, could not renounce his claims until he was twenty-one, 'which he is then sure to do', but it was impossible 'to take him away from his English education for an improbable eventuality'. Moreover the Duke did not want to abandon responsibility for his son's schooling by sending him abroad.

By the time Affie joined the rest of the family at Windsor Castle in May for the Queen's eightieth birthday dinner, the problem was nearing a solution. The Duke of Connaught finally renounced the claims of both himself and his son, and the fourteen-year-old Duke of Albany was chosen as Affie's heir. It was said that Prince Arthur of Connaught had helped to bring this about by going to see his fellow Etonian cousin Charles and threatening him with a good thrashing if he did not submit himself forthwith as the Coburg candidate, although they younger boy must have realised that there had always been the possibility of his becoming heir, like it or not. In June the matter was confirmed, with a proviso that should Charles have no heir or die unmarried the succession would revert to Arthur of Connaught.

Affie wanted to adopt Charlie as his heir, but his mother Helen, the widowed Duchess of Albany, would not consider the idea. Her doubts about her brother-in-law's suitability were confirmed when she, Charlie and her daughter Alice joined him for tea one afternoon at Rheinhardsbrunn and they were shocked to discover him drinking champagne already. Affie would not offer them a home nearby, as he wanted the boy to live with him. As the Diet insisted on the new heir living and being educated in Germany, and as Helen would not allow her son to be separated from her, they based themselves in a suite of rooms at Stuttgart Palace lent to them by King William of Württemberg. Charlie left Eton, and after some family argument Emperor William arranged for him to attend Leichterfelde military cadet school. Sandra's husband Ernest Hohenlohe was appointed Charlie's co-guardian in the duchies, and his regent in the event of Affie's death before he attained his majority.

That Christmas Affie and Marie had Missy under their roof again, but it was not for the happiest of reasons. Missy had been forced to employ a governess for her eldest son, an ugly and brusque-mannered British woman who rejoiced in stirring up trouble in the palace. Between them, she and Queen Elizabeth did all they could at court to keep alive the gossip about and scandal of the Crown Princess's affair with Zizi Cantacuzino, which was only terminated when King Carol exiled him and sent Missy away from Roumania on indefinite leave. As she was carrying her third child, Marie suggested that she should come to Germany for her confinement, and at Gotha she gave birth to a second daughter on 9 January 1900. Named Marie after her mother and grandmother, the thriving baby was the last great joy that Affie was to know.

By this time his health had deteriorated to a serious degree. Princess Alice of Albany, who later became Countess of Athlone, described his violin performances at this time in her memoirs some sixty years later:

> Full of confidence and old vintage, Uncle Alfred would succumb to [his guests'] flattery and oblige with a few of his favourite selections. Those who were adequately anaesthetized by his wine applauded at the wrong moment. Others, who had been more abstemious, suffered all they deserved from the erratic movements of the bow over the strings, which he fingered with exuberant originality but with little regard for the score.[15]

Such a description of the ducal soirees would have been comic if it was not so cruel, for during his last two years Affie was a very sick man, paying the price for years of heavy drinking and smoking.

On 17 January he left Gotha for a four-week visit to the Russian court at St Petersburg, accompanied by his daughter Sandra and her husband Ernest, while Marie stayed behind at Gotha with Missy, Ducky and Ernie. After undertaking cures in Egypt and Hungary, he returned to Coburg in the spring of 1900, but it was evident to those close to him that there could be little hope. Though they had drifted apart and seen little of each other in recent months, Marie was shocked to see the physical state he was in, and even more so when she realised that they were close to bankruptcy. She had been warned about a year earlier of 'new and terrible financial troubles' in his affairs, and to her it was 'an absolute *cauchemar* (nightmare)'.[16] Later she learned that his creditors were planning to descend on them and claim the Palais Edinburg. In order to forestall such a humiliating occurrence she bought the property from her husband – who by this time was too unwell to care very much – and settled his debts, with the generous assistance of Queen Victoria, who contributed £95,000.[17]

In May 1900 he went to take the waters at Herculesbad. The reason given was that he had been advised to do so for the sake of his rheumatism, but the closest members of his family knew that the trouble went deeper than that. Soon after he arrived, he began to suffer from severe throat problems. By the end of the month he was unable to swallow, and he could only be fed by tube. On 22 June a group of eminent specialists held a consultation at Vienna and discovered a growth of carcinomatous type at the root of the tongue, so advanced as to render any operation useless.

Thirteen years before, doctors and laryngologists had diagnosed cancer of the larynx in Affie's brother-in-law, Crown Prince Frederick William, who had at the time been only a few months older than Affie was now. Affie was probably kept in ignorance of the true state of his health, but Marie and the others who were informed knew only too well the physical anguish that had marked Fritz's last few months and would undoubtedly blight Affie's remaining days as well. His breathing would become progressively more difficult, the heart would have to work twice as hard, eating and drinking would be agonising exercises of persuasion on the one hand and great courage on the other, and his senses of taste and smell would gradually disappear. Even as late as June, the newspapers were speculating about a family visit to England by the Duke of Saxe-Coburg, and while staying in Paris Marie wrote to her daughter to say that she was expecting him to join them in London, though in view of his state of health she did not know when he would be well enough to travel.

However, early in July, three months after returning to Roumania, Missy was warned that he was dying. At the end of the previous month she had been bitterly distressed at his refusal to receive her or anyone in the immediate family. Marie warned her that his condition had made him very irritable and unwilling to see people at all, although he assured her by letter that he was recovering and had been advised by an Austrian doctor that he needed another three weeks to do so. A few days later, Affie surprised them all by sending a message that he wished Nando to go and visit him instead. Marie believed that it was because he wanted to have a last opportunity of telling him that he and others at the Roumanian court would have to treat Missy better in future – 'but it is so unlike him!'[18] Although he might have been a rather remote husband and father, now that he knew he did not have long to live, he probably wanted to take this chance of performing one last service for his daughter.

The Crown Prince of Roumania duly went to Coburg to see his father-in-law, and found him being fed by a tube. The doctors told him that even if they operated on him and removed the tongue, it would still be too late to save him. Desperate to try and reconcile her parents, Missy asked her mother if she would write him a cheerful letter, but not try to see him, as that 'would only excite him more'.[19]

At Windsor and Osborne the summer had been one of almost unrelieved gloom. Britain was at war with the Boers in South Africa, and as British military reverses gradually gave way to victory, so her popularity plunged on the continent. The Queen had been forced to abandon her customary spring holiday on the French Riviera because of European hostility, while on a train journey through Brussels in April the Prince and Princess of Wales had been fortunate to escape an attempt on their lives. Meanwhile, at Friedrichshof, Vicky was spending much of her time in bed, slowly dying from a painful disease which proved to be cancer of the spine.

With these sorrows weighing heavily on her, the Queen's family were anxious to spare her further upsets in her increasingly frail old age. Not until 25 July did she receive a telegram from the physicians, initially withheld from her, saying that her second son's condition was hopeless. 'The malady is incurable, and alas! One can only too well guess at its nature!'[20]

While Affie himself was kept in ignorance as long as possible, he knew that his case was hopeless. With the pitiful example of his brother-in-law, the late German Emperor Frederick, never far from his mind, he probably longed for a speedy release from the constant excruciating pain. Fritz had borne and fought against the merciless disease for a very long time, but as the imperial German Crown Prince on whose survival so much had depended, he had everything to live for. In Affie's case, there was no reason to cheat the grave in the same way. He no longer served in the Royal Navy he had so loved; his only son had died in miserable circumstances; his marriage had not been happy for a long time; and he was no longer well enough to take his guests hunting in the magnificent ducal forests, one of the few solaces of his oppressively dull life in Germany.

Those who had commented on the close resemblance between Affie and the Prince Consort, had they still been alive in 1900, would have appreciated yet another similarity. 'I do not cling to life,' Albert had confessed to Queen Victoria. 'I am sure, if I had a severe illness, I should give up at once.'[21] Now, such words might just have surely been said by his second son. The immediate family were warned that he had no more than six months left to live, and maybe much less than that. Marie and Baby Bee had recently spent a month at Windsor as guests of the Queen, only returning to Coburg on 17 July. They were shocked to hear that he was so ill.

Ten days later Affie returned to his duchy, a brave but pathetic figure gasping for breath. It was fitting that he should ask to be taken to the Rosenau, that beloved place in which his father had been born. Here he could sit in the garden when sunshine permitted, gazing fondly at – but now unable to smell – the roses which Marie had planted and tended so lovingly.

That weekend he was racked with the agonies of semi-suffocation, and the doctors prepared to operate; a tracheotomy, or incision in the windpipe, would be vital to facilitate his breathing. On the Sunday night he slept fairly well, but woke feeling weak and drowsy next morning. Monday proved to be a fine summer's day, remaining warm for much of the evening. Affie had been taken out to sit on the garden terrace with his family, loath to leave this haven of peace and happy memories until the very last moment. As dusk began to fall, he was carried in a bath chair to the guardhouse, a small lodge on the estate where it was easier to nurse him. Here he had his supper, taken as had been the case with all his meals for the last two months through a tube, and then retired to rest with the minimum of assistance. His personal physician left him briefly to get his own supper, but was immediately called back by a valet.

On his return the doctor noticed that the patient's breathing was already slower. He summoned the family, and in their presence at about ten o'clock Affie passed away quietly in his sleep. His face, it was said, bore 'the expression of amiability and kindness which it wore all his life'.[22] He had died just seven days short of what would have been his fifty-sixth birthday. His wife Marie and their daughters Ducky, Sandra and Baby Bee were by his deathbed. Only Missy was too late to be with them at the very end.

Just one day before, Europe had been appalled by the assassination of King Humbert of Italy. Now this fresh and scarcely less-expected sorrow burst on England, Germany and above all on the grieving relations at Osborne. 'Oh, God! My poor darling Affie gone too!' mourned Queen Victoria, when Helena and Beatrice broke the news to her on Tuesday morning. 'My third grown-up child...it is hard at eighty-one!'[23]

As the news broke early that day, the Lord Mayor of London ordered that the great bell of St Paul's should toll, just as it had done many years before when the Prince Consort died. Within less than six months it would do so again for the passing of Queen Victoria herself, and a little more than six months after that, for her eldest daughter Vicky, the Empress Frederick, as well. Flags were flown at half-mast over government offices, public buildings, clubs and institutions throughout London and other cities. At Windsor the Union Jack on the Round Tower was also flown at half-mast, while the blinds of the private apartments in Victoria Tower, were drawn. At Berlin, the German court went into mourning for a fortnight, and warships in harbour at Kiel likewise lowered their flags to half-mast.

'What a mercy darling Alfred did not know the true nature of his illness, and the utter hopelessness of it,' the Empress Frederick wrote to Queen Victoria two weeks later. 'Dear Alfred was spared mental pain and anxiety and like Fritz was convinced that he *would* improve!'[24]

The funeral was held at Coburg on the morning of Saturday, 4 August, at the Church of St Moritz, where Affie had lain in state in a verdant bower of summer palms and flowers. His orders, medals and regalia were spread around the raised coffin on black velvet cushions; the chancel was draped with black crêpe, and there was an overwhelming décor of the palms so beloved by interior decorators of the age. One of the guards of honour standing watch at one corner of the catafalque was his brother Arthur, Duke of Connaught, resplendent in Guards uniform, his bearskin standing out among the formidable array of German *pickelhaubes* and the varied headgear of foreign royalties. Among them were Emperor William II; sixteen-year old Charlie, who now found himself Duke of Saxe-Coburg far sooner than he had imagined; Affie's son-in-law Ernest of Hohenlohe-Langenburg, now Prince Regent; George, Duke of York, Affie's favourite nephew; Prince Arthur of Connaught, who had so nearly ended up becoming the next Duke of Saxe-Coburg himself; the Duke of Sparta, heir to the throne of Greece; and representatives from nearly all the German courts. Few grieved more bitterly than Bertie, who had left for Coburg with Alix and their son Georgie almost as soon as the news reached England, and who returned home afterwards in one of his increasingly familiar moods of black depression which so dismayed his entourage. Grief at the loss of his beloved brother was exacerbated by discovering that at Friedrichshof his favourite sister was seriously ill, and perhaps by a foreboding that these bereavements were taking their toll on their increasingly frail mother.

The Times correspondent faithfully reported that 'the chancel had been transformed into a veritable grove of palm trees. The spacious Gothic church presented a most harmonious appearance. The steps of the sanctuary were covered in a black carpet and the same draped the walls, the gloom of which was relieved at intervals by fresh green pine sprays and a silver frieze'. The nave and galleries were 'hung with drapery embossed with ermine' – an unmistakable sign that they were in the presence of a Peer of the Realm.[25]

Somehow the wreaths rather pathetically showed their givers' character down to the last petal. The one consisting of scarlet geraniums, white stocks and heliotrope, arranged in a scheme of red, white and blue, was 'From his sorrowing Mother', and was placed at the head of the coffin. Bertie and Alix presented one made of white lilies, nestling in garlands of white ribbon with a small verse attached: 'Sleep on beloved and take thy rest. Now comes peace. Goodnight.' Too ill to attend herself, Vicky sent a tribute of pine and fir sprays. A great parterre of lilies, lily-of-the-valley and white carnations round an immense anchor was inscribed:'The Navy mourns for its gifted Admiral of the Fleet'.

At ten o'clock that night a battalion of the 96th Prussian Regiment lined up outside the church. In deep silence, against the flickering light of a sea of torches held by citizens of the duchy, the hearse arrived, drawn by four black horses. The coffin was brought out on the shoulders of twelve NCOs who placed it on the hearse, which moved slowly away to the throb of the funeral march and the muffled roll of drums. The route was lined with silent townsfolk, dark shadows between the stakes of pine torches perfuming the warm summer night.

So, like his father, Affie lies in his adopted land. It would not have been right to bring him home to Windsor, since he was now officially a federal German prince. In death his birthright became null and void. His last resting place is the vault in the family mausoleum in the cemetery on the hillside overlooking Coburg. There young Alfred was also laid to rest beside him, and many years later his widow as well. Over the vault are two large blocks of marble ordered by the grieving Queen Victoria. Affie's tomb is very simple, containing merely his names, titles, dates and places of birth and death, all in German, and at the foot a crowned anchor entwined with a rope.

Several memorial services were held in England on the same day as the funeral, at St Paul's Cathedral, York Minster, Devonport, Portsmouth, and Edinburgh. The one held at Osborne, attended by the Queen and her daughters Helena and Beatrice, was the most pathetic. It took place in the private chapel, while minute guns were fired from the guardship HMS *Australia*, anchored off Cowes. Everyone who attended was affected by the sight of the grieving Queen, old and bent in her chair, dressed as ever entirely in black. That same day another service was held in the Chapel Royal, Windsor, attended by the Princess of Wales and her unmarried daughter Victoria, as well as the Duchess of Argyll, the Duchess of York, and various dignitaries including Lord Salisbury and Lord Rosebery. At Devonport dockyard chapel, naval and military commanders in the south west paid their tributes in person, while at nearby St Andrew's Church, Plymouth, the mayor, corporation and other civic dignitaries were present. At noon a 55-gun salute was fired by ships of war in the harbour at Plymouth.

Only one memorial to Affie is to be seen in England. It is a plaque in relief of his profile in the parish church at Sandringham, placed there by command of his brother, by then Edward VII. A granite Celtic cross was erected to his memory, bearing the dedication 'by his sorrowing mother' in the grounds of Balmoral in 1901, but she did not live to see it.

Many kind tributes appeared in the press. An officer who had served under him wrote that his brother seamen esteemed him as a capable officer who never shirked his own work or permitted others to shirk theirs, but it was his kindly nature and thorough honesty that won their affections. It has been truly said that the Duke loved the Navy and the Navy was proud of him.[26]

A perceptive journalist added his comments in a graceful manner which Affie would have surely appreciated:

Naturally it was a sore trial for Prince Alfred to give up the sea and the life which he really enjoyed, and to settle upon a Principality, with the entire absence of adventure and initiative which must necessarily mark that position in the existing state of things in Germany. That the Duke could make himself so good a German Prince, after his life of travel and excitement as an English Admiral, says much of his strength of will and his sense of duty.[27]

Another called him 'a man of many gifts, an accomplished musician, a discerning connoisseur in art', while admitting than 'in disposition he was less accessible as he grew older than his brothers, though as a boy he was accounted quite the brightest of the Royal Family'. He also gently suggested that the Duke's ill-health 'may be taken as the explanation of his gradual withdrawal within himself; he aged outwardly with a rapidity that was sad to look upon'.[28]

The independent spirit which the court painter Franz Xaver Winterhalter had seen in two-year-old Affie, staggering across the carpet and making his own way across the family group in the celebrated family group portrait of 1846, was to become a recurring theme throughout his life. For most of his fifty-five years he led an energetic, colourful existence; he was his 'own man' through and through. That he was not well-known in the land of his birth was not merely due to his reserved nature and a tendency, much exaggerated by other writers, to be arrogant. He had considerable strength of character, marked intellectual gifts, and a practical mind which made him extremely proficient in his job; he was sagacious and careful in business; and, above all, he possessed the foremost requisite of a Prince of the Blood Royal – the capacity and opportunity to be a worthy ambassador for Britain.

Appendices

Charles, Duke of Saxe-Coburg Gotha

For nearly five years, the duchies of Saxe-Coburg and Gotha were under the regency of Prince Ernest of Hohenlohe-Langenburg. Duke Charles assumed control of the administration on his twenty-first birthday, 19 July 1905. Three months later he married Princess Victoria Adelaide, eldest daughter of the Duke of Schleswig-Holstein and niece of the German Empress Victoria Augusta. Their eldest daughter Sybille married into the Swedish royal family and her son Prince Carl Gustav ascended the throne in 1973. Their youngest son Frederick-Josias, born in 1918, succeeded Charles as Hereditary Head of the House of Coburg.

Although Charles's marriage was happy, the rest of his life was scarcely less miserable than that of other contemporary German princes. In 1914 he found himself compelled to fight for the Fatherland against his English cousins, and was forced to abdicate after the downfall of the Second Reich. When Hitler rose to power he showed some temporary sympathy with Nazism. After the Second World War he was tried *in absentia*, being in hospital with an eye ailment at the time, for pro-Nazi activities, found guilty and heavily fined. He died in March 1954 aged sixty-nine, broken in spirit and crippled by arthritis.

Dukes of Edinburgh

Prince Alfred was the fifth prince to bear the title Duke of Edinburgh. It had first been conferred in 1726, on Prince Frederick Lewis, eldest son of George II. He was made Prince of Wales three years later and died in 1751; his eldest son bore both titles until his accession to the throne as George III in 1760. Four years later George's brother Prince William Henry became Duke of Gloucester and Edinburgh. On the latter's death in 1805, he was succeeded by his son Prince William Frederick, who died in 1834. The title remained unappropriated until conferred on Affie in 1866.

After his death there was no Duke of Edinburgh for forty-seven years. On 19 November 1947 the title was conferred on Lieutenant Philip Mountbatten, RN, who married Princess Elizabeth, heiress to the throne, the next day. Philip was the son of Prince Andrew of Greece, and therefore the grandson on his father's side of George I of Greece, who had been chosen for the vacant throne instead of Affie. On his mother's side, Philip was the grandson of Prince Louis of Battenberg, who had been encouraged by Affie to join the Royal Navy. In 1917, the year that anti-German feeling reached new heights, the name of Battenberg was anglicised to Mountbatten.

By a further coincidence, the first married home of Philip, Duke of Edinburgh, was Clarence House, which had been Affie's official London residence. On the accession of Philip's wife as Elizabeth II in 1952, it became the home of Queen Elizabeth the Queen Mother, who had been born on the day of Affie's funeral. She lived there until her death in 2002.

Marie, Duchess of Edinburgh

Marie stayed in England for a while after her husband's death. She was at Osborne at some stage during the final days of Queen Victoria's life, and the court circular of 16 January 1901 reported a little inaccurately that Her Majesty had 'driven out' the previous afternoon, accompanied by the Duchess of Saxe-Coburg and Gotha.[1] In fact the Queen had been placed in the carriage beside Marie as they sat in the porch waiting for the rain and fog to clear, but after it became apparent that the weather was not going to improve, the seriously ill sovereign was taken back to her bed, and never left it again.[2] After Affie's death, Marie spent more and more time at her charming house of Tegernsee, near Munich. The Sengerschloss stood on a hill overlooking the lake; although close to the Bavarian capital with its cornucopia of art galleries, museums and opera houses, it was a place of peace, similar to the Rosenau but more exclusively Marie's, free from memories of the past. She stayed there every summer, when not visiting friends and relations throughout Europe.

Though only forty-six when she was widowed, she had already become stout and elderly before her time. Nobody could persuade her to wear anything but her customary drab old-fashioned clothes, and she was merciless in reproving her smart daughters – not only grown-up, but also mothers themselves – for their 'sinful' love of finery. To Marie Buchanan, whose father Sir George was British Ambassador to St Petersburg early in the twentieth century, she was an awe-inspiring old lady, 'who was terrifyingly dictatorial, and shot questions at me in a gruff, abrupt voice, always making me feel inarticulate and self-conscious'.[3]

Marie's last journey to imperial Russia was undertaken just before the First World War, when she visited Ducky. Within a year of Queen Victoria's death in 1901 the then Grand Duchess of Hesse had scandalised most of the European courts by divorcing her husband, but both soon made happy second marriages, and in 1905 Ducky became Grand Duchess Kyril of Russia. Marie and Missy were also guests of Nicky and Alix at Tsarskoe-Selo, but the contrast with happy days of old was painful. Gone were the colossal family parties, picnics, receptions and reviews. There were no longer any friendly public appearances, with all the pomp and glitter that had been synonymous with the Romanovs. Instead, the imperial family lived a solitary and nervous life on their country estates, haunted by the ill-health of the haemophiliac Tsarevich Alexis, only appearing in St Petersburg when absolutely vital. They hardly ever entertained and only showed themselves 'outside' to a small faithful and trustworthy circle. Missy and her Mama came away sad and disturbed.

Thankfully Marie did not long survive the horrors of the Russian revolution and the cold-blooded butchering of so many of her relations. The few who were spared, more by accident than from any mercy on the part of the Bolsheviks, had to leave as quickly as possible with barely any luggage apart from such jewels as they could hide. The loss of her Russian income dealt her finances a major blow, and for a while she feared that she would not only be obliged to sell everything, including her horses, carriages, properties and houses, but she would also be declared bankrupt. Unaware of just how much the situation in Russia had altered after the collapse of the Romanov Empire, she asked Missy to seek the help of King George V in persuading the Soviet government to honour the provisions of her marriage treaty.

After severe gastric trouble and general declining health, she died in her sleep after a heart attack at the Hotel Dolder in Zurich on 25 October 1920, eight days after her sixty-seventh birthday. Her end was hastened, it was said, by receiving a letter scantily addressed to 'Frau Coburg'.

The Clarence House Sale

Marie had had to move out of Clarence House with little delay to make room for the Duke and Duchess of Connaught, but she had never been really happy in London, had described the house as 'hideous', and needed no persuasion to leave it all behind her. Moreover, after coming into his inheritance Edward VII wasted little time in ordering the sale of most of his brother's souvenirs, just as he was clearing out from Osborne and Windsor the accumulation of sixty years, as he probably could not bear to see all those reminders from happier and younger days. Marie must have made a clean sweep of her excess bric-á-brac then, or else when they had moved to Coburg. Few Russian items are mentioned in the 79-page auction catalogue of Affie's valuables and souvenirs, material witness of a royal life all over the world – unique in the nineteenth century.

The 'COLLECTION OF PORCELAIN, BRONZES, ARMS, JAPANESE LACQUER, AND OTHER SPECIMENS OF ORIENTAL ART, formed by H.R.H. The Duke of Edinburgh, K.G.' was made 'During his Cruise in H.M.S. Galatea'. The bottom of the title page reads: 'Also, the Collection of European China, Marbles, Bronzes, Pictures, Water-colour Drawings, and other Objects of Art and Vertu'. This catalogue, undated, is probably a copy for the use of the public at the 1901 sale. Some of the prices fetched are pencilled faintly in the margins. Both this and another catalogue, dated 1975, are in the British Museum. The prices marked may be those paid by the Museum, or possibly an unknown collector.

The first few pages list fifteen silver and nine gold trowels used for laying foundation stones, mostly from the Australian tour. Of particular interest is the one 'used in depositing the first stone of the Breakwater, Table Bay, the 17th of September, 1860'; it sold for 30 gns. There were costly presents from the Kherafa of Dacca, Maharajahs and Rajahs, princes and corporations and native communities and Indian railways and municipalities – from North India to Ceylon. From these, a 'Vase formed from an Emu's egg mounted in gold' fetched 125 gns; a 'Bison Horn mounted in gold as a cup, the lid set with a large topaz' 60 gns; and a 'Silver Hookah with tube of gold abroad, velvet holder and silver mouthpiece' 50 gns. From closer to home, an 'Ivory Paper-Knife mounted with engraved gold, surmounted by an enamelled crown, and set with diamonds, emeralds and other stones', presented by the Board of the Mersey Docks on 21 June 1866, was sold for 70 gns. The Victorian *piece de resistance* from among the trowels and caskets was 'A Cabinet of polished wood, mounted in frosted silver, with a group of native ferns, kangaroos, emus and fern wreaths, and with glazed recesses on each side, the front one containing a model of H.M.S. *Galatea* in Holdfast Bay; containing an address mounted in gold and silver, from the Civil Service of the Colony, the 1st November 1867'. Significantly no price is marked.

Next comes the group of Silver, with a few Russian items; a silver-gilt cup (8 gns), a knife and fork (30 gns), a silver-gilt salt pot (10 gns). A small cup with a view of the Kremlin went for 3 gns. In this section too are gifts such as Cowell's small gilt vase for matches, and the nostalgic 'Gold Cigarette case and Matchbox inscribed Jugenheim 11 July 1873', commemorating the engagement of Affie and Marie (30 gns).

There are four pages of Chinese porcelain but only a few prices, the highest (20 gns) being for 'A pair of White Crackle Jars with masks and ring handles and horses in blue in slight relief, mounted with bronze for lamps – on curved wood stands'. No dates or dynasties are mentioned.

Porcelain from Japan was apparently much more popular, at least with the owner of this catalogue. Practically every item on the three pages listed is priced, from 1 gn. For seven eggshell cups painted blue and covered with wickerwork, to 45 gns for 'a Pair of Large Japanese Jars...painted with dragons and male and female heads with crimson, black and gold borders'.

The nine Chinese enamels sold well, with a Ming square vase depicting birds and flowers on a turquoise ground selling for 10 gns. A 'Large Japanese Incense-burner in three stages each with representations in high relief, with cascades, trees, flowers and birds; in the middle a man on shore invoking a dragon', presented to Affie by the Mikado, went for 150 gns. A pair of 'Japanese Cisterns inlaid with silver' fetched the same.

One may pass over the pages of carvings in ivory and wood, all given by eastern potentates, only mentioning what would be almost worth their weight in gold today as historical curios of a lost empire; 'A photograph album of sandalwood containing numerous photographs of Indian celebrities' (50 gns), and another, embossed with 'an ivory medallion portrait of H.R.H. containing views of India' (40 gns). Both were originally presented by the Maharajah of Vizianagram.

Jade comes next, with a set of carved agate chess men fetching 4 gns; a folding stand of green jade inlaid with gold and enamel 40 gns; and a green agate cup with silver gilt feet 10 gns. A page and a half list Medals and Coins, most of which sold for only 5 gns and 10 gns in small lots. The highest price, for three gold Japanese coins and '6 gold and 12 silver coins' was 19 gns. A specimen of 'Native Gold in Quartz 22 ozs. From the Mine at Ballarat' (Victoria, Australia) fetched 26 gns, as did twenty-eight assorted nuggets; a piece of Quartz 'containing Gold' 2 gns. Eleven 'Indian Marbles' went for 12 gns, an Embroidered White Crape Shawl 5 gns, and a 'white Satin Coverlet embroidered with birds and flowers' 20 gns. 'A carriage Clock ingraved ormolu case, presented 6th August 1846', a gift on Affie's second birthday, is unpriced.

Among the most picturesque items of porcelain were a pair of Berlin plates, each with pink and gold borders and painted with a view of Rheinhardsbrunn (6 gns), and 'A large Punch-Bowl painted with the Modern Midnight Conversation, the cover surmounted by a cut melon' (12 gns). There were several small examples of Naples, Venice, Sevres, Tornay, Vienna, English, French and Majolica ware, mostly unexceptional apart from a dish painted with an 'Indian Nautch girl in pink' (25 gns). Ten pieces of glass, one Venetian, all fetched modest prices – less than five guineas each.

'Bijouterie etc.' was delightfully varied. Eleven small charms went for 15 gns; an enamelled watch-key formed a pistol lavishly set with enamels and diamonds only fetched 5 gns. A small gold pencil-case with chain 'inscribed and dated Malta Dec. 27th 1858' sold for 1 gn, a silver-gilt ring chased with the Crucifixion inscribed 'D. Martino Luthero Caterina V. Boren 1525' 10 gns (which seems a modest price), and two filigree cigar cases 50 gns. Among decorative furniture, the most remarkable was a 'Louis XVI library table of black wood mounted with mouldings and ornaments of chased or-molu' (250 gns).

Five miniatures fetched very varied prices. One of George, Prince of Wales, painted in 1794, was sold for 4 gns; one by Conway of William, Duke of Clarence (1791) 20 gns; and a rather incongruous pair, one portraying the Duchess of Kent and the other Mrs Fitzherbert, 40 gns altogether. A group of eighteen photographs, then of almost negligible value, remained unpriced. Engravings portrayed various admirals, ships, members of the family, the Great Exhibition, and 'The Galatea among icebergs in the Southern Ocean' (2 gns). More in demand were the Watercolours. 'Galatea reefing topsails' sold for 60 gns; 'Acropolis at Athens' 50 gns; a set of twenty 'Costumes of the British Army' 60 gns. These prices pale into insignificance beside the 500 gns for fifteen drawings by Mr Brierley, the artist who illustrated *The Cruise of the Galatea*.

Seven terracotta busts were sold for 5 gns apiece, among them one of Affie by Stede of Edinburgh. Four marbles, one of Marie, were unpriced.

There are eight pages of arms, each item enthusiastically marked, but the prices have worn away. At the end of the last page is penciled 2,500 gns, presumably the total for items bought, perhaps all purchased by one buyer. They include 'A dagger with horn handles, massive chased gold sheath...and gold lace belt...' and a 'Sword with enamelled gold handle set with diamonds, watered blade, cross-guard damascened with gold and gold-mounted sheath', let alone 'the Dagger with walrus-tooth handle and blade set with pearls', another sword with 'a gold handle set with turquoises and rubies', and a Scimitar with an ivory handle mounted with massive gold tigers' heads, jeweled...channelled throughout to receive pearls which flow from hilt to point'.

The last page is headed Natural History, first being 'Heads set with Horns'. There were fourteen items from Africa, including hartebeest, gnu, eland, kudu, gemsbok and buffalo from the Free State; two from India; twenty-two red deer from the Highlands; and one American elk. 'Horns mounted, not Heads', were mainly rhino horns from India. 'Skins and

Rigs' brought the sale to a close, with six Indian tigers, one African lion, one Australian kangaroo, and one Russian wolf, making the total for this section £850.

The total of the whole sale, according to the jottings by this unknown owner of the catalogue, was £14,429.

The Children of the Duke and Duchess of Edinburgh

Alfred Alexander William Ernest Albert, Hereditary Prince of Saxe-Coburg Gotha. Born 15 October 1874 at Buckingham Palace; died 6 February 1899 at Meran, Tyrol.

Marie Alexandra Victoria ('Missy'). Born 29 October 1875 at Eastwell Park, Kent; died 18 July 1938 at Sinaia, Roumania. 10 January 1893, married Ferdinand of Hohenzollern-Sigmaringen, Crown Prince of Roumania (1865-1927, King of Roumania 1914-27). Three sons, including King Carol II of Roumania, and three daughters.

Victoria Melita ('Ducky'). Born 25 November 1876, at San Antonio, Malta; died 2 March 1936 at Amorbach, Germany. 19 April 1894, married Ernest, Grand Duke of Hesse and the Rhine (1868-1937). One daughter (and one stillborn son). Marriage dissolved 1901. 8 October 1905, married Grand Duke Kyril Vladimirovich of Russia (1876-1938), One son, Grand Duke Vladimir, later head of the house of Romanov, and two daughters.

Alexandra Louise Olga Victoria ('Sandra'). Born 1 September 1878 at Coburg; died 16 April 1942 at Schwabisch-Hall, Germany. 20 April 1896, married Ernest of Hohenlohe-Langenburg (1863-1950), Two sons, and three daughters.

Stillborn son, born 13 October 1879 at Eastwell Park.

Beatrice Leopoldine Victoria ('Baby Bee'). Born 20 April 1884 at Eastwell Park; died 13 July 1966 at Sanlucar de Barrameda, Spain. 15 July 1909, married Don Alfonso, Infante de Orleans y Bourbon (1886-1975), three sons.

Genealogical Tables

The House of Guelph, 1714–1840;
The House of Saxe-Coburg Gotha, 1840–1917.

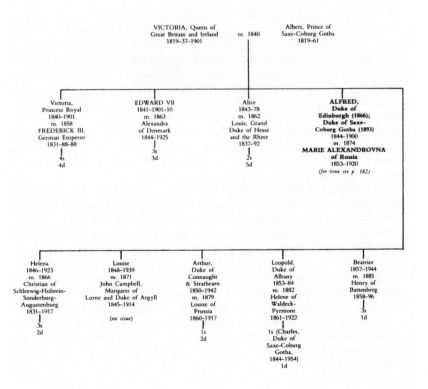

VICTORIA, Queen of
Great Britain and Ireland
1819–37–1901   m. 1840

Albert, Prince of
Saxe-Coburg Gotha
1819–61

Victoria,
Princess Royal
1840–1901
m. 1858
FREDERICK III,
German Emperor
1831–88–88
4s
4d

EDWARD VII
1841–1901–10
m. 1863
Alexandra
of Denmark
1844–1925
3s
3d

Alice
1843–78
m. 1862
Louis, Grand
Duke of Hesse
and the Rhine
1837–92
2s
5d

ALFRED,
Duke of
Edinburgh (1866);
Duke of Saxe-
Coburg Gotha (1893)
1844–1900
m. 1874
MARIE ALEXANDROVNA
of Russia
1853–1920
(for issue see p. 182)

Helena
1846–1923
m. 1866
Christian of
Schleswig-Holstein-
Sonderburg-
Augustenburg
1831–1917
3s
2d

Louise
1848–1939
m. 1871
John Campbell,
Marquess of
Lorne and Duke of Argyll
1845–1914
(no issue)

Arthur,
Duke of
Connaught
& Strathearn
1850–1942
m. 1879
Louise of
Prussia
1860–1917
1s
2d

Leopold,
Duke of
Albany
1853–84
m. 1882
Helene of
Waldeck-
Pyrmont
1861–1922
1s (Charles,
Duke of
Saxe-Coburg
Gotha,
1844–1954)
1d

Beatrice
1857–1944
m. 1885
Henry of
Battenberg
1858–96
3s
1d

The House of Holstein-Gottorp-Romanov

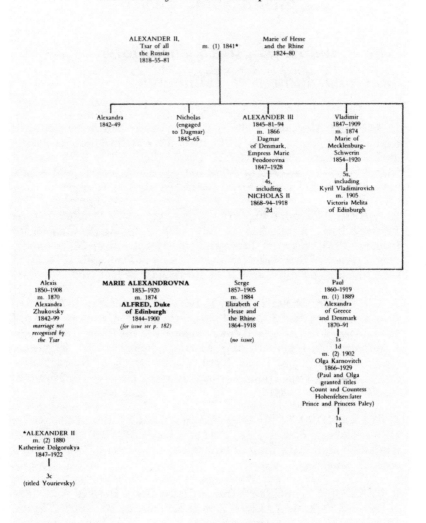

ALEXANDER II,
Tsar of all
the Russias
1818–55–81

m. (1) 1841*

Marie of Hesse
and the Rhine
1824–80

Alexandra
1842–49

Nicholas
(engaged
to Dagmar)
1843–65

ALEXANDER III
1845–81–94
m. 1866
Dagmar
of Denmark,
Empress Marie
Feodorovna
1847–1928

4s,
including
NICHOLAS II
1868–94–1918
2d

Vladimir
1847–1909
m. 1874
Marie of
Mecklenburg-
Schwerin
1854–1920

5s,
including
Kyril Vladimirovich
m. 1905
Victoria Melita
of Edinburgh

Alexis
1850–1908
m. 1870
Alexandra
Zhukovsky
1842–99
*marriage not
recognised by
the Tsar*

MARIE ALEXANDROVNA
1853–1920
m. 1874
**ALFRED, Duke
of Edinburgh**
1844–1900
(for issue see p. 182)

Serge
1857–1905
m. 1884
Elizabeth of
Hesse and
the Rhine
1864–1918

(no issue)

Paul
1860–1919
m. (1) 1889
Alexandra
of Greece
and Denmark
1870–91

1s
1d
m. (2) 1902
Olga Karnovitch
1866–1929
(Paul and Olga
granted titles
Count and Countess
Hohenfelsen:later
Prince and Princess Paley)

1s
1d

*ALEXANDER II
m. (2) 1880
Katherine Dolgorukya
1847–1922

3c
(titled Yourievsky)

Acknowledgements

I wish to acknowledge the gracious permission of Her Majesty The Queen to republish certain material of which she owns the copyright; and the generous help of Earl Mountbatten of Burma; Lady Elizabeth Millicent, Duchess of Sutherland; Lady Zia Wernher; His Imperial Highness Grand Duke Vladimir of Russia; and Lord Hampton.

For access to, and permission to publish, from other unpublished journals and correspondence and illustrations, and general assistance, I wish to thank Gerhard Schreier, Coburg Historical Society; Wolfram Trötsch, Coburg State Tourist Office; Freiherr von Adrian-Werberg, Bayerisches Staatsarchiv, Coburg; the Trustees of the Broadlands Archives, Romsey, Hampshire; the staffs of the Imperial College of Science and Technology, British Library, Naval Historical Library, Public Record Office, Royal College of Music, National Portrait Gallery, Victoria and Albert Museum, Royal Commission on Historical Manuscripts, Royal Society of Medicine, and National Maritime Museum, London; Scottish National Portrait Gallery, Edinburgh; the University Libraries of Birmingham and Reading; Staffordshire Record Office; County of Hereford & Worcester Record Office; State Library, Pretoria; Public Library, and Cape Provincial Library Service, Cape Town, Johannesburg Public Library, and Knysna Museum, Cape Province; Det Kongelige Bibliotek, Rigsbibliotheket, Risarkivet, and Tøjhusmuseet, Copenhagen; Vejen Public Library, Askov High School Library, and Slavisk Institut, Aarhus, Denmark; National Library of Australia, Canberra; and National Library of Malta.

I would also like to acknowledge the friendly advice and generous help of E. M. Almedingen; Theo Aronson; Alan Barnard; Georgina Battiscombe; Arturo Beeche; Daphne Bennett; Juliet Burton; Claudia Craig-Potter; Marlene Eilers-Koenig; F. S. Fitzgerald-Bush; Sir Roger Fulford; Paul Goudime; Rear-Admiral Wilfred Graham; Coryne Hall; Richard Hough; Irma Jordaan; Anita Leslie; Elizabeth Longford; Marvin Lyons; Arnold McNaughton; John Marriott; Paul Minet; Hugie Negus; John A. S. Phillips; Robin Piguet; Eric Rosenthal; Karen Roth-Nicholls; J. B. Sultana;

Joris van den Worm; Wing Commander Guy and Kate Van der Kiste; Dr Igor Vinogradoff; Ian Vorres; Katrina Warne; Gerrit Wessels; Barrie White; Sue Woolmans; and Charlotte Zeepvat. In particular I would also like to thank my wife Kim for all her help and support.

Sir Roger Fulford, CVO, died on 18 May 1983, while the first version of this book was being completed. On its first publication, Bee Jordaan and I took the opportunity not only to acknowledge the generous assistance he gave each of us in his last years and his keen interest in the work while under progress, but also to place on record our considerable debt to his books on the Victorian royal family, without which our knowledge today of the period would be very much the poorer.

Reference Notes

Abbreviations

BDC Beloved and Darling Child, edited by Agatha Ramm
DC Dearest Child, edited by Roger Fulford
Dg C Darling Child, edited by Roger Fulford
D Ma Dearest Mama, edited by Roger Fulford
D Mi Dearest Missy, edited by Diana Mandache
EFS The Empress Frederick writes to Sophie, edited by Arthur Gould Lee
FL Further Letters of Queen Victoria, edited by Hector Bolitho
MR The Story of My Life, by Marie, Queen of Roumania
PA Prince Alfred, Duke of Edinburgh
PC Letters of the Prince Consort, edited by Kurt Jagow
QV Letters of Queen Victoria (with series and volume number)
YDL Your Dear Letter, edited by Roger Fulford

Authors (and titles, where necessary to avoid confusion) of books, or names of
   manuscript sources and periodicals, are given in every other case. All are fully
   cited in the bibliography.

Chapter 1

1. *The Listener* 20.11.1975, Lord Mountbatten interviewed by Kay Evans BBC
   Radio 4
2. Lyttelton 348
3. Bolitho, Prince Albert to Duke Ernest 6.8.1844, 72
4. *DC*, Queen Victoria to Princess Victoria 4.5.1859, 191
5. Woodham-Smith 268
6. Lyttelton 364
7. Ibid. 384
8. Ibid. 409-10
9. PA's Journal 14.1.1851
10. Ibid. 5.1.1852
11. Ibid. 23.6.1852
12. Ibid. 14-20.8.1852
13. Ibid. Nov 1852
14. Ibid. 18.4.1855
15. Magnus 14

16. *DC*, Queen Victoria to Princess Victoria 26.5.1858, 108
17. Bennett *Queen Victoria's Children* 81
18. *PC*, Prince Albert to Baron Stockmar 13.9.1855, 34

Chapter 2

1. Bolitho, Prince Albert to Duke Ernest undated, 169-70
2. Coburg MSS. PA to Alexandrine 6.12.1857
3. Corti *English Empress* 40
4. *DC*, Queen Victoria to Princess Victoria 10.2.1858, 38
5. Ibid. Queen Victoria to Princess Victoria 31.5.1858, 110
6. Martin IV 300-1
7. As 5 above
8. Coburg MSS. PA to Alexandrine 5.9.1858
9. *DC*, Queen Victoria to Princess Victoria 16.9.1858, 130
10. Ibid. Queen Victoria to Princess Victoria 1.10.1858, 134
11. Martin IV 30
12. *The Times* 30.12.1858
13. Mills 117
14. Coburg MSS. PA to Alexandrine 6.4.1859
15. *DC*, Queen Victoria to Princess Victoria 27.5.1859, 185
16. Ibid. Queen Victoria to Princess Victoria 5.4.1860, 243
17. Martin V 88
18. Johannesburg MSS
19. Martin V 232-3
20. *QV* I iii Queen Victoria to King Leopold 15.11.1860, 413

Chapter 3

1. Bolitho, Prince Albert to Duke Ernest 6.8.1861 217
2. *D Ma*, Queen Victoria to Crown Princess Frederick William 19.4.1862, 55
3. Ibid. Crown Princess Frederick William to Queen Victoria 6.9.1862, 104-5
4. *The Times* 24.1.1862
5. *QV* II i, Queen Victoria Memorandum 25.11.1862, 48
6. *The Times* 6.1.1863
7. Coburg MSS. PA to Alexandrine 16.3.1863
8. *DM*, Queen Victoria to Crown Princess Frederick William 19.5.1862, 213
9. Swartz 80
10. Fulford *Hanover to Windsor* 100
11. Kennedy, Lord Clarendon to the Duchess of Manchester 217
12. Bodleian MSS. PA to Lord Alfred Paget 27.11.1863
13. Zeepvat 42
14. Dormer, Queen Victoria to Howard Elphinstone 17.4.1864, 158
15. *D Ma*, Queen Victoria to Crown Princess Frederick William 6.5.1864, 328
16. Ibid. Queen Victoria to Crown Princess Frederick William, 12.9.1863, 267
17. Ibid. Queen Victoria to Crown Princess Frederick William, 11.5.1864, 331
18. *YDL*, Queen Victoria to Crown Princess Frederick William, 4.8.1866, 94
19. McClintock 95
20. Battiscombe 78

Chapter 4

1. Pakington MSS. PA to Sir John Pakington 22.9.1866
2. Ibid. 16.11.1866
3. *YDL*, Queen Victoria to Crown Princess Frederick William 9.2.1867, 120, 123
4. Ibid. Queen Victoria to Crown Princess Frederick William 15.2.1867, 123
5. Sutherland MSS. PA to Duchess of Sutherland 8.9.1867
6. Milner & Brierley 88-9
7. McKinlay 82
8. *Australian Dictionary of Biography*
9. *Reynolds's Newspaper* 24.5.1868
10. Dorner 219
11. Sanderson and Melville II 92
12. *YDL*, Queen Victoria to Crown Princess Victoria 30.5.1868, 192

Chapter 5

1. *YDL*, Queen Victoria to Crown Princess Frederick William 7.7.1868, 200
2. Ibid. Queen Victoria to Crown Princess Frederick William 10.7.1868, 201
3. Ibid. Crown Princess Frederick William to Queen Victoria 5.8.1868, 204
4. Ibid. Queen Victoria to Crown Princess Frederick William 29.9.1868, 207-8
5. Ibid. Crown Princess Frederick William to Queen Victoria 2.11.1868, 210
6. *The Times* 19.4.1869
7. Lee I 371
8. *QV* II i, Earl of Mayo to Queen Victoria 27.11.1869, 637
9. *YDL*, 279
10. Gladstone MSS. PA to Gladstone 13.7.1870
11. *Morning Post* 24.7.1871

Chapter 6

1. Longford *Victoria RI* 385
2. Cullen 144-6; Longford *Victoria RI* 386
3. Ponsonby, Arthur 87
4. Weintraub *Importance* 177-8
5. Battiscombe 116-7
6. Gladstone MSS. PA to Gladstone 27.11.1871
7. Stanley *Later Letters* 10.12.1871, 147-8
8. Ibid. 17.12.1871, 150-1
9. Marie of Erbach-Schonberg 110
10. *YDL*, Queen Victoria to Crown Princess Frederick William 7.8.1867, 147
11. *Dg C*, Queen Victoria to Crown Princess Frederick William 22.1.1873, 74-5
12. Ibid., Queen Victoria to Crown Princess Frederick William 23.5.1873, 92
13. *QV* II ii, Queen Victoria's Journal 11.7.1873, 261
14. *Dg C*, Queen Victoria to Crown Princess Frederick William 12.7.1873, 101; Longford, Victoria RI 393
15. *FL*, Queen Victoria to Empress Augusta 16.7.1873, 195
16. *Dg C*, Queen Victoria to Crown Princess Frederick William 19.7.1873
17. Sutherland MSS. PA to Duchess of Sutherland 6.7.1873
18. Longford *Victoria RI* 394
19. *Reynolds's Newspaper* 3.8.1873

Chapter 7

1. *Dg C*, Queen Victoria to Crown Princess Frederick William 2.8.1873, 105
2. Stanley *Later Letters* Jan. 1874, 200
3. Ibid. 203-4
4. Ibid. 205
5. Ibid. 210
6. Ibid. 23.1.1874, 215
7. Loftus 88
8. Stanley *Later Letters* 23.1.1874, 217
9. Ibid. 27.1.1874, 220
10. *Dg C*, Queen Victoria to Crown Princess Frederick William 2.2.1874, 17
11. *Daily News* 6.3.1874
12. Dg C 131-2; QV II ii 328
13. Longford *Victoria RI* 404
14. Buchanan, Meriel 115
15. Kuhn, Henry Ponsonby to Lady Ponsonby 8.9.1874, 169
16. *FL,* Queen Victoria to Empress Augusta 25.11.1874, 202
17. Ridley 97
18. *D Mi*, Duchess of Edinburgh to Crown Princess Marie 17.7.1893, 129
19. Cornwallis-West 181
20. Ponsonby, Mary 100-1
21. Sullivan & Flower 71
22. Jacobs 74
23. *Dg C*, Queen Victoria to Crown Princess Frederick William 23.9.1874, 153-4
24. MR I 47
25. *Ibid.* 34-5
26. *Vinogradoff MSS.* Grand Duchess Marie to Prince Vladimir Meschersky 24.2.1875

Chapter 8

1. *QV* II ii, PA to Queen Victoria 31.7.1876, 473
2. *Malta Times & United Services Gazette* 2.12.1876
3. Ibid. 20.1.1877
4. *United Services Gazette* 1.6.1878
5. Chilston 123-4
6. *The Times* 12.12.1878
7. Coburg MSS. PA to Alexandrine 4.1.1879
8. Chilston 137
9. Sutherland MSS. PA to Duchess of Sutherland 6.7.1880
10. Ibid. 11.7.1880
11. Dormer 11-3
12. Marie Louise 18
13. Cornwallis-West 182
14. Millar 233
15. *The Times* 13.12.1881
16. Private information
17. *The Times* 19.11.1883
18. Weintraub *Victoria* 475
19. Hough 84

Chapter 9

1. Ripon MSS. PA to Lord Ripon 8.3.1886
2. Ibid. 30.3.1886
3. Ibid. 2.5.1886
4. Broadlands MSS. PA to Louis of Battenberg 11.7.1886
5. Cornwallis-West 186
6. *QV* III i, PA to Henry Ponsonby 21.4.1888, 399-400
7. *MR* I 24
8. Private information – John A. S. Philips
9. Ponsonby, Arthur 349-50
10. Ibid. 350
11. *Dg C*, Queen Victoria to Crown Princess Frederick William 2.6.1872, 47

Chapter 10

1. Broadlands MSS. PA to Louis of Battenberg 2.10.1890
2. *Naval & Military Record* 25.10.1890
3. *Royal Cornwall Gazette* 23.10.1890
4. *D Mi*, Duchess of Edinburgh to Princess Marie of Edinburgh 20.4.1890, 60
5. Ibid. Duchess of Edinburgh to Princess Marie of Edinburgh 30.1.1891, 62
6. Gill, 'Duchess was too grand...' *Western Morning News* 8.4.1985
7. *MR* I 208
8. *Morning Post* 3.7.1891
9. *Reynolds's Newspaper* 25.10.1891
10. Ibid. 1.11.1891
11. *D Mi*, Duchess of Edinburgh to King Carol 24.6.1892, 67
12. Ibid. Duchess of Edinburgh to King Carol 10.10.1892, 68
13. *The Times* 25.1.1893
14. *D Mi*, Crown Princess Marie to Duchess of Edinburgh 1/12.4.1893, 92
15. *Naval & Military Record* 8.6.1893
16. Ibid. 21.8.1893
17. Coburg MSS. PA to Alexandrine 6.8.1893
18. *D Mi*, Duchess of Edinburgh to Crown Princess Marie 9.8.1893, 135
19. Ibid. Duchess of Edinburgh to Crown Princess Marie 15.8.1893, 136

Chapter 11

1. *MR* I 208
2. *The Times* 26.8.1893
3. *D Mi*, Duchess of Saxe-Coburg to Crown Princess Marie 30.8.1893, 138
4. James 290
5. Gladstone MSS. PA to Gladstone 19.11.1893
6. Ibid. 26.12.1893
7. *The Times* 6.2.1894
8. Ibid. 9.2.1894
9. *EFS* 150
10. *D Mi*, Duchess of Saxe-Coburg to Crown Princess Marie 30.8.1893, 138
11. *BDC*, Empress Frederick to Queen Victoria 2.9.1893, 161-2
12. *MR* I 224
13. Reid 140
14. St Aubyn 296
15. *EFS* 182
16. Reid 108

17. Longford *Darling Loosy* 242-3
18. *D Mi*, Duchess of Saxe-Coburg to Crown Princess Marie undated but probably December 1893, 147
19. Private information
20. *D Mi*, Duchess of Saxe-Coburg to Crown Princess Marie 13/25.1.1895, 208
21. Ibid. Duchess of Saxe-Coburg to Crown Princess Marie 10.9.1895, 246
22. Ibid. Duchess of Saxe-Coburg to Crown Princess Marie 13.1.1896, 247
23. Pope-Hennessy 325
24. *MR* II 237
25. Ibid. 241-2

Chapter 12

1. *D Mi*, Duchess of Saxe-Coburg to Crown Princess Marie 22.10.1897, 320
2. Reid 108
3. *D Mi*, Duchess of Saxe-Coburg to Crown Princess Marie 15.2.1898, 329
4. Ibid. Duchess of Saxe-Coburg to Crown Princess Marie 11.4.1898, 336
5. *MR* I 200-1
6. RA Add U32, Queen Victoria to Empress Frederick 9.2.1899
7. Beeche 50
8. MR II 145
9. *Miami Herald* 2.10.1981
10. Private information
11. *BDC*, Queen Victoria to Empress Frederick 8.2.1899, 225
12. *QV* III iii, Journal 15.3.1899, 347
13. Ibid. 347-8
14. Mallet 156
15. Alice, Princess 86
16. *D Mi*, Duchess of Saxe-Coburg to Crown Princess Marie 24.12.1898, 370
17. Ridley 340n
18. *D Mi*, Duchess of Saxe-Coburg to Crown Princess Marie, 7.7.1900, 435
19. RA V2431/1900, Crown Princess Marie to Duchess of Saxe-Coburg 7.7.1900; Pakula *The last romantic* 127
20. *QV* III iii, Journal 25.7.1900, 576
21. Martin V 415
22. *Manchester Times* 3.8.1900
23. *QV* III iii, Journal 31.7.1900, 579
24. RA Z 60/89, Empress Frederick to Queen Victoria 15.8.1900; Pakula *An uncommon woman* 588
25. *The Times* 6.8.1900
26. *Ibid.* 1.8.1900
27. *Ibid.* 6.8.1900
28. *Pall Mall Gazette* 3.8.1900

Appendices

1. *The Times* 16.1.1901
2. Rennell 74
3. Buchanan, Meriel 119

Bibliography
(PA – Prince Alfred)

Letters

Bodleian MSS (Department of Western Manuscripts), Oxford, letter from PA to
   Lord Alfred Paget, 1863
Broadlands MSS (Southampton University), letters from PA to Prince Louis of
   Battenberg, 1875-90
Coburg MSS (Bayerisches Staatsarchiv, Schloss Ehrenburg, Coburg), letters from PA
   to Alexandrine, Duchess of Saxe-Coburg Gotha, 1857-93, and PA's journal, 1851-
   5
Gladstone MSS (Department of Manuscripts, British Library), letters from PA to
   W.E. Gladstone, 1866-94
Johannesburg MSS (Johannesburg Public Library Archives), one anonymous letter
   describing PA in Port Elizabeth, 1860
Pakington MSS (Hereford & Worcester Record Office, Worcester), letters from PA
   to Sir John Pakington, 1866-71
Playfair MSS letters from PA to Sir Lyon Playfair, 1865-86 (Imperial College of
   Science & Technology Archives, London)
Ripon MSS (Department of Manuscripts, British Library), letters from PA to George
   Frederick Samuel Robinson, 1st Marquis of Ripon, 1886
Royal Archives (Windsor), letter from Queen Victoria to the Empress Frederick,
   1899
Sutherland MSS (Staffordshire Record Office, Stafford), letters from PA to Anne, 3rd
   Duchess of Sutherland, 1864-83
Vinogradoff MSS (private collection), one letter from Grand Duchess Marie to
   Prince Vladimir Meschersky, 1875

Books

The place of publication is London unless otherwise stated

Airlie, Mabell, Countess of, *Thatched with Gold: Memoirs*; ed. Jennifer Ellis,
   Hutchinson, 1962
Albert, Prince Consort, *Letters of the Prince Consort, 1831-1861*; sel. and ed. Kurt
   Jagow, John Murray, 1938
Aronson, Theo, *Grandmama of Europe: The Crowned Descendants of Queen
   Victoria*, Cassell, 1973

— *Royal Ambassadors: British Royalties in Southern Africa 1860-1947*, Cape Town, David Phillip, 1975

— *Victoria and Disraeli: The Making of a Romantic Partnership*, Cassell, 1977

Ashdown, Dulcie M., *Victoria and the Coburgs*, Robert Hale, 1981

Aston, Sir George, *HRH the Duke of Connaught and Strathearn: A Life and Intimate Study*, Harrap, 1929

Australian Dictionary of Biography

Battiscombe, Georgina, *Queen Alexandra*, Constable, 1969

Beavan, A.H., *Popular Royalty*, Sampson Low, 1897

Beéche, Arturo E., ed., *The Grand Duchesses: Daughters and Granddaughters of Russia's Tsars*, Oakland, CA, Eurohistory, 2004

Bennett, Daphne, *King Without a Crown: Albert, Prince Consort of England, 1819-1861*, Heinemann, 1977

— *Queen Victoria's Children*, Victor Gollancz, 1980

— *Vicky, Princess Royal of England and German Empress*, Collins Harvill, 1971

Beresford, Charles William, 1ˢᵗ Baron, *The Memoirs of Admiral Lord Charles Beresford*, Methuen, 1914

Blake, Robert, *Disraeli*, Eyre & Spottiswoode, 1966

Bolitho, Hector, ed., *The Prince Consort and his Brother: Two Hundred New Letters*, Cobden-Sanderson, 1933

Bramsen, Bo, *Huset Glucksborg*, 2 vols, Copenhagen, Gyldendal, 1976

Buchanan, Sir George, *My Mission to Russia*, Cassell, 1923

Buchanan, Meriel, *Queen Victoria's Relations*, Cassell, 1954

Bülow, Prince Bernhard von, *Memoirs*, 4 vols, Putnam, 1931-2

Bury, Lady Charlotte, *The Diary of a Lady-in-Waiting*, ed. A. Francis Steuart, John Lane, 1905

Chilston, Viscount, *W. H. Smith*, Routledge & Kegan Paul, 1965

Cornwallis-West, Mrs George, *The Reminiscences of Lady Randolph Churchill*, Edward Arnold, 1908; Bath, Cedric Chivers, 1973

Corti, Egon Caesar Conte, *Alexander von Battenberg*, Cassell, 1954

— *The Downfall of Three Dynasties*, Cassell, 1934

— *The English Empress: A Study in the Relations Between Queen Victoria and her Eldest Daughter, Empress Frederick of Germany*, Cassell, 1957

Cullen, Tom, *The Empress Brown: The Story of a Royal Friendship*, Bodley Head, 1969

Diesbach, Ghislain de, *Secrets of the Gotha*, Chapman & Hall, 1967

Dormer, P.G., *The Edinburghs at Eastwell*, Privately printed, n.d.

Downer, Martyn, *The Queen's Knight: The Extraordinary Life of Queen Victoria's Most Trusted Confidant*, Bantam, 2007

Duff, David, *Hessian Tapestry: The Hesse Family and British Royalty*, Frederick Muller, 1967; Newton Abbot, David & Charles, 1979

— *The Shy Princess: The Life of HRH Princess Beatrice, the Youngest Daughter and Constant Companion of Queen Victoria*, Evans, 1958; Frederick Muller, 1974

— *Victoria Travels: Journeys of Queen Victoria Between 1830 and 1900, with Extracts from her Journal*, Frederick Muller, 1970

Eilers, Marlene, *Queen Victoria's Descendants*. Falkoping, Sweden, Rosvall Royal Books, 1987

Elsberry, Terence, *Marie of Romania: The Intimate Life of a Twentieth-Century Queen*, Cassell, 1973

Epton, Nina, *Victoria and her Daughters*, Weidenfeld & Nicolson, 1971

Erbach-Schonberg, Marie, Princess, *Reminiscences*, Allen & Unwin, 1925

Ernest II, Duke of Saxe-Coburg Gotha, *Memoirs*, 4 vols, Remington, 1888

Fisher, John Arbuthnot, Lord Fisher of Kilverstone, *Fear God and Dread Nought: The Correspondence of Admiral of the Fleet Lord Fisher of Kilverstone*; sel. and ed. Arthur J. Marder, 3 vols, Jonathan Cape, 1952-9

Fulford, Roger, *Hanover to Windsor*, Batsford, 1960

Gavin, Charles M., *Royal Yachts*, Rich & Cowan, 1932

Gelardi, Julia P., *From Splendor to Revolution: The Romanov Women, 1847-1928*, New York, St Martin's, 2011

Gernsheim, Helmut & Alison, *Edward VII and Queen Alexandra: A Biography in Word and Picture*, Frederick Muller, 1962

— *Queen Victoria: A Biography in Word and Picture*, Longmans, 1962

Gilliard, Pierre, *Thirteen Years at the Russian Court: A Personal Record of the Last Years and Death of the Czar Nicholas II and his Family*, Hutchinson, 1921, Bath, Cedric Chivers, 1972

Gore, John, *King George V: A Personal Memoir*, John Murray, 1941

Gower, Lord Ronald Charles Sutherland, *Old Diaries, 1881-1901*, John Murray, 1902

Grant, Sir Alexander, *The Story of the University of Edinburgh During its First Three Hundred Years*, Longmans, 1884

Hall, Coryne, *Little Mother of Russia: A biography of the Empress Marie Feodorovna (1847-1928)*, Shepheard-Walwyn, 1999

Hamilton, Lord Frederick Spencer, *The Vanished World of Yesterday*, Hodder & Stoughton, 1950

Hampshire, A. Cecil, *Royal Sailors*, Kimber, 1971

Hough, Richard, *Louis and Victoria: The First Mountbattens*, Hutchinson, 1974

Ileana, Princess of Roumania, Archduchess of Austria, *I Live Again*, Victor Gollancz, 1952

Jacobs, Arthur, *Arthur Sullivan: A Victorian Musician*, Oxford University Press, 1984

James, Robert Rhodes, *Rosebery: A Biography of Archibald Philip, Fifth Earl of Rosebery*, Weidenfeld & Nicolson, 1963

Kennedy, A.L. ed., *'My Dear Duchess': Social and Political Letters to the Duchess of Manchester 1858-1869*, John Murray, 1956

Keppel, Henry, *A Sailor's Life under Four Sovereigns*, 3 vols, Macmillan, 1899

Kerr, Mark, *Prince Louis of Battenberg, Admiral of the Fleet*, Longmans, Green, 1934

King-Hall, L., *Sea Saga*, Victor Gollancz, 1935

Kuhn, William M., *Henry and Mary Ponsonby: Life at the Court of Queen Victoria*, Duckworth, 2002

Kyril, Grand Duke of Russia, *My Life in Russia's Service – Then and Now*, Selwyn & Blount, 1939

Lee, Sir Sidney, *King Edward VII*, 2 vols, John Murray, 1925-7

Loftus, Lord Augustus, *The Diplomatic Reminiscences of Lord Augustus Loftus 1862-1879*, 2nd series, 2 vols, Cassell, 1894

Longford, Elizabeth, *Victoria R.I.*, Weidenfeld & Nicolson, 1964

— (ed.) *Darling Loosy: Letters to Princess Louise 1856-1939*, Weidenfeld & Nicolson, 1991

Lyttelton, Sarah, *The Correspondence of Sarah Spencer, Lady Lyttelton*; ed. Mrs Hugh Wyndham, John Murray, 1912

McClintock, Mary Howard, *The Queen Thanks Sir Howard: The Life of Major-General Sir Howard Elphinstone*, John Murray, 1945

MacDonnell, Freda, *Miss Nightingale's Young Ladies: The Story of Lucy Osburn and Sydney Hospital*, Angus & Robertson, 1970

McKinlay, Brian, *The First Royal Tour, 1867-1868,* Robert Hale, 1971

MacNaughton, Arnold, *The Book of Kings: A Royal Genealogy,* 3 vols, Garnstone, 1973

Magnus, Philip, *King Edward the Seventh,* John Murray, 1964

Mallet, Victor, ed., *Life with Queen Victoria: Marie Mallet's Letters from Court, 1887-1901,* John Murray, 1968

Marie, Duchess of Edinburgh, *Dearest Missy: The Correspondence between Marie, Grand Duchess of Russia, Duchess of Edinburgh and of Saxe-Coburg and Gotha and her Daughter, Marie, Crown Princess of Roumania, 1879-1900,* ed. Diana Mandache, Falkoping, Sweden, Rosvall Royal Books, 2011

Marie, Queen of Roumania, *The Story of My Life,* 3 vols, Cassell, 1934-5

Marie Louise, Princess, *My Memories of Six Reigns,* Evans Bros, 1956

Martin, Theodore, *The Life of HRH The Prince Consort,* 5 vols, Smith, Elder, 1875-80

Massie, Robert K., *Nicholas and Alexandra,* Victor Gollancz, 1968

Metelerkamp, Sanni, *George Rex of Knysna,* Cape Town, Howard Timmins, nd, c. 1956

Millar, Oliver, *The Victorian Pictures in the Collection of H.M. The Queen,* Cambridge University Press, 1992

Mills, A.R., *Two Victorian Ladies: More Pages from the Journals of Emily and Ellen Hall,* Frederick Muller, 1969

Milner, Revd John, & Brierley, Oswald W., *The Cruise of HMS Galatea, Captain HRH The Duke of Edinburgh, KG, in 1867-1868,* W. H. Allen, 1869

Nevill, Ralph H., *The Gay Victorians,* Eveleigh, Nash & Grayson, 1930

Nicholas, Prince of Greece, *My Fifty Years,* Hutchinson, 1926

Nicolson, Harold, *King George V: His Life and Reign,* Constable, 1952

Oxford Dictionary of National Biography

Paget, Lady Walburga, *In My Tower,* 2 vols, Hutchinson, 1924

Pakula, Hannah, *An Uncommon Woman: The Empress Frederick,* Weidenfeld & Nicolson, 1996

— *The Last Romantic: A Biography of Queen Marie of Roumania,* Weidenfeld & Nicolson, 1985

Pless, Princess Daisy of, *From my Private Diary,* John Murray, 1931

— *What I Left Unsaid,* Cassell, 1936

Plumb, J. H., & Wheldon, Huw, *Royal Heritage: The Story of Britain's Royal Builders and Collectors,* BBC, 1977

Ponsonby, Arthur, *Henry Ponsonby, Queen Victoria's Private Secretary: His Life from his Letters,* Macmillan, 1942

Ponsonby, D. A., *The Lost Duchess: The Story of the Prince Consort's Mother,* Chapman & Hall, 1958

Ponsonby, Sir Frederick, *Recollections of Three Reigns;* prepared for press with notes and an introductory memoir by Colin Welch, Eyre & Spottiswoode, 1951

— *Sidelights on Queen Victoria,* Macmillan, 1930

Ponsonby, Mary, *Mary Ponsonby: A Memoirs, Some Letters and a Journal,* ed. Magdalen Ponsonby, John Murray, 1927

Pope-Hennessy, James, *Queen Mary, 1867–1953,* Allen & Unwin, 1959

Prothero, Rowland E., *Life and Correspondence of Arthur Penrhyn Stanley, Late Dean of Westminster,* 2 vols., John Murray, 1884

Reid, Michaela, *Ask Sir James: Sir James Reid, Personal Physician to Queen Victoria and Physician-in-Ordinary to Three Monarchs,* Hodder & Stoughton, 1987

Rennell, Tony, *Last Days of Glory: The Death of Queen Victoria,* Viking, 2000

Ridley, Jane, *Bertie: A Life of Edward VII,* Chatto & Windus, 2012

Romanovsky-Krassinsky, Marie, Princess, *Dancing in Petersburg: The Memoirs of Kschessinska*, Victor Gollancz, 1960

St Aubyn, Giles, *Edward VII, Prince and King*, Collins, 1979

Sanderson, Edgar, & Melville, Lewis, *King Edward VII: His Life and Reign, the Record of a Noble Career*, 6 vols, Gresham, 1910

Sinclair, Andrew, *The Other Victoria: The Princess Royal and the Great Game of Europe*, Weidenfeld & Nicolson, 1981

Stanley, Lady Augusta, *Letters of Lady Augusta Stanley, A Young Lady at Court, 1849-1863*; ed. Dean of Windsor & Hector Bolitho, Gerald Howe, 1927

— *Later Letters of Lady Augusta Stanley, 1864–1876*; ed. Dean of Windsor & Hector Bolitho, Jonathan Cape, 1929

Stuart, Mrs Arthur T., *Chronicle of Service Life in Malta*, Edward Arnold, 1908

Stuart, Vivian, *The Beloved Little Admiral: The Life and Times of Admiral of the Fleet The Hon, Sir Henry Keppel, GCB, OM, DCL, 1809–1904*, Robert Hale, 1967

Sullivan, Herbert, & Flower, Newman, *Sir Arthur Sullivan: His Life, Letters and Diaries*, Cassell, 1927

Swartz, Helen M. & Marvin, ed., *Disraeli's Reminiscences*, Hamish Hamilton, 1975

Van der Kiste, John, *Childhood at Court, 1819-1914*, Stroud, Sutton, 1995

— *Princess Victoria Melita, Grand Duchess Cyril of Russia*, Stroud, Sutton, 1995

Victoria, Consort of Frederick III, German Emperor, *The Empress Frederick writes to Sophie*, Faber, 1955

— *Letters of the Empress Frederick*, ed. Sir Frederick Ponsonby, Macmillan, 1928

Victoria, Queen, *The Letters of Queen Victoria: a Selection from Her Majesty's Correspondence Between the Years 1837 and 1861*, ed. A. C. Benson & Viscount Esher, 3 vols, John Murray, 1907

— *The Letters of Queen Victoria, 2nd Series: a Selection from Her Majesty's Correspondence and Journal Between the Years 1862 and 1885*, ed. G. E. Buckle, 3 vols, John Murray, 1926–8

— *The Letters of Queen Victoria, 3rd Series: a Selection from Her Majesty's Correspondence and Journal Between the Years 1886 and 1901*, ed. G. E. Buckle, 3 vols, John Murray, 1930-2

— *Further Letters of Queen Victoria, from the Archives of the House of Brandenburg-Prussia*; ed. Hector Bolitho, Thornton Butterworth, 1938

— *Dearest Child: Letters between Queen Victoria and the Princess Royal, 1858–1861*; ed. Roger Fulford, Evans Bros, 1964

— *Dearest Mama: Private Correspondence of Queen Victoria and the Crown Princess of Prussia, 1861–1864*; ed. Roger Fulford, Evans Bros, 1968

— *Your Dear Letter: Private Correspondence of Queen Victoria and the Crown Princess of Prussia, 1865–1871*, ed. Roger Fulford, Evans Bros, 1971

— *Darling Child: Private Correspondence of Queen Victoria and the Crown Princess of Prussia, 1871-1878*; ed. Roger Fulford, Evans Bros, 1976

— *Beloved Mama: Private Correspondence of Queen Victoria and the German Crown Princess of Prussia, 1878–1885*; ed. Roger Fulford, Evans Bros, 1981

— *Beloved and Darling Child: Last Letters Queen Victoria and her Eldest Daughter, 1886–1901*; ed. Agatha Ramm, Stroud, Sutton, 1990

— *Advice to a Grand-daughter: Letters from Queen Victoria to Princess Victoria of Hesse*, ed. Richard Hough, Heinemann, 1975

Vorres, Ian, *The Last Grand Duchess: Her Imperial Highness Grand Duchess Olga Alexandrovna*, Hutchinson, 1964

Weintraub, Stanley, *The Importance of Being Edward: King in Waiting 1841–1901*, John Murray, 2000

— *Victoria: Biography of a Queen*, Unwin Hyman, 1987
Whittle, Tyler, *Victoria and Albert at Home*, Routledge & Kegan Paul, 1980
Woodham-Smith, Cecil, *Queen Victoria, her Life and Times: Volume One, 1819–1861*, Hamish Hamilton, 1972
Youssoupoff, Felix, *Lost Splendour*, Jonathan Cape, 1953
Zeepvat, Charlotte, *Prince Leopold: The Untold Story of Queen Victoria's Youngest Son*, Stroud, Sutton, 1998

Articles

Abrash, Merritt, *A Curious Royal Romance: The Queen's Son and the Tsar's Daughter*, In *Slavonic and East European Review*, July 1969
Campbell-Jones, Sheila, *Eastwell - the Joy of Romania's Queen Marie*, In *Kent Life*, April 1978
Christie, Ian, *The Family Origins of George Rex of Knysna*, In *Notes and Queries*, January 1975
Eagle, Judith, *For Dearest Mama and Papa: Queen Victoria's Children as Artists*, In *Country Life*, 8 September 1977
Gill, Crispin, *Duchess was 'too grand' for Plymouth*, In *Western Morning News*, 8 April 1985
Goliczov, Roman Ilmar, *Grand Duchess Marie Alexandrovna and Music*, In *Royalty Digest*, January 1979
Leyland, John, *Country Houses: Eastwell Park*, In *Country Life*, 10 April 1897
Marriott, John, *Early Collectors in the Royal Family*, In *Journal of the Royal Philatelic Society*, August-September 1971
Montague, Bee, *The Battenbergs of Swellendam – a Link with Royalty?* In *Personality*, 15 September 1966
Spencer-Warren, Mary, *The Duke of Saxe-Coburg's Palaces*, In *The Strand Magazine*, July 1894
Van der Kiste, John, *Devonport's Royal Commander*, In *Devon Life*, August 1977
Zeepvat, Charlotte, *Young Alfred*, In *Royalty Digest*, January 1999

Journals

All published in Great Britain unless stated otherwise

Army & Navy Gazette
Army & Navy Illustrated
Cape Argus (Republic of South Africa)
Cape Times (Republic of South Africa)
Daily Telegraph
Daily News
European Royal History Journal
Hampshire Advertiser
Illusteret Tidende (Denmark)
The Illustrated London News
The Listener
Malta Times & United Services Gazette (Malta)
Manchester Guardian
Manchester Times

Miami Herald (USA)
Morning Post
Naval & Military Record
Neue Züricher Zeitung (Germany)
The Observer
Pall Mall Gazette
Personality (Republic of South Africa)
Punch
Reynolds's Newspaper
Royal Cornwall Gazette
Royalty Digest
The Scotsman
The Times
United Services Gazette
Western Morning News